How Americans Use Time

John P. Robinson

How Americans Use Time

A Social-Psychological
Analysis of
Everyday Behavior

PRAEGER

PRAEGER SPECIAL STUDIES • PRAEGER SCIENTIFIC

Library of Congress Cataloging in Publication Data

Robinson, John P.
How Americans use time.

(Praeger special studies in U.S. economic, social, and political issues)
Bibliography: p.
Includes index.
1. Time allocation surveys—United States.
I. Title.
HN90.T5R6   301.5   76-58838
ISBN 0-275-24200-5

PRAEGER PUBLISHERS
PRAEGER SPECIAL STUDIES
383 Madison Avenue, New York, N.Y. 10017, U.S.A.

Published in the United States of America in 1977
by Praeger Publishers,
A Division of Holt, Rinehart and Winston, CBS, Inc.

9   038   98765432

© 1977 by Praeger Publishers

Printed in the United States of America

To Nancy,
My ideal partner
for sharing time.

ACKNOWLEDGMENTS

The research in this volume was made possible by grants from the National Science Foundation. The original research would not have been possible without the pioneering foresight of both Professor Alexander Szalai of the Hungarian Academy of Sciences whose dynamic efforts generated the original multination project, and Professor Philip Converse of the University of Michigan. Professor Thomas Juster of the University of Michigan contributed several insights and critical ideas in the analytic and experimental phase of this research. All of these fine gentlemen should be absolved of any responsibility for the final composition and editing of this book, however.

The painstaking care of the Sampling and Field Sections of the Survey Research Center ensured that the data were collected with maximal accuracy, and the Coding Section invariably dealt precisely, yet creatively, with the unique coding problems presented in time-use research. The versatile computer programs available through the Center permitted the application of rather advanced and sophisticated analyses of time-use data.

While the number of individuals who contributed to the various phases of the time-use project numbered in the hundreds, several deserve particular mention. Peppy Linden and Dorothy Kempter skillfully organized the methodological studies, computer tapes, and statistical analyses with important contributions from Virginia Marrash. Edward Yesser directed the time-diary coding operation with careful attention. Tom Sanders and Steve Hendricks developed special computer programs for time-use analysis. Sue Yellen and Kris Westrum prepared the final manuscript under difficult deadlines and circumstances. Nancy Robinson provided her usually excellent editorial comments and skills.

The author gratefully acknowledges permission to reprint the following material:

Tables 1.1-1.4 which will appear in a forthcoming monograph, Studies in the Measurement of Time Allocation, edited by F. Thomas Juster and published by the Institute for Social Research of the University of Michigan.

Plans are under way to publish the study questionnaire and detailed statistical tables, on which much of the discussion in this book is based, as part of the Monograph Series of University Microfilms International, 300 Zeeb Road, Ann Arbor, Michigan 48106.

CONTENTS

LIST OF TABLES

LIST OF FIGURES

BACKGROUND AND ANALYSIS MODEL

1

BACKGROUND AND METHODOLOGY

INTRODUCTION

What people do with their time is of ultimate concern to every society. Even if it only enters indirectly or unconsciously into policy deliberations, the matter of whether time is wisely or unwisely spent bears heavily on the quality of societal life. This is especially true in industrial societies where the dependence on the clock is paramount and where the use of time has become so central to judgments about successful societal functioning.

This book examines a unique body of empirical data on what Americans do with this basic and valuable resource. These time data comprise something of a societal time-and-motion study, in which social planners and social scientists can observe quantitatively the functioning of individuals within their total environment. Time use gives insights into the values society, and the individuals in it, place on work, on raising future generations, on mobility, or on the search for the better life.

In addition to providing accurate and detailed quantitative estimates of where our time goes, considerable attention in this book is devoted to interpreting what these time allocations mean to people. Time periods vary, both across activities and across people, in the gratifications they provide, in the degree of psychological constraint involved, in the human energy expended, and in their connection with large life purposes.

The most straightforward interpretations of time-use data can be made by economists who take at face value Benjamin Franklin's maxim "time is money." With their central concern about productivity, it seems only natural that economists would recognize the function of time to capture many of the "productive" transactions

of daily life (for example, housework, voluntary organizations) that
occur outside of the marketplace. In rethinking their discipline,
viewing both time and money as the basic resources available to the
households that make up society, much empirical effort has been
devoted by economists to placing monetary values on units of time,
particularly that spent on maintenance of the household. This
exercise generates more complete estimates of our country's gross
national product, GNP (Morgan et al., 1966; Walker and Gauger,
1973). Recently more serious attention has been given to general
production models of the household, in which time is a major
resource (for example, Becker, 1965; Hill and Stafford, 1974).
Nerlove (1974) noted some lines of a revised Malthusian Model of
family decision making emerging from this literature:

> The main link between household and economy is the
> value of human time; the increased value of human
> time results in fewer children per household, with
> each child embodying greater investments in human
> capital which in turn result in lower mortality and
> greater productivity in the economically active years
> . . . as long as the investment occurs which increases
> the amount of human capital per individual, the value
> of a unit of human time must continue to increase.
> (p. S217)

The increased value of time was also a central feature of
Linder's (1970) treatise on The Harried Leisure Class, although
he started from a different set of premises. Linder also chastised
his fellow economists at the time for failing to recognize the
importance of time scarcity as a problem for their discipline to
confront.

However, the profundity of our dependence on time goes beyond
those aspects of time captured in econometric models. Indeed,
concern about time is also considered one of the earmarks of a
"postindustrial society," with Americans characterized as a nation
of "clock-watchers" (Bell, 1975). Here more social concern is
voiced about the availability of leisure time, or how much of it is
squandered on television, or its relationship to the shorter and
more transitory nature of human interactions and social movements.

It is not surprising then to find the groundwork for the quantitative study of time in this country to have been primarily laid by
sociologists, such as, Bevans (1913), Lundberg et al. (1934),
Sorokin and Berger (1939), and Reiss (1959). Despite the attention
given it by such prominent sociologists, however, the empirical
potential of time to function as a "currency" for sociology–

representing a "hard" measure of human preferences and values—is mostly an unfulfilled aspiration. Linder (1970, p. 6) claims that this inability of sociologists to use their own results is due to their failure to recognize the time-scarcity problem.

Perhaps more promise for the time variable in sociology lies in treating time as a measure of "territoriality." Melbin (1976) developed this analogy most extensively, noting parallels in human and animal behavior and distinguishing three major mechanisms—queuing, phasing, and scheduling—by which humans use time to communicate with one another or to compete with one another. In examining sex-role differences in time use (see Chapter 5), we have also found the concept of territoriality a useful analogue.

Considerable sociological progress is also evident in theoretically relating time to social change (for example, Moore, 1963; Heirich, 1964). With the incorporation of time-use data into the social indicator movement, with its heavy emphasis on the processes of social change (Sheldon and Parke, 1975), empirical findings may soon catch up to the theoretical advances. Some impressive starts in this direction have been made with the publication of the results of the 1965-66 multinational time-use study (Szalai et al. 1972), and the incorporation of American results of this study into the landmark U.S. government publication <u>Social Indicators 1973</u>.

Time measurements have become far more central in the planning processes in the socialist countries of Eastern Europe where the impetus for the multination study started. It is not uncommon to find policy directives to increase factory production of washing machines or to decrease the length of the workweek being derived from extensive data on time use, often collected as a standard part of the census in these countries. Staikov (1972) presents several examples of advanced policy deliberations in socialist planning using time-diary data. In the societies of Western Europe and in Japan, extensive time-use data have been collected to guide the more modest policy aims of the governmental institutions concerned with the mass media and transportation.*

Despite the "postindustrial" era into which the United States supposedly entered and in which profitable uses of time are of more central concern, research has been surprisingly fragmented and sporadic. Nevertheless, major deliberations about policy and planning often center around standard available data and uses of

---

*In this country, elaborate models using time data for transportation and land use policy deliberations have been developed by F. Stuart Chapin and his associates (see, for example, Chapin, 1974; Zehner and Chapin, 1974).

time for particular purposes, such as the length of the workweek, time spent commuting, watching television, and other uses of leisure time for recreation. As we shall see, our research indicates that available estimates of time spent on such activities, as given by government and industry sources, often give inaccurate and misleading pictures of how Americans spend their time. We believe that the methodological advantages provided by the time diary, the core instrument analyzed in this monograph, afford the analyst a unique opportunity to observe accurately how Americans spend their time.

The term "time budget" is used to refer to logs or diaries of activities that groups of individuals keep over a specified period, usually the full 24-hour day. The sample page in the diary form used in our 1965-66 study in Figure 1.1 shows how the diary is intended to capture all activities during the day, as well as the "secondary activities" that accompany them, the place where they occur and the social partners present during the activity.

The term "budget," however, implies the presence of an underlying rationale for people's planning, and our suspicions about how little of daily life is fully planned in advance is reinforced both by casual inspection of individual time diaries and by the individuals themselves when direct questions are asked on the topic. Nevertheless, collections of time budgets do provide analysts with a highly rational and intriguing perspective on how societal time is allocated, particularly with reference to such questions of social concern as how daily life is changed by marriage or the arrival of children, how much reduced work time gets translated into leisure, or what kind of activities people give up to watch television. It is to such questions at the aggregate level that this book is addressed, as well as to those that concern economists, such as the value of time and time "invested" in children.

The use of the full 24-hour day in time-diary research utilizes the unique value of time as an indicator of social welfare. Unlike most measures in the social sciences, there is little debate about what one is basically measuring. The unit of analysis is as familiar to the public as it is to the researcher, and the 24 hours of the day, unlike almost any other societal resources, are equally distributed to all members of society. As Gutenschwager (1973) has cogently observed, one can visualize these 24 hours as available input to all members of a population, with the output, in the form of choice of activities, representing a combination of preferences and constraints within the population. This output, particularly for the less-constrained uses of time, comprises rather solid behavioral evidence of the preferences and values of individuals. This 24-hour feature furthermore allows the researcher to observe at first hand some of the trade-offs of time that occur when individuals decide to spend their time in one way rather than another.

FIGURE 1.1

Sample Time–Diary Page Used in the 1965–66 Study
(midnight to 9 a.m. only)

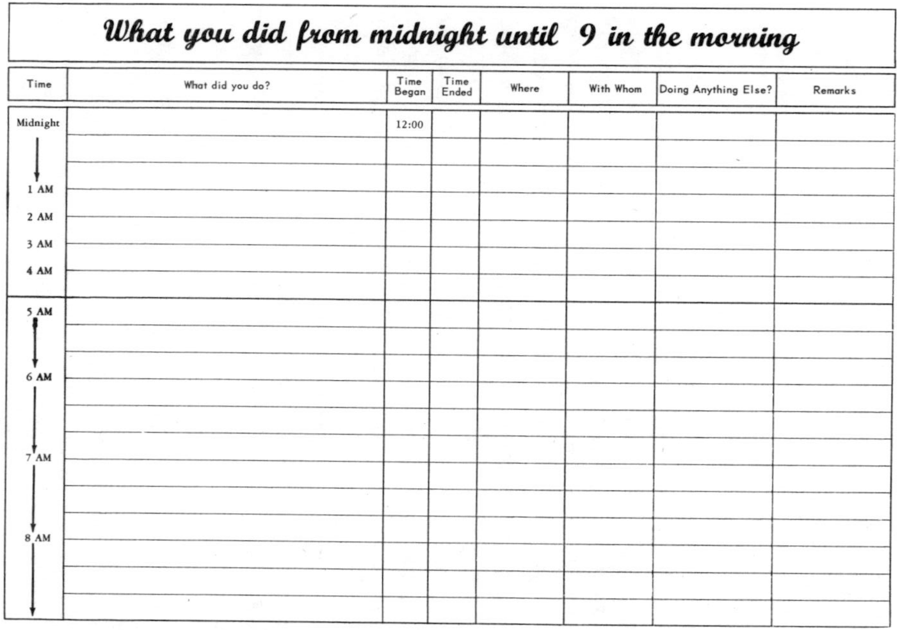

What you did from midnight until 9 in the morning

Time	What did you do?	Time Began	Time Ended	Where	With Whom	Doing Anything Else?	Remarks
Midnight		12:00					
1 AM							
2 AM							
3 AM							
4 AM							
5 AM							
6 AM							
7 AM							
8 AM							

Source: Study of Americans' Use of Time (1965–66).

The potentials of such dynamic analyses of time fall well short of the actual output of results from previous time-diary studies of a single day's activities. First of all, computer modeling exercises with time-use data are quite complicated and expensive to conduct; they require extensive "fine tuning" to map into social reality, even with the availability of computers having large storage and analytic capabilities. There are complex definitional problems given the richness of the data—should "housework" include child care, shopping for durables or related travel; should playing with children, eating, or organizational activity be considered part of "free time?" Should the analytic interest be focused on average duration of time spent on the activity, or percent participating, or duration per participant? Or, say in the case of child care, is the real interest in combining child care as a primary and secondary activity, or in the "with whom" dimension in which the total time spent in the company of one's children is presumably tabulated?

Often the researcher may have been unable to measure or may have forgotten to include a crucial analytic variable; for example in our 1965-66 study, the employment status of the respondent's spouse and the age and sex of individual children were not included as part of the original coding and had to be added to the analysis tape some years later. Moreover, while time diaries do give a glimpse of individuals interacting with their total environment, the one-day glimpse is tantalizingly brief, and often superficial or dehumanized. As many individuals in our surveys complain, the particular day on which they have kept the diary is atypical. The worker recuperating from a hard day at work is made to look listless, while the housewife caught on her busy day appears even more harassed than her busier counterpart with a full-time job. Outside of weekends, individuals have little chance to demonstrate how creatively or productively they use their leisure time. Quantitatively, the J-shaped distribution of daily participation figures for most leisure activities rules out straightforward application of statistical tests based on the assumption of normally distributed variables.

To a great extent, these individual idiosyncracies can be expected to cancel each other when the attention of the research focuses on how aggregates of individuals spend their time (see later chapters). Nevertheless, analyses of time use are always haunted by the spectre of Parkinson's (1957) famous law, namely, activities expand to fill the time available for their completion. Two individuals (or the same individual at two time points) are classified as "working," "preparing meals," or "watching television" when one is doing so to kill time and the other to transcend the level of his environment; or when one is actively enjoying the activity and the other performing it perfunctorily. Some attempts to overcome these shortcomings and to provide greater insight into the psychological meanings of activities are provided—although again at the aggregate level—in Chapters 5 and 6.

METHODOLOGICAL QUESTIONS

It might be supposed that the measurement of time use by the public is a relatively simple process, since time is a measure that people use so often and so readily in planning their daily lives. Our experience with time diaries, however, has alerted us to the many subtleties and sources of bias inherent in time-use measures available to policy makers in government and industry and to various social commentators and critics. While almost everyone who has thought about the matter would agree that some sort of direct observation would be the ideal method of gathering time-use data, systematic observation becomes prohibitively expensive and unwieldy for any large cross-section sample. Perhaps more importantly, direct observation is apt to change the observed person's behavior, making it inaccurate as well as expensive.

The most common, convenient—and unfortunately often misleading—alternative has been to rely on figures from surveys in which respondents are asked to estimate how much time they spend on this or that activity over some specified period. Thus, surveys have asked for estimates of the yearly time spent on housework (Morgan et al., 1966), or voluntary organizations (ACTION, 1975), yearly participation in outdoor recreation (U.S. Bureau of Outdoor Recreation, 1972), and daily television viewing (Roper, 1971). In each of these instances, our experience has been that the estimates generated appear to exceed significantly the time reported on such activities on a daily basis (Robinson, forthcoming). When asked to report on almost any not socially undesirable activity, it appears that respondents oblige interviewers and researchers by providing overly generous participation rates for that activity.

The alternative of the diary has been used less often—perhaps because of the much greater expense involved—but has significant advantages. Respondents are asked to record all of their activities, and the times when the activities began and ended, for only the previous day. Thus, the diary approach does have the advantage of asking people to report activities for a single day and when that period is still fresh in their minds. Hence recall bias and exaggeration of socially acceptable activities are both likely to be minimized.

Still, far fewer people report sexual activity, gambling, fighting, or criminal behavior than we know empirically to be the case. Do we have any basis for assuming that activities recorded in diaries

are more accurate than those recorded by other survey techniques?
To explore this possibility, we have conducted a series of small-
scale validity studies applying direct (that is, TV cameras) and
indirect (namely, beepers that go off at random intervals to signal
respondents to write down what they are doing) observational methods
for comparison with diary entries over the same time period. The
samples of individuals used in these experiments are small, usually
less than 100, but cross-sectional and the sample of behaviors is in
the thousands. Generally these results give us considerable confidence in the ability of the diary measures to reflect the aggregate
behavior of such groups as people under age 30, the unemployed,
people without television sets, or women not in the labor force
(Robinson, forthcoming).*

The ability of time-diary figures to capture the unique character
of the everyday lives of aggregates was apparent in the 1965-66 study,
when separate data from a national sample and from the single city
of Jackson, Michigan, were compared; Jackson was chosen for its
convenience and its similarity in sociological structure to the urban
industrial European sites in the multinational study of Szalai et al.
conducted in 1965 and reported in 1972.

The correlation, across the 96 categories of time use, between
the Jackson and national time-use aggregates, as measured by
Yule's Y, was .95.† In fact, one of the most striking findings of

---

*We are much less certain of the validity of time-use diary data
at the level of the individual respondent, since we are only observing
a single sample of time use for one 24-hour period out of 365 such
periods during the course of a year. Thus for estimation of national
aggregates, where one is not concerned about the accuracy of microlevel observations, our data suggest that time diaries are a reasonably accurate way of making those measurements. But to the extent
that social scientists are interested in accurate observations of
particular behavior at the microlevel, individual entries in a person's
single time diary exhibit considerable instability and clearly need
to be supplemented with other recall questions or direct observation.

†The formula for Yule's Y is reported in Goodman and Kruskal
(1959). The use of the correlation coefficient to denote correspondence between aggregates of time-use data across the 96 categories
of time use (as in Table 1.1) is somewhat misleading because certain
activities, such as work and sleep, by necessity consume the lion's
share of time, while less frequent activities like going to the movies
or hobbies will be reported far less often. While it is true that there
is considerable correspondence between these entries, these correlation coefficients probably give an exaggerated picture of this correspondence.

the multinational study was the strong correspondence in the aggregate results found in three other countries in which data from two separate sites were available. Such correspondence formed the basis of the intriguing "national life style" mappings that so uniquely and parsimoniously characterized daily life across the 12 countries in the multinational study (Converse, 1972).

The multinational study also introduced an interesting experiment in diary-keeping methods. In each survey site, a randomly chosen 10 percent of the sample was instructed to fill out a "yesterday" time diary for the day prior to the interview; this was in addition to the "tomorrow" diary for the following day, the "tomorrow" approach being the only method by which respondents in the remainder of the sample accounted for their time. The comparison of the aggregate "yesterday" and "tomorrow" estimates for the American portion in this study is shown in Table 1.1, and the overall correlation (Yule's Y) of .85 again suggests the strong degree of correspondence between estimates generated from "yesterday" diaries and the more elaborate and expensive "tomorrow" approach used in the 1965-66 study. When an equivalent experiment was conducted with a small Jackson sample in 1974, the correlation obtained was slightly higher, .88.

These two comparison studies yield few consistent cross-method differences in activities. The "yesterday" approach did pick up more religious organization activities, more visiting, and less work than the more elaborate "tomorrow" method in both studies. However, it is difficult to explain these differences in terms of the greater experience, conscientiousness or requisite awareness of what is required in accounting for a day's activities—which are the main advantages that the respondents in the "tomorrow" condition have over those in the unrehearsed "yesterday" condition.

Differences in the expected direction were found in diary detail, however, as indexed by the number of activities reported in the diaries under the different conditions. In the 1965-66 study, respondents in the experimental 10 percent of the sample reported 27.7 activities in their "tomorrow" diaries compared to 25.0 in their "yesterday" diaries, and they reported more secondary activities (8.6 vs. 7.7) as well. Differences of this magnitude were also found in the other multinational sites taking part in the study and were replicated in the later Jackson study (Robinson, forthcoming). While it is clear that the "tomorrow" approach does generate more detailed diaries and undoubtedly makes the respondent more aware of the day's activities, gains in the order of 10 percent in activities hardly seem worth the accompanying 50-75 percent greater field costs and higher refusal rates. This is particularly true given the lack of evidence of serious systematic bias as reflected in Table 1.1.

TABLE 1.1

Comparison Between Aggregate Time Estimates
for Activities Reported "Yesterday" versus "Tomorrow"
(percent of time)

	1965-66 National and Jackson Study Data Combined	
Activity	Day before (N = 192)	Day after (N = 2024)
00. Work	14.4	14.9
01. Work at home	.2	.3
02. Overtime	−*	.1
03. Travel at work	.5	.2
04. Waiting	−	.1
05. Moonlighting	.3	.3
06. Meals at work	.6	.7
07. Other	.2	.3
08. Coffee breaks	.3	.5
09. Travel to and from work	2.1	1.5
Total	18.6	18.9
10. Preparing food	2.9	3.1
11. Meal cleanup	1.5	1.5
12. Indoor chores	2.1	2.2
13. Outdoor chores	.3	.3
14. Laundry	1.5	1.6
15. Mending	.1	.1
16. Other repairs	.5	.4
17. Animal and plant care	.3	.2
18. Heat and water upkeep	.1	.1
19. Other	.4	.8
Total	9.7	10.3
20. Baby care	1.0	.9
21. Child care	.7	.6
22. Helping homework	.2	.1
23. Reading to children	.2	.1
24. Indoor entertaining	.3	.2
25. Outdoor entertaining	.1	−
26. Medical care	.0	−
27. Other (baby-sitting)	.2	.1
28. No activity	.0	.0
29. Related travel	.3	.3
Total	3.0	2.3
30. Everyday needs	.8	1.0
31. Durable goods	.3	.1
32. Personal care	.1	.1

Activity	1965-66 National and Jackson Study Data Combined	
	Day before (N = 192)	Day after (N = 2024)
33. Medical care	—	.1
34. Government service	.1	.1
35. Repair services	.1	.2
36. Waiting	.1	.1
37. Other services	.8	.8
38. No activity	.0	.0
39. Related travel	1.3	1.3
Total	3.6	3.8
40. Washing and dressing	3.5	3.4
41. Medicinal care	.6	—
42. Helping adults	.3	.4
43. Meals at home	4.5	4.1
44. Restaurant meals	.6	.7
45. Night sleep	32.2	32.1
46. Naps	.8	.8
47. Resting	.3	.4
48. Private, other	.5	.9
49. Related travel	.8	.6
Total	44.1	43.4
50. Full-time classes	.6	.2
51. Other classes	.0	.1
52. Special lectures	.0	—
53. Political and union courses	.0	—
54. Homework and research	.4	.3
55. Technical reading	.0	—
56. Other	.1	.2
57. No activity	.0	.0
58. No activity	.0	.0
59. Related travel	.1	.1
Total	1.2	.9
60. Organization work	.0	.1
61. Work as officer	.0	—
62. Other activity	.0	—
63. Volunteer work	.1	—
64. Religious clubs	.4	.2
65. Religious services	.3	.6
66. Union-management	.0	—
67. PTA, VFW, etc.	.1	.1
68. Other	.1	.1

(continued)

(Table 1.1 continued)

	1965–66 National and Jackson Study Data Combined	
Activity	Day before (N = 192)	Day after (N = 2024)
69. Related travel	.3	.3
Total	1.3	1.4
70. Sports events	.0	.1
71. Nightclubs, fairs	.0	.2
72. Movies	.1	.2
73. Theatre, concerts	.1	—
74. Museums	.0	—
75. Visits with friends	3.3	2.8
76. Parties with meals	.8	.9
77. Bars, tea rooms	.3	.3
78. Other gatherings	.1	.1
79. Related travel	.9	1.0
Total	5.6	5.6
80. Playing sports	.6	.4
81. Hunting, fishing	.5	.2
82. Taking a walk	.1	.1
83. Hobbies	.1	.1
84. Sewing, canning	.6	.5
85. Artistic work	.0	.1
86. Making music	.1	.1
87. Games, cards, etc.	.3	.4
88. Other active leisure	.1	.1
89. Related travel	.2	.1
Total	2.6	2.1
90. Radio	.1	.2
91. Television	6.6	6.6
92. Records	.1	.1
93. Reading books	.2	.3
94. Reading magazines	.1	.4
95. Reading newspapers	1.2	1.7
96. Talking (on phone)	1.1	1.2
97. Letters	.2	.4
98. Relaxing, thinking	.3	.3
99. Related travel	—	—
Total	9.9	11.2
Grand Total	99.6	99.9

*A dash indicates less than .05 percent.

Source: Studies in the Measurement of Time Allocation, ed.
F. Thomas Juster (Ann Arbor, Mich.: Institute for Social Research, University of Michigan, forthcoming).

A second comparison of interest involves a significant departure from this common-method theme. Not only is the diary method somewhat different but so are the research investigators and the sample investigated. The point of comparison is the intensive study by Walker and Woods (1976) of the use of time for household-related obligations, which was completed about two years after our study. This research was conducted only in upstate New York communities, with samples purposely stratified to capture the effects on housework of number and age of children and wife's employment. Most importantly, the diary approach differed in that respondents recorded activities only for those portions of the day in which they were doing housework; thus the coding categories of Walker and Woods can be matched up with ours only with difficulty and arbitrariness.*

The data in Table 1.2, which compare our results with theirs, involve the sum of primary and secondary activities rather than primary activities alone. They are shown separately for employed men, employed women, and nonemployed women.

The only major discrepancy apparent in Table 1.2 is the 17 percent higher housework times recorded by employed women in the Walker and Woods sample, which seems to stem mainly from the greater amounts of time their employed women recorded on food and laundry activities. Nevertheless, considering the many methodological divergences, the two sets of figures in Table 1.2 are remarkably similar.

Nonetheless, as noted earlier, collection of time-use data by the single-day dairy is not only expensive, but analytically limiting. Investigators interested in public participation in a particular type of behavior—be it work, religious activity, or mass media usage—often find the single-day diary duration too short to provide realistic assessments of the long-range personal context of such behavior. Surveys in which public participation is of interest, therefore, usually rely on simple direct questions in which respondents estimate their behavior for far longer time periods. How many weeks of work did the respondent put in during the last year? How often does the

---

*In Table 1.4, meal clearing in the 1965-66 study is coded under "food activity" rather than house chores, yard and repair work under "care of house," and care to adults under "care of family members." Walker (1970) also found a strong convergence between the "yesterday" and "tomorrow" approach, with the following comparisons for wives: food activities (124 minutes "yesterday" vs. 134 "tomorrow"); house care (100 vs. 91); clothing care (42 vs. 43); family care (115 vs. 112) and marketing management (82 vs. 84). For husbands the respective figures were 23-23; 91-83; 28-24; 50-57; and 60-57.

TABLE 1.2

Comparative Daily Hours Spent on
Household Work
(primary and secondary activities)

	Men	Women	
		Employed	Not employed
1. All food activities	.2(.2)	1.6(1.2)	2.3(2.2)
2. Care of house	.6(.5)	1.2(1.2)	1.6(1.9)
3. Care of clothing	—*	.9(.6)	1.3(1.1)
4. Care of family members	.4(.4)	.8(.7)	1.8(2.0)
5. Marketing and record keeping	.4(.5)	.8(.8)	1.0(1.0)
Total	1.6(1.6)	5.3(4.5)	8.0(8.2)

*A dash indicates less than .05 hours per day.

Source: Studies in the Measurement of Time Allocation, ed.
F. Thomas Juster (Ann Arbor, Mich.: Institute for Social Research,
University of Michigan, forthcoming). Data came from Walker and
Woods (1976), pp. 50-51, 62; 1965-66 time study in parentheses.

respondent attend church services? How many hours a week does
the person watch television? Analysis of such data is, moreover,
much simpler than the multiple steps involved in constructing activity
participation from diaries.

We did include some annual estimate questions in our 1965-66
study, making it possible to compare data using the two different
methods. In the survey, respondents were presented with a list of
18 activities (mainly leisure) and were asked to estimate how often
they had participated in each activity in the previous year, using
one of five participation rates:
1. Once a week or more.
2. Every two or three weeks.
3. Between six and twelve times a year.
4. One to five times a year.
5. Not at all this year.
It should be possible to construct synthetically a reasonable estimate
of daily participation using these data. One should be able to assume
that the probability of participation for the last group is zero (that is,
0/365, 0 participation days divided by 365 total days), for the fourth
group three participation days 3/365, for the third group 9/365, and
for the second group 25/365. The estimate for the first group must

be arbitrary, since there is no upper limit—a person who, for example, goes to church every day is in the same category as one who goes but once a week. This group was given a weight of 60 to reflect the fact that participation may have occurred more than once a week for these respondents.

The comparisons of these two sets of estimated participation rates is given in Table 1.3. In contrast to our comparisons of diary data with estimates from surveys by other investigators of time spent on housework, volunteer organizations or television viewing, Table 1.3 mostly shows that the annual estimate figures generally underestimate their closest diary counterparts. This underestimation is found for both obligatory (such as shopping) and leisure activities (such as visiting, nightclubbing, sports), and for frequent (such as visiting, shopping) and infrequent activities (such as sports, night-clubbing). However, evidence of overestimation is also evident in Table 1.3 for fishing, other outdoor recreation, and attendance at sports events, theater, and exhibitions. There are three features of these latter activities that set them apart from the others in Table 1.3:

1. Each of them is a leisure activity.
2. They are more likely to be performed in the summer months when no diary data were collected, our interviewing being mainly conducted in the late fall.
3. They tend to be the most infrequently performed activities on the list.

Thus, respondents in this survey gave estimates that over-estimated their participation in less frequent events and under-estimated participation in more frequent events. While the range of daily participation for the diary data in Table 1.3 runs from 0.3 to 23 percent, the extrapolations from the annual estimates have a more restricted range of 1 to 11 percent. Nonetheless, the fact that the least frequent activities were also those more likely to be a feature of summer living confounds any firm conclusion along these lines.*

———————

*It should also be kept in mind that the figures in Table 1.3 could be brought more closely into line by differentially weighting the open-ended first category depending on its participation rate. In other words, the "once a week or more" category could be weighted at over 60 participation days for activities like gardening, shopping, or visiting and at under 60 days for less frequent activities of attending sports events or the theatre—which would seem most difficult to participate in more than 20 or 30 times a year in many locations.

TABLE 1.3

Comparison of Daily Figures with
Annual Estimates on Daily Participants

	Percent Participating Daily	
Activity	Diary	Annual estimate
Obligatory		
l. Gardening and working around the yard	9	6
m. Making and fixing things around the house	10	7
n. Shopping, except for groceries	12	6
o. Helping relatives, neighbors, friends	10	7
Leisure		
d. Going to classes or lectures	3	2
c. Going to church (or religious activities)	11	9
b. Going to club meetings or activities (PTA, union, etc.)	4	3
e. Going to watch sports events	1	2
i. Going to nightclubs, bars, etc.	4	2
j. Going to concerts, plays, etc.	0.4	1
k. Going to fairs, museums, exhibits, etc.	0.3	1
a. Going to the movies	2	2
p. Visits with relatives, neighbors, friends	23	11
h. Playing active sports (bowling, softball, etc.)	6	3
f. Fishing, hunting, camping, hiking	1	2
g. Boating, swimming, picnics, pleasure drives	—*	—
r. Working on hobbies, painting, or music	6	6
q. Playing cards, other indoor games	5	5

*Data not calculated.

Note: The following weights were assigned to derive the daily figures from estimates: 0 = not at all, 3 = 1-5 times per year, 9 = 6-12 times per year, 25 = every 2-3 weeks, 60 = once a week or more.

Source: Studies in the Measurement of Time Allocation, ed. F. Thomas Juster (Ann Arbor, Mich.: Institute for Social Research, University of Michigan, forthcoming).

While time-diary figures do not match up well with data from studies in which respondents have been asked to provide estimates of their participation in activities over a year's time, a more direct and perhaps more sensitive methodological check on the estimate approach is possible with the estimate data in Table 1.3 from the 1965-66 time-diary study. This check does not involve the application of weights and also brings us to the individual rather than aggregate level of analysis. It is possible on an individual basis to compare the amounts of time recorded in people's diaries for each of the 18 activities listed in Table 1.3 for people who said they participated in that activity frequently and for people who estimated they participated less often or not at all. Such a set of calculations is presented in Table 1.4.

Table 1.4 generally demonstrates a reassuring degree of correspondence. The relations are generally monotonic, or reasonably close to monotonic, and proceed in the exponential order implied in the estimate categories. The totals for all activities at the bottom of Table 1.4 do indicate better discrimination at the higher participation end of the scale than at the lower, that is, between those who participate once a week vs. every two or three weeks (compared to those who participate one to five times a year vs. six to twelve times.

Furthermore, one does find a disturbing amount of daily participation among respondents who said they had not participated at all in the activity during the year. This indication of confusion on the part of respondents is most apparent for the activity of helping others. It at least indicates that respondents need clearer instruction on what is to be included when questions about this activity are asked; another activity appearing to require better definition is nongrocery shopping. The explanation for remaining discrepancies in Table 1.4 may lie more in instabilities due to their infrequency of occurrence, that is, going to fairs and exhibits, to classes or lectures, and hunting or fishing. The almost textbook correspondence for movie attendance data in Table 1.4 indicates it to be the most clearly defined activity of the 18 presented to respondents.

There is further reassurance in the similar pattern of demographic correlates of these activities found for both diary and estimates. Thus both data sets agree, for example, that older people attend church more regularly and that the more affluent make greater use of their free time for participation in organizations or attendance at lectures or concerts. Thus, such estimate data do appear to provide a useful background of general life style, accurately distinguishing frequent from infrequent participants or nonparticipants in particular activities. Nonetheless, when one wants time-use figures that correspond fairly closely to how people actually spend their time, particularly if one wants to attach monetary values to

TABLE 1.4

Comparison of Daily-Diary Participation
with Annual Participation Estimated by Respondents

Activity	Primary Activity, Average Minutes on Day of Diary[a]				
	Not at all[b]	1–5 year[b]	6–12 year[b]	Every 2–3 wks[b]	Once a wk or more[b]
Obligatory					
l. Gardening and working around the yard	1	—[c]	1	2	3
m. Making and fixing things around the house	4	6	5	11	10
n. Shopping, except for groceries	8	10	7	13	14
o. Helping relatives, neighbors, friends	10	3	5	4	8
Leisure					
d. Going to classes or lectures	—	8	4	0	36
c. Going to church (or religious activities)	1	1	3	4	15
b. Going to club meetings or activities (PTA, union, etc.)	3	4	9	17	26
e. Going to watch sports events	0	2	2	2	5
j. Going to concerts, plays, etc.	0	1	0	5	17
k. Going to fairs, museums, exhibits, etc.	0	—	0	7	0
a. Going to the movies	0	2	4	10	26
p. Visits with relatives, neighbors, friends	5	8	19	25	34
i. Going to nightclubs, bars, etc.	2	7	7	12	37
h. Playing active sports (bowling, softball)	1	2	3	5	29
f. Fishing, hunting, camping, hiking	1	3	1	2	7
g. Boating, swimming, picnics, pleasure drives	d	d	d	d	d
r. Working on hobbies, painting, or music	3	8	9	11	22
q. Playing cards, other indoor games	1	1	3	4	15
Total[e]	40	66	82	134	304

[a]In 1965–66 Time-Use Study.
[b]Estimated annual frequency.
[c]A dash indicates less than .5 minutes per day.
[d]Data not calculated.
[e]All activities.

Source: Studies in the Measurement of Time Allocation, ed. F. Thomas Juster (Ann Arbor, Mich.: Institute for Social Research, University of Michigan, forthcoming).

such time figures, then the diary seems the most reasonable source
of such data.

DATA BASES

The research reported in this treatise was supported by several
grants from the National Science Foundation. The major data
resource cited throughout this work is the 1965-66 Survey Research
Center survey of <u>Americans' Use of Time</u>, a survey whose results
have not been fully published to date–although monograph-length
articles outlining the research design and key findings can be found
in Robinson and Converse (1972) and Szalai et al. (1972), which are
recommended to readers interested in more details of this study.

Briefly, the study involved a sample of over 2,000 American
adults aged 18-65 who kept complete diaries of their activities for
a single day mainly between November 1 and December 15, 1965
but also in the winter and spring of 1966. The sample was deliberately
chosen to be an urban and employed one, conforming to the guidelines
of the multinational study of which it was a part. Thus, residents of
non-SMSAs (viz. areas with no city greater than 50,000 population)
were excluded, as well as residents of households in which no member aged 18-65 was part of the labor force; farmers were also
excluded. Respondents were randomly assigned to fill out diaries
on a weekday or on a weekend.

Of the total sample, 1,244 adults were part of the national urban
sample and 788 came from the city of Jackson, Michigan, and its
environs. In order to increase the sample sizes, and because the
time estimates from the two samples were so similar, the two
samples are often combined in the analyses that follow.

The field procedures involved the "tomorrow" approach, that is,
the interviewer contacted the respondent and conducted a brief "warm-
up" interview on the first day and left the diary for the respondent
to enter the next day's activities. The interviewer returned to the
respondent's home on the subsequent day (that is, the day after
"tomorrow") to ensure that the diary had been filled out correctly
and to fill in any missing parts if it had not. At that time the interviewer also completed the remainder of the interview, which dealt
with the highlights, interesting conversations, and mass media usage
on the diary day, as well as activity satisfaction and traditional
demographic questions.

When the diaries were returned to the Survey Research Center,
they were edited to ensure completeness and consistency. Missing
time periods were noted, as well as trip estimates where these were
not pointed out by respondents. Activities were divided into their

primary and secondary components when several activities were reported for the same time period. When two activities were reported they were split equally. For example, "Eating and reading between 8 and 9 p.m." was coded as 30 minutes of eating as the primary activity and reading as the secondary activity together with 30 minutes of reading as the primary activity and eating as the secondary activity.

Primary activities were coded into one of 96 categories in Table 1.1 the complete detailed description being given in the Appendix and in Szalai et al. (1972). In addition to primary and secondary activities, the social company involved in the activity (with whom) and the location (where) were also coded in connection with the duration of the activity.

These durations were then summarized and deviations of greater than 10 minutes from the 1,440 minutes total were noted and the diaries recoded to be within that 10 minute limit. Deviations of less than 10 minutes were added or subtracted from the activity of maximum durations, that activity usually being sleep.

As an illustration of the coding procedures, take the following entries recorded in one respondent's diary:

Time	Primary Activity	Where	With Whom	Secondary Activity
Midnight–5:55 a.m.	Went to bed, sleep	At home	Alone	Nothing else
5:55–6:20 a.m.	Made breakfast for husband	At home	Husband	Talked
6:20–6:45 a.m.	Talked with husband	At home	Husband	Nothing else
6:45–8:00 a.m.	Back to sleep	At home	Alone	Nothing else
8:00–8:20 a.m.	Washed and dressed	At home	Alone	Radio
8:20–8:31 a.m.	Made beds	At home	Alone	Radio
8:31–9:00 a.m.	Made breakfast	At home	Children	Dressing children

Each entry in the diary was coded into five blocks: time, primary activity, location, with whom, and secondary activity. Thus, the first entry in the diary is sleep (code 45 in the Appendix). No secondary activity, by definition, accompanied sleep so "nothing else" is entered for secondary activity. The sleeping was done alone, so this is the entry under "with whom" (code 00) and it was done at home, which is entered under location (code is also 0). Finally, the activity took place between midnight and 5:55 a.m., which is five hours and 55 minutes or an elapsed time of 355 minutes.

The next activity was starting breakfast (coded 10 as meal preparation), with talking as the secondary activity (code 96). Since it was done with her husband, the with-whom code is 1 (for husband) and 0 (for no other person); the at-home location is again coded 0. The elapsed time here is 25 minutes. The same coding procedures were followed for the rest of the activities reported during the 24-hour day. The coding for the seven activities above in terms of primary activity, secondary activity, with whom, location, and time duration is as follows:

45	—	00	0	355
10	96	10	0	025
96	—	10	0	025
45	—	00	0	075
40	90	00	0	020
12	90	00	0	011
10	21	20	0	029

Total: 540 minutes between midnight and 9 a.m.

2

SOCIAL-PSYCHOLOGICAL CONSIDERATIONS IN THE ANALYSIS OF TIME DATA

TIME USE AS A SOCIAL INDICATOR

Social indicators can be considered indexes of social or economic status or process that indirectly reflect social welfare. As indirect measures they need to be integrated or aggregated with other measures of welfare. How people allocate their time can be considered to be such a measure. In reflecting on the organization of his volume, Social Indicators 1973 (U.S. Office of Management and Budget 1975) Tunstall contends that time was the most frequent common denominator of the social indicators available at the time.

Thus, a national time-use survey, designed to represent a "census" of typical everyday behavior across the country, will naturally interest a broad academic and policy-making audience. Data from the first comprehensive time-budget study in the United States, conducted by the Survey Research Center in 1965-66, have been utilized by a wide variety of government and private organizations interested in accurate data on public allocation of time to transportation, child care, housework, volunteer activities, and the mass media. Our time-use data have been employed to estimate the accumulated radiation hazards from nuclear-powered pacemakers, the accumulated noise pollution to which an average American may be exposed on a typical day, the departures from "normal day's activities" caused by accidents or injuries (in legal cases involving injuries), the effect of household technology on housework, the amounts of leisure time available to people in various social and economic classes, and the inaccuracies in the standard rating service figures on television and other mass media exposure.

Tunstall's comment that time may be the most attractive social indicator "when we have no obvious direct measurement for a social concern," does highlight a major limitation of time data. Analyses of time use require some identification of the extent to which activity patterns involve time use as outputs or as inputs. As economists have long argued, it is sometimes difficult to tell whether an activity is an input and when it should be viewed as an output, or as a combination of some input and some output. For example, is television viewing an output reflecting the consumption of leisure time, or is it an input to the viewer's stock of cultural and educational capital? Is housework time an input that is essential to the production of a set of outputs, or is it principally an input into the maintenance of family role expectations or obligations? These are not simple questions, and in part the answers clearly depend on the perceptions of the individual engaging in the activity.

Some researchers, like Gutenschwager (1973), have suggested that time be treated solely as an input, with the output in the form of choice of activities, being some combination of preferences and constraints within the population. As such, time can be viewed as a basic human resource with the attractive property noted earlier that, unlike other national resources, it is equally distributed to all members of society (after correcting, of course, for differences in life expectancy). Inequalities thus only arise from the energy levels people invest and the productivity they derive from these constant amounts of time; this is also reflected in the phenomenon of secondary activities such as the use of time to simultaneously accomplish two or more objectives, for example, housework and television.

To the degree that respondents in a time-diary study do not attach any underlying motive to their daily activities, time data share many of the properties of an "unobtrusive" measure, that is, one in which the act of measurement does not systematically bias the recorded observation. While time-budget survey data are essentially neutral, this neutrality appeals to social scientists in many disciplines, with economists being able to attach "hard" monetary value to various uses of time, and psychologists and sociologists "soft" value such as personal satisfactions and enjoyment.

Four major types of social-psychological comparisons of time-use data, illustrating their widespread societal implications, can be distinguished: cross-time, cross-sectional, cross-national, and cross-activity. The cross-time focus is central to social indicator interests and the availability of properly sampled time diaries provides a most systematic perspective on social change. Szalai (1966) presented a pioneering exercise of this type which compared time-budget data from the Soviet Union between 1924 and 1959. The most extensive cross-time analysis of U.S. data was made by Robinson and Converse (1972), when the 1965-66 data provided the opportunity to examine quantitatively such questions as: Do people now have more free time available than they did 30 or 50 years ago? Have housewives benefited from reductions in the workweek of their husbands? With the collection of future time-use data we will be in the position to judge how the influx of better educated young people will affect the use of recreational and educational facilities. How will our "nation on wheels" be affected by energy shortages? To what extent can one explain trends in birth rate and labor force participation by considerations of the value of time?

The other three types of time-use comparisons also provide insights into questions raised in the context of social indicators:

1. Cross-sectional: How is time spent differently by older and by younger people? What is the impact of having a child or additional children on a person's daily life? Are differentials in social and economic well-being decreased or increased by taking nonmarket activities into account? What are the societal consequences of people having too much or too little free time available?

2. Cross-national: The availability of standardized time data from 2,000 residents in each of 12 countries in the Szalai et al (1972) volume has made it possible to identify objectively distinctive features of American daily life. How are our methods of raising children different from societies in which there is more dependence on day-care facilities and grandparents? Are Americans so rushed that they get less sleep or spend less time eating than people in other countries? Is social life more constrained or less active in this country? How much has television been responsible for this state of affairs?

3. Cross-activity: A unique property of time as an indicator is that, if time is saved or lost on one activity, time devoted to other activities will either increase or decrease as a result. Gutenschwager (1973) has contended that "Recurrent inventories of time use patterns may be the only way, ultimately, to assess the effects of public policy on behavioral patterns in time and space."

Thus, comparison of time-use data of household appliance owners and nonowners—or better still, of the same people before and after they purchase appliances—can indicate whether appliances do indeed save time and, if they do, what use is made of the time thus saved. Similarly, one can assess the impact of the four-day workweek or flexible work hours on leisure and other uses of time. With regard to a more vital issue currently facing the country, how will Americans adjust to energy shortages, particularly to the time that may be lost because of 55 m.p.h. speed limits and higher fuel costs?

A brief review of findings from the 1965-66 study that illustrates time-use data of these four types of comparisons is provided in Chapter 7.

Such a set of results, of course, represents only a highlighting of the portrait of American daily life that has been generated by time-budget research. A general analysis model underlying these analyses is examined next.

A SOCIAL-PSYCHOLOGICAL
CONCEPTUAL FRAMEWORK

In order to put into perspective and to gain a greater understanding of the myriad factors that determine the allocation of time, interest in time use shifts rapidly away from the single distribution of time figures to more detailed analysis of their internal structure. We have been guided in our analyses of the 1965-66 time-use data by the general social-psychological model in Figure 2.1. In this conceptual framework, time use is portrayed as being determined by four sets of factors: personal, role, resource, and environmental. No attempt has been made to specify the mathematical functions related to these sets of factors, although in Chapters 3 and 4 several multiple regression analyses are undertaken that rest on certain assumptions about the additive nature of the influence these factors have on time use.

Most basic of the factors in the model are the personal factors, such as the person's sex and age. These, in turn, are linked closely to the social role requirements that people assume, the main time-relevant ones being imposed by the responsibilities of employment, marriage, and parenthood.

Role factors, in turn, interact with two other sets of factors: (1) environmental factors, such as societal scheduling or ecological location, and (2) resources, such as income and home technology. While one can cite a host of examples to the contrary, environmental factors may be seen for the most part as constraints on the individual's use of time, and resources may be seen as largely providing more options for the use of time.

All four sets of factors are treated as mutually interacting. Thus the role factor of employment may relate to the personal factor of sex (or age) differentially in that women (or younger people) are less likely to be employed than men (or the middle aged). In the same way, the resource factor of income may affect time use directly by allowing the individual to purchase leisure goods or services, for example, or it can act indirectly through the personal factor of education, or in fact be affected by the factor of education in its relation to time use. The greater participation in reading and culture by high income individuals is an example of the latter processes, particularly when this difference is shown to be primarily

FIGURE 2.1

Schematic Model of Factors Affecting
Time Use

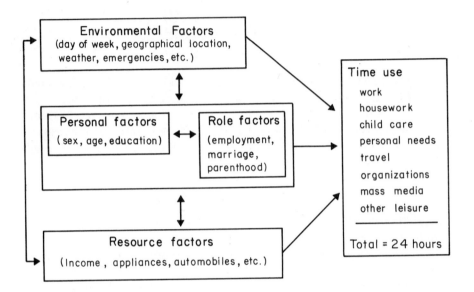

Source: Compiled by the author.

a function of more education of high income people rather than a
correlate of income per se.

While personal, role, resource, and environmental factors
all directly affect the way time is spent, so does time itself. For
example, quite apart from the effects of these four factors, individual decisions about time allocation, for example, how long to work
or whether to go out for an evening of entertainment, ultimately
determine how much time is available for other activities. As
Linder (1970, p. 12) notes, work time "affects both the supply and
the demand for time on other activities." Ultimate answers to the
question of how much time is determined by these first four factors,
as opposed to the fifth factor of basic time choices themselves, may

have to await an ingenious field study designed to assess and control the workings of Parkinson's famous law.

Nonetheless, it is possible in the meantime to examine, with the data at hand, variations in uses of time in the 1965-66 study associated with, and perhaps attributable to, the four sets of factors on the left in Figure 2.1. The full list of available background variables from the 1965-66 study is listed in Table 2.1, with those employed in the analysis in the next section of this chapter under- lined. One major impression about the impact of the four sets of factors, based on the analysis presented in the tables of this chapter, is that personal factors explained surprisingly little variance in how time was spent. Presumed differences by age, racial background, religion, area of upbringing, and attitudinal factors by and large did not materialize.

The major exceptions are the factors of education and sex. The better educated, for example, put their leisure time to more active uses, as reflected most notably in their aversion to television. Sex, moreover, was associated with greater differences in time use than any other variable in Table 2.1 except the day of the week. The woman's bond to the household can be no more clearly documented than in time diaries, a topic examined in particular detail in Chapter 6. Here it is found that, even if employed and single, more women than men find themselves (1) working shorter hours, (2) taking less advantage of continuing education opportunities, and (3) otherwise confined to the household for one or two more hours every day. At the same time, many of the differences associated with sex are induced by the different role demands that women undertake, again pointing to the frequent interactions between the various sets of factors in Table 2.1.

As a group, however, role factors exercised more control over time use than any other set of factors in Figure 2.1. Of the three major factors in this group, employment predominated over marriage and parenthood; becoming employed can commit up to half of one's total waking hours to job-related matters. Of the other two factors (and perhaps not surprisingly to anyone who has been through the cycle), becoming a parent had slightly more effect on time use than becoming a spouse. Both parental and marital roles demanded proportionately more from women than from men, particularly in the matter of child rearing—a phenomenon examined in detail in Chapter 3.

Other role-related factors, such as type of occupation or employment status of the spouse, are generally associated with minimal differences in time-diary figures. One exception, of course, is the role of student, although its main effect is directly on education-related activities rather than obligatory or leisure activities.

TABLE 2.1

Variables Included in the 1965–66 Study
According to Type of Factor*

Personal Factors	Role Factors	Environmental Factors	Resource Factors
Job satisfaction (11–13)	Employment (1)	Season of year (P1)	Workweek hours (9)
Housework satisfaction (14–20)	Variable work schedule (4)	Day of week (P1)	Friends (P32–36)
Annual leisure (27)	Self-employment (6)	Weather (P2a)	Own home (R7)
Feel rushed (P29)	Work shift (7)	Day unusual (P9, P11)	Plumbing facilities (R9)
New friends (P37)	Other jobs (8)	Vacation days (P10)	Telephone (R10)
Leisure satisfaction (P38)	Marital status (R4)	Geographic location (cover)	Radio or TV (R11–12)
Life satisfaction (P41)	Number of children (R5)	Size of place (cover)	Watch or clock (R12–14)
Personal competence (P42–44)	Age of children (R5)	Distance to work (R21)	Household help (R15)
Sex (R1)	Spouse's employment (R6)	Type of dwelling (R30)	Books (R16)
Race (R2)	Continuing education (R24)	Type of neighborhood (R42)	Yard or garden (R17–18)
Religion (R22)	Number of adults (R37)	Distance to city center (R43)	Motor vehicles (R20)
Education (R23)			Income (R28–29)
Rural upbringing (R25)			
Rural-urban preference (R27)			
Age (cover sheet)			

*Study question number in parentheses; major analysis variables in this chapter are underlined.

Source: Compiled by the author.

Day of the week is obviously the dominant environmental factor. Also people who reported their day as "unusual" in any way recorded less work and less television in their diaries as a response to unusual social, child-care, or organizational responsibilities. Regional and urban planners might be surprised, however, at how little difference the environmental variables in our 1965–66 study seemed to make in how time is spent. Not only were systematic and consistent differences between metropolitan and suburban areas difficult to detect, but so also were differences by region, weather conditions, and season of the year (although data were not collected during the winter and summer months). No startling differences emerged at the more local ecological level, by variables such as type of dwelling (house vs. apartment), size of the yard, or type of neighborhood (residential vs. primarily commercial). Outside of the expected longer commuting times, distance from work had no patterned impact on other uses of time; neither did distance from the center of the nearest city.

The lack of expected differences by resource factors was even more surprising. One trademark of the 20th century has been the burgeoning technology of household equipment designed to relieve women of the burdens of housework. One may well argue that the meals are better prepared or that the clothes are cleaner due to the use of modern technology, but it is difficult to find evidence that the presence of more sophisticated ovens or washing machines in the household has brought with them lower time input into such activities. Moreover, while automobiles undoubtedly provide their owners with greater mobility and flexibility, the time their owners spend in transit is not much less than that of nonowners. Even those few women who enjoyed the luxury of outside household help appeared to spend just about as much time doing housework as those without help. Finally, while people with higher incomes occasionally seem to have a "richer" or more cultural use of their leisure time, this may be just as well explained by their higher educational levels as by their higher income.

One important exception to the conclusion of the lack of impact of household technology on time use involves television, which has had a tremendous impact on time use as discussed in Chapter 6. Further discussion of the basis for these conclusions can be found in the detailed tables in the next section of this chapter and in the discussion in subsequent chapters.

BASIC SOCIAL AND ECONOMIC PREDICTORS
OF TIME USAGE

People's use of their time is determined by many factors. The list of possible determinants is almost endless, but Table 2.2 lists those we attempted to identify and measure in the 1965-66 study as most common to a cross-section population. While most consisted of standard survey background items, such as marital status, sex, and education, many had not been used often in survey analysis, such as day of the week, season of the year, life satisfaction, and availability of household help. In this section, we attempt to isolate the more important bivariate predictors of the way that people spend their time, enlarging somewhat on the brief discussion of this topic in the earlier sections of this chapter.

The analyses described here again pertain to the aggregate rather than the individual level. Since many of the distributions of time use for a particular activity category are not normally distributed and because so many comparisons will be made, we have not attempted to calculate the usual tests of statistical signifi-

TABLE 2.2

Total Sample: Variation in Time Use by Four Types of Factors

	Personal								Role					
Variable	Sex	Educa-tion	Age	Race	Reli-gion	Life satis-faction	Enjoy house-work	Inter-est in new people	Em-ploy-ment	Mari-tal Sta-tus	No. of Child-ren	Age of Child-ren	Cont. Edu-cation	Shift work
Direction of Variable	Male	More	Old-er	Non-white	Cath.	More	Yes	Yes	Yes	Not mar-ried	More	Young	Yes	Yes
1. Main job	+++	0	0	0	0	0	0	0	+++	0	-	0	0	0
2. Second job	++	0	-	+	0	--	0	++	+++	0	0	0	0	0
3. At work, other	+	-	0	0	0	0	0	0	+++	0	0	0	0	0
4. Travel to job	+	0	0	0	0	0	0	0	+++	0	0	0	0	0
5. Cooking	---	--	+	0	0	0	0	-	---	0	+	0	0	0
6. Home chores	---	--	0	0	0	0	+	0	---	0	+	0	-	0
7. Laundry	---	--	+	0	0	0	0	0	---	+	++	0	-	0
8. Marketing	-	0	0	0	+	-	0	0	--	0	0	0	0	0
9. Garden, animal	-	0	0	--	0	-	-	0	--	-	0	--	0	0
10. Errands, shopping	-	0	+	--	-	+	+	+	-	0	0	--	0	+
11. Other house	-	0	0	--	0	+	0	0	--	0	0	0	-	-
12. Child care	---	0	--	0	+	0	-	0	---	-	+++	+++	-	0
13. Child inter-action	-	0	-	0	0	-	0	0	---	--	+	0	0	+
14. Personal care	--	0	0	+	0	0	0	0	0	+	0	0	0	-
15. Eating	+	0	+	-	0	0	0	0	-	0	0	-	0	0
16. Sleep	0	-	0	-	0	-	0	-	0	0	-	0	0	0
17. Personal travel	-	+	+	-	0	0	0	0	-	0	0	-	+	0
18. Leisure travel	0	+	-	+	0	0	0	0	-	0	0	0	+	-
19. Study	++	+++	--	-	-	+	0	0	0	+	-	--	+++	0
20. Religion	--	0	+	++	0	+	0	0	--	0	0	-	0	--
21. Organizations	-	++	0	--	0	0	0	+	---	0	0	-	+	0
22. Radio	+	+	0	0	0	0	0	0	++	0	0	-	-	--
23. Television	++	--	0	+	0	-	0	-	--	0	0	0	--	0
24. Reading	0	+	0	-	0	0	-	0	--	0	-	0	0	--
25. Read paper	++	0	++	-	0	-	0	-	-	-	-	-	-	-
26. Read magazine	+	+	0	-	0	0	0	0	-	0	0	0	--	0
27. Read books	-	+	0	0	0	-	0	-	-	0	0	-	0	+
28. Movies	++	+	-	-	0	-	-	+	+	+	-	0	++	0
29-30. Visiting	--	0	-	0	0	-	0	+	--	+	0	+	-	0
31. Conversation	--	0	0	0	0	0	0	+	--	0	+	0	0	+
32. Active sports	+++	0	0	-	+	+	0	+	+	0	0	-	0	0
33. Outdoors	+++	0	0	-	0	0	0	0	-	0	0	0	0	0
34. Entertainment	0	++	0	0	0	0	-	+	+	0	0	0	+	-
35. Cultural events	++	+	0	-	0	0	0	0	0	+	-	-	0	0
36. Resting	---	-	0	++	-	0	0	0	-	0	0	0	0	-
37. Other leisure	---	+	++	--	-	0	0	+	--	0	--	--	0	-
Free Time	0	0	-	0	0	0	0	0	---	0	0	-	0	0

+++ Extremely above average
++ Considerably above average
+ Somewhat above average
0 Average (or curvilinear relation)

	Environment										Resource			
Day of week	Sea-son	Wea-ther	Day unusual	Region	City suburb	City size	Dist. to city	Dist. to work	Type of dwel-ling	In-come	House-hold help	TV	Auto
Week-end	Fall	Poor	Yes	South	City	Large	Fur-ther	Fur-ther	Non-house	More	Yes	Yes	> 1
---	0	0	--	0	-	0	0	0	0	0	+	0	+
0	0	0	-	-	-	0	0	0	0	-	-	+	0
--	0	0	-	0	0	0	0	0	0	0	0	0	0
---	-	0	0	+	+	+	0	++	0	+	0	0	0
+	0	0	0	-	0	-	0	0	0	-	0	0	0
+	0	0	0	0	0	0	0	-	0	0	0	0	0
+	0	0	0	0	0	-	0	--	0	-	-	0	-
0	0	0	0	0	+	0	+	0	0	0	0	0	0
0	-	0	0	-	0	0	0	0	-	0	+	0	0
0	+	0	+	-	0	0	0	0	0	+	+	0	0
++	++	0	++	0	0	0	0	0	-	0	0	0	0
0	0	+	++	0	0	0	0	0	0	-	0	0	-
-	0	-	+	0	-	0	0	0	0	0	-	-	--
+	0	0	0	0	0	0	0	0	0	0	0	0	0
0	0	0	0	+	0	+	0	0	0	0	0	0	0
+++	0	0	0	-	0	0	0	0	0	0	0	0	0
+	0	0	0	0	0	+	0	0	0	+	++	0	+
++	+	0	0	0	0	0	0	0	+	+	0	0	-
--	+	0	+	-	0	0	0	0	+	+	+	0	0
+++	0	0	-	0	0	0	0	+	-	0	0	-	-
0	+	+	++	+	0	0	0	0	0	0	-	+	0
0	+	0	0	0	0	0	0	0	0	0	+	0	-
++	-	+	--	0	--	0	0	0	0	--	--	+++	-
-	0	0	0	+	+	+	0	0	++	+	-	0	+
++	0	0	0	0	0	0	0	0	-	+	+	+	+
+	0	0	0	-	-	0	0	0	--	+	0	0	0
0	-	0	0	0	0	+	0	0	+	+	+	0	-
++	0	0	0	+	+	0	-	0	+	0	0	+	---
+++	-	0	++	0	0	0	0	0	+	0	+	-	-
0	0	+	++	0	+	0	+	0	0	-	0	0	0
0	0	+	0	0	0	0	0	0	-	0	-	--	+
++	0	-	+	0	0	0	0	0	-	+	0	0	0
++	0	0	0	-	-	0	0	0	0	+	0	0	0
++	0	-	0	0	0	+	0	0	0	+	+	0	0
+	+	0	-	0	0	0	0	0	0	0	0	0	0
0	+	0	0	0	0	0	0	0	-	0	0	0	+
+++	0	0	++	0	0	-	-	0	+	0	0	--	-

--- Extremely below average
-- Considerably below average
- Somewhat below average
X Data not collected

Source: Compiled by the author from the Study of Americans' Use of Time (1965-66).

33

cance on these data.* The full time-use figures themselves are available in the Statistical Appendix in Szalai et al. (1972).

It will be noted that the 96-category scheme used to code the activity data has been condensed to 37 categories in Table 2.2 to simplify analysis; the exact procedure for doing so is described in the Appendix. The various predictors which appear as columns in Table 2.2 are grouped into four sets: personal, role, environmental, and resource, corresponding to the model outlined in Figure 2.1.

The entries in Table 2.2 are to be read as follows: Depending on the "direction" of the variable, a "+" sign for a particular activity means that individuals with that characteristic spend somewhat more time on that activity than other individuals, "++" signifies notably more time, and "+++" signifies considerably more time. Thus in Table 2.2, there is a "+" sign at the intersection of sex and television, which is reflective of time data that show men reporting 105 minutes per day of television viewing as a primary activity compared to 79 minutes for women. The "++" sign at the intersection of number of children and laundry reflects the 19 minutes spent by those with no children doing laundry as compared to 21 minutes for those with one child, 29 minutes for those with two children, and 38 minutes for those with three or more children.

The "-," "--," and "---" notations have parallel meanings for lower than average time allocations, and a 0 indicates that time that is neither particularly above nor below the allocation for the sample as a whole or that some sort of curvilinear relation exists. Thus the "--" sign at the intersection of day of the week and study reflects the 2 and 4 minutes of average class and homework time reported on Saturday and Sunday as compared to almost 12 minutes for regular days of the week. Thus, these designations were necessarily derived subjectively and readers interested in single comparisons or hypotheses should supplement these judgments with their own, using data in the multinational volume or the tabulations described earlier in the acknowledgments of this book.

The ratings in Table 2.2 actually represent derivations from Tables 2.4, 2.5, and 2.6; here the same judgments were performed separately on time data for men, for employed women, and for

---

*For the reader interested in these significance data, we have provided a list of participation rates and standard deviations of time-use figures in Table 2.3. It should be noted that these figures are weighted to offset the differences of the day of the week in people's diaries, but outside of sex and employment status none of the other factors in Table 2.3 were taken into account; this is what the MCA results in Chapters 3 and 4 provide.

TABLE 2.3

Differences in Time Use by Sex and Employment Status[a]

| | Percent of Time Spent by | | | Total Sample (N = 1,244) | | |
| | Employed Men (N = 520) | Employed Women (N = 342) | House- wives (N = 355) | | | Percent partici- pating |
	All time[b]	All time[b]	All time[b]	Mean	Standard deviation	
1. Main job	.25	.19	—	236.1	239.0	51
2. Second job	.01	—	—	4.8	36.7	2
3. At work, other	.01	.01	—	12.0	22.7	33
4. Travel to job	.03	.02	—	25.9	35.9	51
Total Work	.30	.22	—	278.8		
5. Cooking	.01	.03	.07	43.8	52.7	61
6. Home chores	.01	.05	.09	57.2	74.1	61
7. Laundry	—[c]	.02	.04	25.3	55.1	30
8. Marketing	.01	.01	.01	13.6	30.1	34
Total Housework	.03	.11	.21	139.9		
9. Garden, animal care	—	—	.01	3.3	12.9	12
10. Errands, shopping	.01	.01	.01	17.6	44.1	31
11. Other house	.01	.01	.02	22.7	54.9	38
Total Household Obligations	.02	.02	.04	43.6		
12. Child care	—	.01	.04	22.5	53.8	31
13. Other child	.01	.01	.01	10.0	30.7	19
Total Child Care	.01	.02	.05	32.5		
14. Personal care	.04	.05	.05	67.8	47.4	98
15. Eating	.06	.05	.05	80.8	41.8	98
16. Sleep	.32	.33	.33	459.9	97.1	99
Total Personal Needs	.42	.43	.43	608.5		
17. Personal travel	.02	.02	.03	30.0	39.6	64
18. Leisure travel	.01	.01	.01	17.4	31.2	43
Total Nonwork Travel	.03	.03	.04	47.4		
19. Study	.01	.01	.01	10.5	57.9	5
20. Religion	.01	.01	.01	9.6	34.5	12
21. Organizations	—	—	.01	6.2	32.9	6
Total Study and Participation	.02	.02	.03	26.3		
22. Radio	—	—	—	3.8	18.2	8
23. TV (home)	.07	.05	.07	⎰88.9	⎰98.9	⎰70
24. TV (away)	—	—	—	⎱	⎱	⎱
25. Read paper	.02	.01	.01	22.8	31.6	49
26. Read magazine	.01	—	.01	5.9	21.3	11
27. Read books	—	—	.01	5.6	24.5	7
28. Movies	—	—	—	3.4	25.2	2
Total Mass Media	.10	.06	.10	130.4		
29. Social (home)	.01	.02	.02	⎰62.2	⎰101.7	⎰51
30. Social (away)	.03	.02	.03	⎱	⎱	⎱
31. Conversation	.01	.01	.02	18.2	35.3	41
32. Active sports	.01	—	—	5.4	26.9	6
33. Outdoors	—	—	—	2.6	19.1	3
34. Entertainment	—	.01	—	5.3	30.1	4
35. Cultural events	—	—	—	0.6	8.1	1
36. Resting	—	.01	.01	19.6	45.3	29
37. Other leisure	.01	.01	.02	18.2	45.2	26
Total leisure	.07	.08	.10	132.2		
Total	1.00	1.00	1.00			
Total Free Time (18-37)	.20	.17	.23	306.3		

[a]National data from the 1965-66 study.

[b]Percent of total time.

[c]A dash indicates less than .5 percent.

Source: Compiled by the author from the Study of Americans' Use of Time (1965-66).

TABLE 2.4

Employed Men: Variations in Time Use by Four Types of Factors*

Variable	Personal								Role					
	Sex	Education	Age	Race	Religion	Life satisfaction	Enjoy housework	Interest in new people	Employment	Marital Status	No. of Children	Age of Children	Cont. Education	Shift work
Direction of Variable	Male	More	Older	Nonwhite	Cath.	More	Yes	Yes	Yes	Not married	More	Young	Yes	Yes
1. Main job	+++	-	+	+	-	++	X	0	+++	0	0	+	0	+
2. Second job	++	0	-	+	+	--	X	++	+++	-	0	+	+	0
3. At work, other	+	-	-	+	0	0	X	0	+++	0	0	0	0	+
4. Travel to job	++	0	+	+	0	+	X	0	+++	-	0	0	0	0
5. Cooking	---	0	++	-	-	-	X	-	---	++	0	-	0	0
6. Home chores	---	0	0	-	0	-	X	0	---	+	0	0	-	-
7. Laundry	---	0	++	+	-	0	X	--	---	+++	0	-	0	+
8. Marketing	--	0	+	--	+	-	X	0	--	0	0	+	0	0
9. Garden, animal	--	0	0		0	-	X	0	--	-	-	0	0	0
10. Errands, shopping	--	0	+	--	-	++	X	+	-	0	0	--	-	+
11. Other house	-	0	+	-	0	0	X	-	--	-	0	-	0	--
12. Child care	---	+	--	--	+	0	X	0	---	-	++	++	0	-
13. Child interaction	-	0	--	-	+	0	X	0	---	--	++	+	0	0
14. Personal care	--	0	0	+	0	0	X	0	+	+	0	0	-	-
15. Eating	++	0	0	-	0	0	X	0	-	0	0	0	0	0
16. Sleep	0	0	0	--	0	-	X	-	-	0	0	0	0	0
17. Personal travel	-	0	+	-	0	0	X	+	-	-	0	-	0	0
18. Leisure travel	0	0	-	+	0	0	X	+	-	+	0	0	0	-
19. Study	++	+++	--	0	0	0	X	0	0	+	0	-	+++	-
20. Religion	--	-	+	++	+	+	X	+	--	0	0	--	0	--
21. Organizations	+	++	-	--	0	-	X	++	---	0	+	-	++	0
22. Radio	+	0	0	--	0	0	X	++	++	0	-	0	--	0
23. Television	+	--	0	0	0	--	X	-	-	--	+	+	--	0
24. Reading	0	++	-	--	-	0	X	+	--	++	-	0	0	--
25. Read paper	++	0	++	0	0	0	X	-	-	-	-	0	-	0
26. Read magaz.	+	++	+	--	-	0	X	--	-	-	-	-	-	-
27. Read books	-	++	0	0	+	-	X	-	--	+	0	-	--	+
28. Movies	++	++	-	--	+	--	X	++	+	+	--	0	++	0
29-30. Visiting	-	-	-	++	0	--	X	++	--	++	0	+	0	0
31. Conversation	--	0	0	+	0	-	X	0	-	-	+	0	0	+
32. Active sports	+++	+	0	0	+	0	X	++	+	+	-	0	+	0
33. Outdoors	+++	0	0	0	-	0	X	0	-	--	+	-	0	+
34. Entertainment	0	++	0	0	0	+	X	0	+	+	-	-	0	0
35. Cultural events	++	++	0	--	-	-	X	0	0	++	-	-	0	0
36. Resting	---	--	0	++	-	+	X	0	-	-	0	0	--	0
37. Other leisure	---	++	0	--	-	-	X	+	-	0	--	0	-	--
Free Time	0	0	--	+	0	-	X	0	---	+	0	0	0	0

	Environment										Resource			
Day of week	Sea-son	Wea-ther	Day unusual	Region	City suburb	City size	Dist. to city	Dist. to work	Type of dwel-ling	In-come	House-hold help	TV	Auto
Week-end	Fall	Poor	Yes	South	City	Large	Fur-ther	Fur-ther	Non-house	More	Yes	Yes	>1
---	0	0	--	0	0	0	0	0	0	0	0	+	+
0	-	0	-	0	0	0	-	-	0	-	-	+	0
--	-	0	-	0	0	0	0	0	-	0	-	+	0
---	-	0	0	+	++	++	0	++	-	+	0	+	0
++	+	0	0	-	0	0	0	0	+	0	+	-	0
+++	+	-	0	0	0	0	0	-	0	0	+	0	+
++	+	+	0	0	0	-	-	--	+	-	0	0	0
++	0	0	0	0	0	0	+	+	0	0	0	0	--
-	-	0	0	-	0	0	0	+	-	-	0	+	+
++	+	0	++	--	0	0	0	0	0	0	++	-	0
+++	+	+	+	0	0	0	+	0	0	+	--	+	0
++	0	+	+	0	0	0	+	0	+	0	0	0	-
+	0	0	++	0	0	0	0	0	0	0	-	0	--
+	0	0	+	0	0	0	0	0	+	0	0	0	0
0	0	0	0	0	0	+	0	0	0	0	0	0	0
+++	0	0	0	0	0	0	0	0	0	0	+	0	0
++	0	0	0	0	+	++	0	+	+	+	++	-	0
++	0	+	+	0	+	0	0	0	0	0	0	--	-
--	++	0	++	-	0	0	0	0	+	0	+	--	-
+++	0	+	0	+	0	0	-	0	-	-	0	--	--
0	0	++	++	0	-	0	+	0	+	0	--	++	0
+	+	0	0	0	+	+	0	0	0	0	0	0	0
++	-	0	-	0	--	0	0	0	0	--	--	+++	-
-	0	0	-	0	+	++	+	-	++	++	0	-	+
++	0	0	0	+	0	0	0	0	-	+	+	++	0
+	0	0	0	0	-	0	0	0	0	++	++	++	0
0	-	0	-	+	+	++	0	0	++	+	0	0	--
+++	++	0	--	+	+	+	--	--	+	0	0	++	--
+++	-	+	++	0	0	0	0	0	0	0	++	--	0
0	0	++	++	0	++	0	++	0	0	0	0	0	0
-	0	++	0	0	+	0	0	+	0	+	--	---	+
+++	++	--	++	-	0	--	0	0	--	0	0	+	0
++	0	0	0	--	0	0	0	0	0	+	++	-	0
++	+	--	0	+	+	+++	0	0	+	0	++	+	0
0	+	0	--	0	0	-	0	0	0	0	-	+	0
0	+	0	-	-	-	0	0	0	0	0	0	--	0
+++	0	0	++	0	--	-	-	0	0	0	0	--	--

*See Table 2.2 for key of symbols.

Source: Compiled by the author from the
Study of Americans' Use of Time (1965-66).

TABLE 2.5

Employed Women: Variations in Time Use by Four Types of Factors*

	Personal								Role					
Variable / Direction of Variable	Sex / Male	Education / More	Age / Older	Race / Nonwhite	Religion / Cath.	Life satisfaction / More	Enjoy housework / Yes	Interest in new people / Yes	Employment / Yes	Marital Status / Not married	No. of Children / More	Age of Children / Young	Cont. Education / Yes	Shift work / Yes
1. Main job		++	0	--	+	--	-	0		0	--	--	--	--
2. Second job		0	-	++	-	--	0	++		+	0	-	0	-
3. At work, other		-	0	0	0	0	-	0		+	-	-	0	0
4. Travel to job		0	0	0	0	-	0	0		+	-	-	0	0
5. Cooking		--	+	-	0	0	0	--		--	++	0	+	0
6. Home chores		--	+	++	0	0	+	-		--	+	+	0	+
7. Laundry		--	0	0	0	+	0	0		--	++	0	0	0
8. Marketing		0	0	0	0	0	0	+		0	0	-	0	+
9. Garden, animal		+	0	--	-	-	-	+		-	0	--	0	-
10. Errands, shopping		-	0	-	0	-	+	+		0	+	0	0	++
11. Other house		0	0	--	0	++	0	+		-	+	++	0	0
12. Child care		--	--	+	0	0	-	0		-	+++	+++	-	++
13. Child interaction		-	++	+	-	-	0	-		0	-	+		+++
14. Personal care		0	0	+	0	0	0	0		+	0	-	0	-
15. Eating		0	+	-	0	-	+	0		0	0	-	0	-
16. Sleep		-	0	-	0	0	0	-		0	-	+	+	0
17. Personal travel		+	-	-	-	-	0	0		++	0		+	+
18. Leisure travel		+	--	++	0	+	0	0		+	+	+	+	--
19. Study		++	--	--	-	++	++	++		+++	--	-	++	0
20. Religion		0	0	+	-	+	0	0		++	0	-	0	-
21. Organizations		++	++	--	+	0	0	0		++	0	+	--	+
22. Radio		++	++	++	+	--	0	---		++	0	--	0	---
23. Television		--	++	++	0	0	0	-		0	-	0	--	0
24. Reading		0	0	-	0	0	--	0		+	--	0	+	---
25. Read paper		0	++	-	-	--	0	0		-	--	--	-	--
26. Read magazine		+	0	+	-	0	0	0		-	-	0	0	
27. Read books		+	++	+	-	--	+	0		0	0	-	0	+
28. Movies		0	--	+	-	0	-	0		++	++	--	++	-
29–30. Visiting		+	--	-	-	++	+	-		++	0	++	-	0
31. Conversation		0	-	0	-	0	0	+		0	+	+	0	++
32. Active sports		++	0	--	0	++	0	0		0	+	-	-	0
33. Outdoors		0	-	-	0	-	0	+		-	-	-	-	
34. Entertainment		++	--	++	-	--	-	++		+	+	+	+	--
35. Cultural events		-	-	-	+	0	-	0		0	-	0	-	-
36. Resting		-	++	++	--	0	0	0		++	-	-	+	--
37. Other leisure		0	++	--	0	-	0	+		0	0	-	0	0
Free Time		++	0	++	-	++	0	+		++	--	-	0	0

38

				Environment							Resource			
Day of week	Sea-son	Wea-ther	Day unusual	Region	City suburb	City size	Dist. to city	Dist. to work	Type of dwel-ling	In-come	House-hold help	TV	Auto
Week-end	Fall	Poor	Yes	South	City	Large	Fur-ther	Fur-ther	Non-house	More	Yes	Yes	> 1
---	0	0	--	-	--	-	0	0	0	0	+	0	0
-	0	-	-	--	--	-	0	0	0	--	-	+	-
---	0	0	-	0	+	0	0	0	0	0	0	0	0
---	-	-	-	+	+	+	0	++	0	+	-	0	0
++	0	+	-	-	0	-	0	-	0	--	+	0	0
0	0	0	-	0	0	+	0	--	-	0	-	-	-
++	-	0	-	0	--	--	0	--	-	--	-	-	--
0	-	0	0	0	+	0	0	0	-	0	0	+	+
++	0	0	0	0	+	0	0	0	0	+	+	-	0
-	++	0	-	+	0	+	+	0	-	0	0	0	0
++	+++	0	++	-	0	0	0	0	0	0	0	-	0
--	0	++	++	+	--	0	0	0	-	-	0	--	0
--	0	-	0	-	-	0	0	-	-	0	--	--	--
++	0	-	0	0	0	+	0	0	0	0	0	+	0
0	0	0	0	+	+	+	0	0	0	+	0	0	+
+++	0	0	0	-	0	0	0	0	0	0	0	+	-
0	+	0	0	+	0	0	+	0	0	+	++	0	+
+++	+	0	0	+	0	0	0	+	+	+	0	++	-
--	0	-	0	-	0	0	-	0	++	0	0	++	--
+++	+	0	--	0	0	0	0	++	-	0	0	+	-
++	++	0	++	++	++	+	0	-	+	-	0	+	-
-	+	0	+	0	0	-	-	0	-	+	++	++	--
++	-	+	--	-	--	0	0	-	0	--	--	+++	--
-	+	0	0	+	++	0	+	0	0	+	---	+	+
++	0	0	+	0	0	0	-	0	0	++	++	0	+
++	0	0	0	-	-	0	0	0	--	0	0	-	0
-	-	0	+	0	0	+	0	0	0	0	0	++	0
++	-	-	++	+	++	0	0	++	+	0	0	-	-
+++	0	0	++	0	++	0	0	+	++	0	0	+	-
+	0	0	++	0	+	0	0	0	0	0	0	-	0
0	-	+	0	0	0	0	0	0	0	0	+	-	+
++	-	-	0	0	+	++	0	0	+	+	0	0	0
++	+	-	+	0	-	0	0	+	+	+	-	+	0
++	0	0	0	0	0	0	0	0	-	0	0	0	0
+	++	0	0	0	-	0	0	0	0	+	+	0	0
0	+	0	+	0	+	0	0	-	0	+	+	0	++
+++	0	0	+	++	++	0	0	0	+	0	0	0	0

*See Table 2.2 for key of symbols.
Source: Compiled by the author from the
Study of Americans' Use of Time (1965-66).

TABLE 2.6

Nonemployed Women: Variations in Time Use by Four Types of Factors*

Variable	Personal								Role					
	Sex	Educa-tion	Age	Race	Reli-gion	Life satis-faction	Enjoy house-work	Inter-est in new people	Em-ploy-ment	Mari-tal Sta-tus	No. of Child-ren	Age of Child-ren	Cont. Edu-cation	Shift work
Direction of Variable	Male	More	Old-er	Non-white	Cath.	More	Yes	Yes	Yes	Not mar-ried	More	Young	Yes	Yes
1. Main job	0	0	0	+	-	0	0	0	0	0	0	0	+	X
2. Second job	0	0	0	0	0	0	0	0	0	0	0	0	0	X
3. At work, other	0	0	0	0	0	0	0	0	0	0	0	0	0	X
4. Travel to job	0	0	0	0	0	0	0	0	0	0	0	0	+	X
5. Cooking	--	0	+	0	0	0	0		0	+	0		--	X
6. Home chores	-	0	-	0	0	+	0		+	++	-		--	X
7. Laundry	-	+	0	+	0	+	+		0	++	0		--	X
8. Marketing	++	-	0	+	-	-	0		--	0	-		-	X
9. Garden, animal	0	0	--	+	0	-	-		0	0	--		+	X
10. Errands, shopping	+	+	--	-	+	+	0		++	0	--		0	X
11. Other house	0	0	--	0	+	-	0		++	-	0		--	X
12. Child care	0	---	++	+	-	-	+		-		++	+++	-	X
13. Child inter-action	0	--	0	0	-	-	0		---	+	-		0	X
14. Personal care	0	0	0	+	0	0	0	0	0	0	0	0	0	X
15. Eating	+	+	-	0	++	0	0	0	0		-	-	+	X
16. Sleep	-	+	+	0	-	0	0		+	--	-		0	X
17. Personal travel	++	+	-	0	++	0	0		0	0	--		+	X
18. Leisure travel	+	0	+	-	0	0	0		--	--		+	++	X
19. Study	+++	0	--	--	+	-	0		-	-	---		+++	X
20. Religion	0	++	++	-	+	+	0		0	++	-		0	X
21. Organiza-tions	++	0	--	---	++	0	0		--	-	--		++	X
22. Radio	0	0	+	-	0	0	0		-	0	-		0	X
23. Television	---	0	++	0	-	0	0		++	-	0		---	X
24. Reading	0	0	-	0	0	0	0		0	0	+		0	X
25. Read paper	0	++	0	-	0	-			-	0	--		-	X
26. Read magazine	0	0	--	+	+	-	+		--	++	++		--	X
27. Read books	+	0	--	+	+	-			-	0	--		+++	X
28. Movies	+	0	0	-	0	-	0		-	--		++	+	X
29-30. Visiting	0	0	--	0	--	-	+		--	0	+		-	X
31. Conversa-tion	++	+	--	0	0	0	+		0	0	0		0	X
32. Active sports	--	--	-	+	+	0	0		-	++	-		0	X
33. Outdoors	0	0	-	0	+	0	0		++	+	++		0	X
34. Entertain-ment	++	0	0	++	-	--	++		-	+	0		++	X
35. Cultural events	+	0	0	0	+	+	0		0	0	-		+	X
36. Resting	-	0	0	0	0	+	-		0	+	+		0	X
37. Other leisure	0	++	--	-	0	0	0		--	--	--		0	X
Free Time	0	+	--	-	-	-	0		--	0	-		++	X

			Environment							Resource			
Day of week	Sea-son	Wea-ther	Day unusual	Region	City suburb	City size	Dist. to city	Dist. to work	Type of dwel-ling	In-come	House-hold help	TV	Auto
Week-end	Fall	Poor	Yes	South	City	Large	Fur-ther	Fur-ther	Non-house	More	Yes	Yes	> 1
-	0	0	X	+	0	0	0	X	0	0	+	0	+
0	0	0	X	0	0	0	0	X	0	0	0	0	0
0	0	0	X	0	0	0	0	X	0	0	0	0	0
0	0	0	X	0	0	-	0	X	+	0	0	0	0
--	0	0	X	0	0	-	0	X	0	-	--	0	-
0	-	0	X	0	+	0	0	X	0	0	0	+	+
--	0	0	X	0	+	-	0	X	0	0	--	+	-
--	0	+	X	0	++	+	+	X	0	0	+	0	+
--	-	0	X	-	0	0	0	X	-	0	++	0	0
-	+	0	X	0	0	0	0	X	-	++	0	+	+
+	++	-	X	0	0	0	0	X	--	0	+	+	0
--	0	-	X	0	0	0	0	X	0	-	0	+	--
--	+	-	X	0	-	-	-	X	+	0	0	-	--
0	0	0	X	0	0	-	0	X	0	0	+	0	0
-	0	0	X	+	0	0	0	X	0	0	0	+	0
++	-	+	X	-	0	0	0	X	+	-	0	-	0
-	0	-	X	0	0	+	0	X	-	++	0	0	++
++	+	-	X	0	0	0	---	X	+	+	0	-	0
0	-	0	X	0	0	+	0	X	0	+++	++	-	+++
+++	-	-	X	-	0	+	+	X	-	0	0	-	+
---	+	-	X	0	-	-	0	X	--	++	-	+	++
0	0	+	X	0	-	-	0	X	0	-	0	-	0
++	0	+	X	0	0	-	-	X	+	--	--	++	-
0	+	0	X	+	0	0	0	X	++	0	0	+	0
++	0	0	X	0	+	0	0	X	-	+	+	+	+
-	0	0	X	-	0	0	+	X	--	0	-	-	0
0	--	0	X	-	-	-	+	X	+	+	++	-	0
++	0	0	X	+	+	0	+	X	+	+	+	0	-
++	-	0	X	0	0	0	-	X	0	+	+	--	-
--	0	0	X	+	+	0	0	X	+	0	+	+	0
0	0	-	X	0	0	0	0	X	-	--	-	0	0
++	-	0	X	0	0	0	-	X	-	--	0	-	--
++	0	0	X	0	--	-	-	X	-	0	0	+	-
0	0	-	X	0	-	-	0	X	0	++	+	0	+
++	0	-	X	0	+	0	0	X	0	-	0	-	0
-	+	+	X	0	+	+	0	X	--	0	0	0	+
++	0	0	X	0	-	0	--	X	+	+	0	--	+

*See Table 2.2 for key of symbols.
Source: Compiled by the author from the
Study of Americans' Use of Time (1965-66).

housewives. Only in the case where the activity differences for a
factor were consistently found, or where dramatic differences
appeared for one or two groups, was an entry other than 0 registered
in Table 2.2. In the discussion of results which follows in Chapters
3 and 4, as much reliance is placed on the entries in Tables 2.4,
2.5, and 2.6 as on the Table 2.2 entries. The analyses in Chapters
3 and 4 consider the various daily activities in their order of appear-
ance in Table 2.2, Chapter 3 covering "obligatory activities" (the
first 17 activities in Table 2.2), and Chapter 4 "free time activities"
(the last 20 activities in Table 2.2).

Before discussing these analyses, it may be instructive to
examine some breakdowns of time use by two of the most powerful
predictors in Table 2.2, namely sex and employment status. Table
2.3 shows the large percentage differences in time use across the
three sex and employment groups analyzed separately in Tables
2.4, 2.5, and 2.6. Employed men and women dominate the work
categories and housewives the basic housework and child care categories. Other household obligations are split more evenly across
the three groups, and only minor differences in personal care and
travel appear.

Differences in free-time activities are obscured by the very
small percentages of time devoted to individual types of leisure
activities in Table 2.3, and an analysis in Chapter 4 provides a more
sensitive examination of these differences and also a standard for
gauging the substantial differences in the amount of free time available to the three groups—housewives having almost an hour more
per day than employed men and two hours more than employed
women. On a percentage of free-time basis, men are found to
spend more of their time away from home than women, in sports
and attending classes; when they are at home, men spend more time
watching television and reading the newspaper, women more time
entertaining visitors and engaging in women's hobbies.

II

ANALYSIS OF DAILY ACTIVITIES

CHAPTER

3

OBLIGATORY ACTIVITIES

The distinction between work and leisure is one easily made in casual everyday parlance, as in the adage "eight hours for sleep, eight hours for work, and eight hours for play." These distinctions between "obligatory" and "discretionary" time become much more difficult and arbitrary when one is examining the uses of time that people record in their daily diaries. Paid work seems easily classified as obligatory time, even though families could survive for long periods with no members in the active labor force. Moreover, most workers are probably able to squeeze in some discretionary activities or personal business during their time spent at the workplace. But what of the auxiliary activities that accompany work, such as lunch periods, coffee breaks, or most importantly, commuting to and from work? Moreover, how should the work-related activities of job search, waiting in welfare offices, vacations, and holidays be treated?

Much the same arbitrariness is true for unpaid housework. Very little of it is obligatory in the sense that the individual's life would be threatened if it were not performed. Being defined as work that "is never finished" only adds to its nonobligatory character, as does the evidence we will present that suggests that under the pressure of paid employment women complete their housework in much less time and with minimal assistance from their husbands. It is much easier, and more common, to perform housework than other work in combination with pleasurable free-time activities, such as television viewing, telephone conversations, and visiting. Moreover, certain parts of what we include under homemaking are found to be extremely pleasurable and rewarding, such as feeding babies, shopping for new clothes, and cooking. Much the same highlights occur in the world of work, however, and few jobs carry with them the "lows" of housework, such as making beds, washing dishes, and doing the general cleaning along with the simple, if often boring, necessity of being at home. Since these ultimately represent activities "that have to be done," there is little doubt that their classification as obligatory activities is appropriate.

Paid work and all the activities related to the maintenance of family and household are then the major activities of interest in this chapter. Due to the great interest in activities connected with children, child-care activity also receives detailed attention. The other obligatory activities concerned with personal care can also have strong discretionary components. Personal-care activities, however, are of much less interest, both intrinsically and analytically–they seem to be practical "constants" in everyday life as seen in Tables 2.2-2.6. Eating, sleeping, and other personal care consume about 72 weekly hours of the lives of employed men, employed women, and housewives. To a surprisingly large extent, the same blandness of results holds true for travel-related activities.

Work, housework, and child care, then, are the focal activities of this chapter.

WORK TIME

Our estimates of time spent at work do not seriously diverge from figures collected annually by the Bureau of Labor Statistics. These figures indicated, if anything, an increase in the average workweek in 1965 compared to the previous 10 or 20 years. This finding, which is at odds with the common stereotype of an ever-shortening workweek, is accounted for by the spurt in the numbers of those businessmen and professionals who put in workweeks in excess of 50 hours (Wilensky, 1961);* this has offset whatever gains labor unions have made in reducing the workweek for their membership.

These difficulties in bringing our work figures in accord with those obtained by government and other researchers are practically insurmountable. The question time frames differ (for example, weekly vs. daily estimates, "last week" vs. "average week" estimates) as well as the samples examined (all adults vs. adults meeting our sampling criteria, those working over 35 hours per week vs. those

---

*Nor has the shortening of workweeks in some blue-collar jobs resulted in any dramatic increase in moonlighting (Wilensky, 1961). Wilensky also noted the much shorter workweeks prevailing before the industrial revolution as further counterevidence to the projected shorter workweek.

working over 10 hours per week, urban samples vs. full national samples, industrial workers vs. all workers vs. all nonfarm workers).

Our time-diary data are unique in that they refer to aggregated single-day accounts of employed persons in nonfarm occupations residing in metropolitan areas. Offsetting this restricted sampling frame is their advantage of being developed from a much more systematic and detailed (and thereby probably more accurate) empirical base—namely, the entries in time diaries. Time-diary reports require far less complex judgments about work from respondents than the general questions used in most workweek studies, which ask respondents to report their total work hours for the previous week.

We included a general question of this type in our survey in order to examine differences between general estimates and actual work activities recorded in diaries on the same population of respondents. In fact, the figures from the two sources did not diverge widely—time-budget entries averaged 41.9 hours compared to 43.5 hours per week estimated by all workers—but the time-diary figures used a definition of work that encompassed certain "nonwork" activities as well. These nonwork activities and the time they consumed are noted toward the bottom of the list of work-related activities in Table 3.1. They consisted of a weekly total of an hour and a quarter of work breaks,* a quarter of an hour on work delays, and another two-thirds of an hour for other time spent at the place of work (such as changing clothes before or after work or hanging around the place of work). An additional hour and a quarter per week at the workplace is spent eating meals, an activity described in Table 3.9 along with other meals.

Even without specific probing, then, close to 10 percent of all time at work in our diaries should not be considered productive. In other words, from this we can infer that the gross estimates that our respondents made of their weekly work appear padded to a nonnegligible extent. Just how these discrepancies may have been reflected in previous generations' workweek estimates thus becomes of concern in the intricate matter of interpreting historical shifts in the length of the workweek.†

---

*We consider this figure a lower bound of work breaks, because interviewers were not explicitly instructed to have respondents differentiate work activities unless the respondent chose to do so.

†We have summarized the numerous subtleties and difficulties involved in these historical comparisons in Robinson and Converse (1972).

TABLE 3.1

Time Spent Working
(minutes per day)

	Employed Men				Employed Women			
	M-F	Sat	Sun	Total	M-F	Sat	Sun	Total
N =	(374)	(65)	(78)	(517)	(245)	(44)	(51)	(340)
1. Main job								
00. Regular work	434	193	71	348	351	91	51	271
01. Work at home	9	1	8	8	14	3	2	11
02. Overtime	1	8	2	2	0	0	0	0
03. Travel for job	9	5	—*	7	2	0	0	1
04. Waiting, delays	3	5	1	3	2	1	0	2
2. Second job (05.)	10	14	2	10	4	0	4	4
3. At work, other								
07. At work, other	8	7	1	7	5	2	1	4
08. Work breaks	14	8	2	11	14	3	1	10
4. Trip to work (09.)	50	27	15	41	39	8	5	29
Total Work-Related	537	267	102	436	431	107	65	332
Hours per day	8.9	4.4	1.7	7.3	7.2	1.8	1.1	5.6
Hours per participant per day	9.3	7.7	4.6	8.4	8.0	6.6	5.1	7.4
Hours per week	44.8	+4.4	+1.7	=50.9	35.9	+1.8	+1.1	=38.8

*A dash indicates less than .5 minutes per day.

Source: Compiled by the author from the Study of Americans' Use of Time (1965-66).

This does not exhaust the possible problems in interpreting the work-time figures, however. Since we had anticipated ambiguities in the simple diary reports in which work time was considered sufficiently described simply as "work," we asked some general questions about what people did at work; respondents estimated an additional 12 percent of paid work time that was devoted to nonwork activities not described thus far. This figure of 12 percent was derived from the proportion of their workweek that respondents estimated either that they did not "have any work to do" or that they engaged in "talking with people about things not related to work." Because some of the latter activity could be accomplished while performing work, however, this may have the effect of inflating the 12 percent figure.

Work performed at one's regular place of employment still clearly dominates the figures in Table 3.1. Two socially significant aspects of work, "moonlighting" and work done at home, are quite small in comparison to activities performed at one's main work-place. In contrast to the sociological attention paid to it, work on a second job accounts for less than 2 percent of all work performed by our national urban sample.* Slightly more work time, but still only 3 percent, is devoted to work brought home from the office, being almost entirely reported by white-collar business personnel.

Table 3.1 identifies large differences in work-related activities by day of the week and by sex. Overall, employed men put in a workweek at least ten hours longer than employed women. Almost all of this difference is accounted for by regular work itself, although men put more time in on second jobs, had longer trips to work, and even slightly longer times on other activities (such as work breaks); employed women, surprisingly, put in more work at home than men, such as completing typing and secretarial assignments. Even discounting the fact that employed women were less likely than employed men to report work on any given day, among those reporting work, men put in over an hour's longer workday than women.

Table 2.2 in the previous chapter also documents an "unusual day" as related to lower work times.† While children appeared to

---

*Dividing the average times in Table 3.1 by the percentage of the sample engaging in that activity provides a different perspective on these work data. Those who reported regular work reported roughly 7.2 hours of it; those reporting moonlighting on the diary day put in an average of 3.5 hours.

†Unusual days were characterized by more than average household business, child care, organizational matters, and socializing—and less than average television viewing—indicating these to be fairly important matters to respondents.

have little impact on the work hours of men, employed women with younger children or with a large number of children reported considerably shorter work hours in their diaries; Morgan et al. (1966) found the same result. Among female employees, blacks, shift workers, and the less educated recorded much lower than average work hours; again no such differences were found among men. Age did relate to work among men, with older men reporting slightly more work in their diaries.*

Men also reported considerably more time on second jobs. Not surprisingly, respondents with higher income, those with more household help, whites, and older respondents also reported less moonlighting.

Men also reported more nonwork time both in and around the place of work than did women. Work breaks were mentioned more often in the diaries of less-educated men in manual occupations.

The trip to and from work, which is often neglected in calculations of the American workweek, consumed close to five hours a week for employed men and three and a half hours for employed women. The trip to work did vary monotonically with distance to the workplace; more detailed analyses of these data are presented in Lansing and Hendricks (1967).† The trip to work also took longer in the city and in larger cities, but did not vary by distance

------

*One important determinant of work time not considered in our analysis tables is self-employment. Consistent with figures from other surveys, self-employed workers reported about ten hours more work per week than other employed people, while clerical, sales, and household service workers were below average in reported work time.

†Lansing and Hendricks calculated a fairly constant elasticity coefficient from the commuting data in the multination study. This coefficient can be interpreted as follows: For every minute increase in the speed of the transportation system, people will take half of this increment in time to commute to work and the other half for other activities. The coefficient implies a straightforward relation between transportation efficiency and urban migration.

Although the trip to work did rise monotonically with distance from the job, trip times are not directly proportionate throughout the range of trip lengths. That is, the person living 20 miles from work averages 34 miles per hour in making the trip, compared to 21 miles per hour for the person living 10 miles from work and the 16-miles-per-hour figure for those living 5 miles from work. Slightly lower mile-per-hour figures are reported by Lansing and Hendricks in their national sample.

from the city center.* More affluent respondents had longer trips. People who took common carriers to work rather than driving took almost twice as long to get to work for equivalent distances; the "0" entry in Table 2.2 (Chapter 2) for automobile ownership refers to the lack of differences in commuting time of owners of more than one car compared to owners of only one car.

Of the noncorrelates of work time, perhaps the most interesting is income. For neither employed men nor employed women was income systematically related to the amount of time spent at work, suggesting an important failure of time as an input to match up well with money as an output. The most important activities correlated with amount of input and some of the possible consequences of longer workweeks are considered next.

Length of Workweek

Since employment plays such an important role in determining the available free time, its impact on amount and types of free-time activities is worth examining in detail, specifically, using two different analytic strategies with time-use data: (1) comparing the daily time expenditures of employed men and employed women who had workweeks of varying lengths in the 1965-66 study, and (2) examining the daily time expenditures in diaries collected in 1974 from a special sample of blue-collar workers experiencing an innovation intended, among other aims, to increase or reshape their leisure time, namely, the four-day workweek.

Differences in the time spent on various daily activities for various length workweeks in the 1965-66 study are presented in Table 3.2 for employed men and in Table 3.3 for employed women. The length of the workweek was determined by asking how many hours the respondent had worked in the week previous to the interview; answers were divided into five categories: 15-29 hours, 30-39 hours, 40-45 hours, 46-54 hours, and 55 hours and over. The first

---

*These results are also found in Morgan et al. (1966), who explained these results largely on the fact that many more suburban residents work in the suburbs than city dwellers work in the city. The difference according to city size is less surprising; compared to the residents of larger cities in the national sample, those in smaller cities made the trip in less time for equivalent distances. Thus, Jackson residents who lived about 20 miles from work made the round trip in 51 rather than 72 minutes and those about 10 miles away made it in 42 rather than 54 minutes.

TABLE 3.2

Employed Men: Differences in Daily Activities by Length of the Workweek

(minutes per day)

	Estimated Hours Worked*					
	Under 30 (N = 14)	30–39 (N = 51)	40–45 (N = 223)	46–54 (N = 117)	55 or more (N = 103)	All Men (N = 508)
1. Main job	208	321	353	387	424	367
2. Second job	0	3	5	11	17	9
3. At work, other	4	20	19	20	18	19
4. Travel to job	27	44	38	44	47	42
Total Work	239	388	415	462	506	436
5. Cooking	5	10	8	7	4	8
6. Home chores	4	20	10	7	10	10
7. Laundry	0	3	1	4	3	2
8. Marketing	13	15	11	13	5	11
Total Housework	22	47	30	31	21	30
9. Garden, animal care	1	1	3	1	2	2
10. Errands, shopping	20	10	18	10	15	15
11. Other house chores	6	32	20	18	16	19
Total Household Obligations	27	43	42	29	34	36
12. Child care	0	3	4	4	3	4
13. Other child	2	9	8	6	8	8
Total Child Care	2	12	13	10	11	12
14. Personal care	56	67	63	53	53	59
15. Eating	97	89	91	83	88	89
16. Sleep	522	434	464	463	459	463
Total Personal Needs	675	590	618	599	600	611
17. Personal travel	49	33	28	28	22	28
18. Leisure travel	43	19	17	16	13	17
Total Nonwork Travel	93	52	45	44	35	44
19. Study	106	18	6	7	10	9
20. Religion	6	6	10	2	3	7
21. Organizations	3	4	6	4	4	5
Total Study and Participation	116	28	22	14	17	20
22. Radio	10	7	5	4	3	5
23. Television	92	114	108	104	73	100
24. Reading, general	0	8	2	5	3	3
25. Read paper	12	21	27	26	17	25
26. Read magazine	13	5	7	5	4	6
27. Read books	8	4	3	8	4	5
28. Movies	0	14	3	4	1	4
Total Mass Media	136	173	155	155	105	148
29–30. Social	74	51	54	47	64	54
31. Conversation	5	15	12	9	15	12
32. Active sports	18	14	9	4	10	8
33. Outdoors	0	8	3	1	6	4
34. Entertainment	4	6	6	9	0	6
35. Cultural events	0	0	2	1	0	1
36. Resting	2	3	5	5	6	5
37. Other leisure	10	8	9	16	8	10
Total Leisure	113	105	99	91	109	100
Total Free Time (18–37)	408	324	291	276	242	286
Total Travel	119	96	83	88	82	87

*In week preceding interview.

Note: Figures may not add to total due to rounding errors.

Source: Compiled by the author from the Study of Americans' Use of Time (1965-66).

TABLE 3.3

Employed Women: Differences in Daily Activities by Length of the Workweek
(minutes per day)

	Estimated Hours Worked*					
	Under 30 (N = 55)	30–39 (N = 70)	40–45 (N = 152)	46–54 (N = 39)	55 or more (N = 19)	All Women (N = 335)
1. Main job	185	261	313	408	347	285
2. Second job	5	0	4	6	0	4
3. At work, other	5	13	19	18	15	14
4. Travel to job	24	29	33	33	35	30
Total Work	219	303	369	466	397	333
5. Cooking	59	48	47	45	29	48
6. Home chores	95	68	59	51	64	65
7. Laundry	36	20	24	25	34	27
8. Marketing	16	16	12	15	6	14
Total Housework	207	153	142	135	133	154
9. Garden, animal care	2	2	3	2	12	3
10. Errands, shopping	26	17	17	19	10	19
11. Other house	21	19	19	20	38	21
Total Household Obligations	49	37	38	42	60	42
12. Child care	31	13	9	7	20	14
13. Other child	9	11	2	20	7	7
Total Child Care	40	24	10	27	27	21
14. Personal care	76	77	81	65	66	77
15. Eating	64	76	72	75	66	72
16. Sleep	470	465	469	446	453	467
Total Personal Needs	610	619	622	586	584	616
17. Personal travel	38	28	25	23	32	28
18. Leisure travel	19	10	14	13	6	14
Total Nonwork Travel	57	37	39	37	38	42
19. Study	8	7	3	3	2	5
20. Religion	14	7	9	6	0	9
21. Organizations	11	4	0	1	0	3
Total Study and Participation	33	18	12	10	2	17
22. Radio	4	14	2	1	5	4
23. Television	54	68	68	40	41	63
24. Reading, general	0	2	2	9	1	2
25. Read paper	20	21	14	6	18	16
26. Read magazine	3	3	4	8	12	4
27. Read books	6	6	2	4	7	4
28. Movies	3	8	2	0	0	3
Total Mass Media	91	122	93	67	84	96
29–30. Social	59	67	58	39	48	59
31. Conversation	20	24	15	10	26	17
32. Active sports	3	4	5	0	0	4
33. Outdoors	1	0	1	0	10	1
34. Entertainment	13	1	8	5	7	8
35. Cultural events	0	0	1	0	0	0
36. Resting	12	18	7	3	9	10
37. Other leisure	26	11	17	14	15	17
Total Leisure	134	126	112	71	115	117
Total Free Time (18–37)	276	274	230	162	206	242
Total Travel	81	66	74	70	74	73

*In week preceding interview.

Note: Figures may not add to total due to rounding errors.

Source: Compiled by the author from the Study of Americans' Use of Time (1965–66).

(lowest-work) category contains very few employed men and the last
(highest-work) category, very few employed women.

As noted earlier, the respondent estimates for the previous
week matched up relatively well with the diary entries averaged
across the week. The correspondence for all work-related activities
was as follows:

Men who said they worked 15-29 hours the previous week
averaged 24.8 hours in their diaries; those who said 30-39 hours,
40.1 hours; those who estimated 40-45 hours, 44.0; the 46-54-hour
group, 48.7 hours; and the 55-hour-and-over group, 53.5 hours.
For women, the comparable figures were 22.7, 32.0, 39.2, 50.5,
and 42.3 hours, respectively. In other words, even for given estimated lengths of the workweek, men's diaries contained more work-
related activity than women's diaries. Note also that respondents
estimating the longest workweeks recorded less work than they
estimated. Nevertheless, the steady monotonic progression necessary to make inferences about the impact of increasing working
times is present. Moreover, commuting times were not included
in the above diary calculations, and workers with long workweeks
did report more commuting as well, adding to the higher work-
related activities of these longer-workweek groups.

It can be seen in Tables 3.2 and 3.3 that not all activities are
affected proportionately by the lower diary times on other activities
necessarily available due to longer workweeks.* In fact, the specific
nonwork activities that seem to be reduced more often than others
are generally similar for both men and women, namely, television,
leisure travel, active sports, movies, and all organizational activity
(including education and religion). However, there are sex differences, namely, men with longer workweeks show reduced personal
travel, and women show reduced sleep, rest, and visiting.

The interesting direct connection between the length of the
workweek and available free time is examined graphically in
Figure 3.1, which indicates that the relation was indeed strong
and predictably linear, but not a one-to-one relation. In fact, for
every hour of work there was only a corresponding average increase
of .61 hours of free time; the ratio was higher for employed men
(.65) than for employed women (.57).†

---

*Moreover, some activities are higher for employees with longer
workweeks, such as laundry time for men and magazine reading for
women. A parallel analysis to that in Tables 3.2 and 3.3 was conducted for hours of television viewing and is reported in Chapter 4.

†A slightly smaller ratio (.56) was found with the multinational
data, when free time available to workers in countries with longer

FIGURE 3.1

Relation Between Work Hours and Free Time

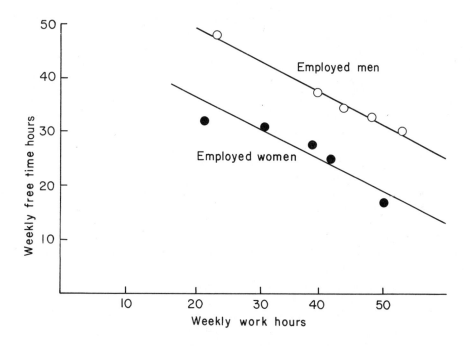

Source: Compiled by the author from the Study of Americans' Use of Time (1965-66).

Since it is not a one-to-one relation, this means that with longer workweeks, an average of .39 hours (1.00-.61) allotted to work must come from other "obligatory" activities, namely household, family, and personal care. In Tables 3.2 and 3.3, it would appear that men are more likely to sacrifice personal care and personal travel time

_____

workweeks was compared to the free time available in countries with shorter workweeks. While people in countries with a short workweek spent more time watching television, they did not spend more time in formal organizations, in leisure travel, or in personal care as found in Tables 3.4 and 3.5. These calculations were made from Szalai et al. (1972, p. 580).

for work, while women sacrifice personal care, sleep, and housecleaning.

On the other hand, this suggests that societal moves toward
shorter workweeks will not be completely translated into correspond-
ingly more free time. On the basis of Tables 3.2 and 3.3, one
would expect that the arrival of shorter workweeks will mean disproportionately more television viewing, organizational activity, and
leisure travel. Whether such changes also occur for a group of
workers with potentials for larger blocks of free time suddenly being
made available is examined next.

Four-Day Workweek*

The four-day workweek issue offers a natural opportunity for combining the diverse time-diary interests of students of work, leisure,
and the family with the practical data requirements of planners.
Not only do questions concerning the impact of this schedule upon
how time is used in the various life domains touch on the most crucial
arguments raised for and against its adoption, but many of these
claims can be most effectively evaluated by using time diaries in
conjunction with more traditional methods of survey research.

Questions examined in this section pertain to the impact upon
time use, both within and outside the work setting, of working an
official week of four 10-hour days. Data derived from an extensive
time-diary survey of 96 four-day and 31 five-day workers in the
Midwest in 1974 were used to explore this and related issues. The
primary activity data summarized in Table 3.4 are arranged according to workday and days off. The table also displays a hypothetical
week, constructed to facilitate comparisons between the two work
groups. Findings from this table are supplemented by results of
auxiliary data analyses when appropriate.

----

*This section was prepared by David Maklan and is drawn from
material contained in his Ph.D. dissertation from the University of
Michigan, 1976, "The Four-Day Workweek: Blue-Collar Adjustment
to a Nonconventional Arrangement of Work and Leisure Time." The
material in this project was prepared under Grant No. 91-26-74-10
from the Manpower Administration, U.S. Department of Labor,
under the authority of Title I of the Manpower Development and Training Act of 1962, as amended. Researchers undertaking such projects
under government sponsorship are encouraged to express freely their
professional judgment. Therefore, points of view or opinions stated
in this section do not necessarily represent the official position or
policy of the Department of Labor.

TABLE 3.4

Time Spent in 39 Primary Activities
(average minutes per day and per week)

| | Minutes per | | | | | |
| | Workdays | | Days off | | Hypoth. week | |
Activity	4-Day Workers (N = 96)	5-Day Workers (N = 31)	4-Day Workers (N = 96)	5-Day Workers (N = 31)	4-Day Workers (N = 96)	5-Day Workers (N = 31)
1. Main job	557	468	NA	NA	2228	2339
2. Meals at work	30	30	5	2	135	154
3. Work breaks	7	6	—[a]	1	28	32
4. Waiting to start	9	8	2	—[a]	42	43
5. At work, other	1	2	3	1	13	12
6. Overtime	20	71	93	57	358	469
7. Second job	1	0	0	13	4	25
8. Travel to/from job	54	53	10	7	246	280
Total Work	679	638	113	81	3054	3354
9. Cooking	2	3	8	11	31	35
10. Indoor home chores	4	1	13	15	58	36
11. Outdoor home chores	6	6	21	10	85	47
12. Marketing	7	15	19	20	84	116
Total Housework	19	25	61	56	258	234
13. Garden, animal care	18	9	37	32	183	110
14. Errands, shopping	6	4	11	6	57	32
15. Other house chores	2	4	30	33	98	86
Total other Household Care	26	17	78	71	338	228
16. Basic child care	6	0	10	2	54	6
17. Other child care	6	2	15	4	69	18
Total Child Care	12	2	25	6	123	22
18. Personal care	52	56	58	78	382	436
19. Eating (except at work)	52	68	84	72	458	485
20. Sleep	393	388	493	495	3053	2932
Total Personal Needs	497	512	635	645	3893	3853
21. Personal travel	14	22	26	34	133	179
22. Leisure travel	11	15	37	45	154	166
Total Nonwork Travel	25	37	63	79	287	345
23. Study	2	6	3	2	17	33
24. Religion	0	0	6	11	18	22
25. Organizations	0	3	1	—[a]	3	17
Total Study and Participation	2	9	10	13	38	72
26. Radio	1	3	1	4	7	21
27. TV	75	97	142	125	726	734
28. Read paper	15	11	22	24	124	105
29. Read magazines	0	0	2	—[a]	5	—[a]
30. Read books	—[a]	3	4	1	13	16
31. Movies	2	0	7	4	29	9
Total Mass Media	93	114	178	158	904	885
32. Social	27	42	99	132	406	475
33. Conversation	13	10	14	25	91	98
34. Active sports	1	8	19	17	60	73
35. Outdoors	5	2	50	30	171	72
36. Entertainment	4	4	10	24	44	68
37. Cultural events	—[a]	5	3	2	11	26
38. Resting, relaxing, doing nothing	11	5	28	17	129	57
39. Other leisure	13	5	41	64	175	154
Total Leisure	74	81	264	311	1,087	1,023
Total Free Time	179	218	489	529	2,183	2,146
Total Travel	78	90	73	86	533	625
Total Unspecified	14	5	14	21	98	66
Total Minutes	1,440[b]	1,440	1,440[b]	1,440	10,080	10,080[b]

[a]A dash indicates less than .5 minutes.
[b]The minutes do not sum to exactly 1,440 per day or 10,080 per week due to rounding.
Note: NA = No activity.
Source: Maklan (1976).

The blue-collar sample consisted of four- and five-day male workers studied as part of an evaluation of selected social-psychological and cultural ramifications of this unconventional work schedule (Maklan, 1976).* The two groups of workers were almost identically distributed on the two basic family variables (number of children living at home and life-cycle stage), as well as length of employment with firm. They were also fairly close with respect to age and education, although the four-day workers tended to be slightly older (3.6 years), to have less formal education (.5 years), to have slightly higher income, and to work afternoon and night shifts.†

The design of the time-diary survey was guided from the outset by three general, sometimes conflicting, purposes: to obtain time-use data which would (1) be representative of the individual's total range of activity, irrespective of work schedule; (2) be reasonably sensitive to fairly small differences in time-distribution patterns of four- and five-day workers; and (3) maintain an acceptable degree of precision and accuracy in the respondents' reports. The following procedure was adopted: Diaries would be collected for a "typical" workday and for each of the worker's days off in the week following

---

*To obtain comparability between the two work groups, the following sample-selection procedure was utilized: A list of organizations within the states of Michigan and Minnesota, which had adopted a 4/40 schedule and employed more than 20 workers, was compiled. Where cooperation was obtained, a similar, but five-day, employer was selected. This second employer had to (a) be in the same industry with workers performing similar functions as those in the four-day plant; (b) be located in the same community, town, or (if in a large metropolitan region) within reasonable proximity to its four-day counterpart; and (c) have approximately the same number of employees. Only when such paired firms could be identified, and the participation of both secured, were workers from either organization included in the sample. Lists of married men holding similar jobs were then compiled from the employee rolls for each firm.

†Some major occupational differences did appear between the two samples. First, the job-matching effort did not prove wholly successful among those workers who participated in the entire study. In particular, there were relatively more truck drivers working a four-day week than the standard five-day schedule (43 vs. 28 percent), and the reverse held for men on an assembly line (6 vs. 26 percent). To account for possible effects of different job structures on attitudes and behavior, the four-day assembly-line workers were weighted by a factor of 4 and the five-day drivers by a factor of 1.5.

the personal interview. Operationally, the typical workday was defined as either the day preceding or the day succeeding the respondent's days off. Practically, this meant that the survey period for four-day workers was four contiguous days and for five-day workers, three contiguous days. While this decision compels the treatment of all respondents within each of the two cells as interchangeable units, it was felt that this period of coverage would be sensitive enough to detect relatively small differences in time usage. It also had the advantage of making possible the construction of a synthetic week for each group of men. To minimize reporting errors, respondents were instructed to record their activities at the end of each day.

The results in Table 3.3 do not support the contention that adoption of the four-day workweek would only lead to additional time on the job rather than opening up new free-time opportunities. Although their official working day exceeded that of five-day workers by two hours, the four-day workers allocated only three-quarters of an hour more to activities related to formal work on these days. In part, this was due to their putting in an actual workday, including paid breaks, shorter than what was officially expected of them. Four-day workers also averaged significantly less overtime. It should be noted, however, that whereas 65 percent of all five-day workers recorded overtime on their workday, only 20 percent of the men on a four-day schedule did so. As expected, four-day workers put in the bulk of their overtime on their days off, largely on their extra free day. When the entire week is considered, then four-day workers did average less formal work (and less overtime) than the men on a five-day schedule.

A second argument, presented in support of widespread adoption of the four-day week, holds that such a switch would be socially beneficial by reducing the number of work trips, thereby helping to relieve traffic congestion and save fuel. This argument can be contested on several grounds, not the least of which is that by having to make fewer work trips the individual may feel less constrained in his selection of residential location. As Table 3.4 shows, there was no significant difference between four- and five-day workers in their daily travel time to and from work. It appears, therefore, that the four-day schedule may bring about these trip-related social benefits, provided some control is kept over the number of men working on their days off.

With regard to "work" performed around the house, the results differ, depending on which of the three components of housework is considered. Differences between four- and five-day workers on core housework are minimal, four-day men spending only about 25 more minutes on core housework. However, when one looks at time allocated to "other household care" activities, four-day workers devoted nearly two more hours to such chores; time spent in "gardening and animal care" accounted for most of the difference.

There was also an important difference between four- and five-day workers in their allocation of time to child care. On the average, men working an official four-day week spent nearly four more hours per week with their children than did their five-day counterparts. Remember that there were minimal family composition differences between the two groups.

Although men working ten-hour schedules should have less free time on their workdays than do men working only eight hours, no difference in their relative amounts of free time is to be expected over the entire week. Recognizing this, advocates of the four-day workweek emphasize the increased opportunity to organize activities in a more concentrated and satisfying manner. Table 3.4 verifies that four-day workers did report less free time for discretionary activities on their workdays, while on weekends these activities accounted for almost seven hours more of their time than for five-day workers. Considering the total week, the differential in free time activities for the two work groups is a scant 37 minutes (2,183 vs. 2,146 min.).

Do four-day workers, then, exhibit patterns of free-time use that are noticeably distinct from five-day workers? This question is taken up with reference to three broad categories of free-time behavior: mass media usage, social interaction, and other leisure participation.

1. Table 3.4 shows strong similarities in the use of media by four- and five-day workers. There is some tendency for four-day workers to make greater use of the media on their days off and less on their workdays, with television accounting for the bulk of this time. Overall, however, no real difference was found between work groups in the amount of television watched per week. A slightly larger percentage of four-day workers did read newspapers, magazines, and books; and they did so for longer periods of time.

2. Social interaction includes nonmedia forms of communication. Five-day workers did spend a few more minutes in conversation, but without reference to "conversation" as a secondary activity, the significance of this finding remains ambiguous. Outside of work and the family, social gatherings constitute the most nearly "organized" setting for informal communication. One of the most commonly stated criticisms directed against the 4/40 schedule is that the longer workday interferes with the individual's social life on week nights. To some extent, the data bear out this contention. The ten-hour day did result in less socializing on workdays, a difference not made up over the longer weekend.

3. The balance of the respondents' free time (excluding associated travel) was distributed among a heterogeneous collection of
activities. Four-day workers did, on the average, report more
than twice as much time per week "resting" or "doing nothing" as
their five-day counterparts, but the amounts of time in question
added up to hardly an hour's difference across the week. Clearly,
any claims of greater participation in formal, hopefully public
service, organizations or educational endeavors find little support
in these data.

Four-day workers did average almost two hours more outdoor
recreation per week. Further analysis showed that almost 13 percent more of them participated in these activities over the weekend.
Significantly, outdoor recreation accounted for almost all of the
weekly discrepancy between the two groups. It does appear that
the longer weekend may have facilitated engagement in activities
requiring extended periods of time.

Conclusions based on a sample of this size serve best as hypotheses for future exploration. Tentatively, these data suggest that
conversion to the four-day workweek yields undramatic results with
respect to the use of time by male blue-collar workers. Overall,
the findings indicate the existence of a tendency toward constancy
and continuity in the workers' patterns of time allocation. Combined
with other personal interview data, the findings presented here
constitute evidence of the need for further evaluation of the four-day
workweek's sociocultural and behavioral implications. In particular,
such efforts are needed before one could confidently adopt any strong
advocacy position based on assumed benefits of this alternative to
existing work-schedule norms.

The differences that do emerge from this analysis, moreover,
do not fit well with the results in the previous section about the
activities workers appear to trade off with longer work hours.
Four-day workers did not spend more time watching television,
traveling, or participating in organizations. They did spend more
time on child care and in outdoor recreation, but these activities,
if anything, attracted more interest among people working longer
workweeks. The identification of activities that are traded off with
work will require additional testing.

HOUSEWORK

Given the current concern about liberating women from the
drudgery of housework, we have found more immediate interest in
housework than in other activities of the day. Time-use data provided
unique but not definitive perspective on the current controversy over

sex roles. First, simple time expenditure data do not reflect those
subtle role demands that are involved in the performance of housework; that is, the constant attention required throughout the day,
week, or year; the continual changes and decisions about scheduling
and priorities; the monotony and inevitability; and the unsettling
combination of the hectic and the menial. A second consideration
is that, like most statistical data, our time diaries contain ample
ammunition for those on either side of the sex-role controversy.

There are, moreover, the analytic ambiguities about how
inclusive a definition of housework ought to be. At the outset of
the current discussion, only the activities listed separately in
Tables 3.5 and 3.6 will be considered, including basic housework
(cooking, laundry, and house cleaning), other household chores
(shopping, repairs, care to pets or plants), child care (the components of which are detailed in Table 3.6), and all related travel.
Among some of the activities omitted, therefore, are household
information-gathering activities via the mass media and conversation,
and contributions to the household accruing from women's hobbies,
such as sewing and canning, and the continual vigilance that even
accompanies the family's free-time activities. Altogether, these
activities might add 2, 5, or even 20 hours per week to the housework totals discussed here. For example, the inclusion of "secondary" activity housework and child care in Tables 3.4 and 3.5 would
increase housework and child care totals by up to five hours a week.

Tables 3.5 and 3.6 document quantitatively the sex and employment status differences that dominate each component of housework
identified in Table 2.2 of the previous chapter. To provide an over-
view of sex-role differences, the total housework figures at the
bottom of Table 3.5 show housewives performing 53.2 hours of
housework per week, which is almost double the 28.1 hours for
employed women. By comparison, the 11.3 hour contribution of
employed men seems paltry indeed, and this total was dominated
by auxiliary household care and shopping. Moreover, it hardly
increased at all (even for child care) on Saturdays and Sundays,
when employed men had much more time available to help around
the house. Note, for example, that men performed only two more
minutes of child care and six more minutes of basic housework on
Saturday than on weekdays.

Sex differences were most dramatic for basic housework and
child-care activities. Housewives spent over ten times as much
time cooking, cleaning, and doing laundry than employed men.
With regard to child care, housewives spent seven times as much
time as employed men, and employed women twice as much time
as men. Only for play activities did men begin to spend time with
children comparable to that of women. To put this figure into

TABLE 3.5

Time Spent on Basic and Other Housework
(minutes per day)

	Employed Men				Employed Women				Housewives			
	M-F	Sat	Sun	Total	M-F	Sat	Sun	Total	M-F	Sat	Sun	Total
Basic Housework												
5. Cooking (10)	6	8	15	8	44	56	66	49	97	82	89	94
6. Home chores												
11. Meal cleanup	3	3	6	3	22	32	28	24	47	40	37	44
12. Clean house	2	4	8	3	34	63	49	41	81	69	33	72
13. Outdoor chores	2	4	11	4	1	1	2	1	4	10	1	4
7. Laundry												
14. Laundry, ironing	1	1	5	1	22	38	35	26	67	49	10	56
15. Clothes upkeep	—*	1	0	—	2	0	2	2	5	5	1	5
8. Marketing (30)	9	18	12	11	13	25	5	13	22	17	6	19
Total Hours per Week	1.9 +	.6 +	1.0 =	3.5	11.4 +	3.6 +	3.1 =	18.1	26.8 +	4.5 +	2.9 =	34.2
Other Housework												
9. Garden, animal care (17)	2	1	2	2	2	3	4	3	6	4	2	5
10. Errands, shopping												
31. Shopping	1	4	—	1	1	2	0	1	1	0	0	1
34. Admin. service	1	—	—	—	1	—	0	1	1	1	0	1
35. Repair service	1	6	2	2	3	6	1	3	2	—	—	2
36. Waiting in line	1	6	0	2	1	2	0	1	1	1	0	1
37. Other service	8	17	7	9	16	19	3	14	18	27	2	17
11. Other house												
16. Other upkeep	6	12	17	9	—	1	0	—	4	14	4	5
18. Heat, water	—	2	2	1	—	—	0	—	—	0	0	—
19. Other duties	5	11	7	6	10	28	18	13	18	17	21	19
42. Care to adults	—	12	5	3	7	6	6	7	8	7	11	9
Total Hours per Week	2.3 +	1.2 +	.7 =	4.2	3.4 +	1.1 +	.5 =	5.0	5.0 +	1.2 +	.7 =	6.9
Grand Total of Hours per Week				7.7				23.1				41.1

*A dash indicates less than .5 minutes per day.

Source: Compiled by the author from the Study of Americans' Use of Time (1965–66).

TABLE 3.6

Time Spent on Child Care

(minutes per day)

	Employed Men				Employed Women				Housewives			
	M-F	Sat	Sun	Total	M-F	Sat	Sun	Total	M-F	Sat	Sun	Total
12. Basic child care												
20. Baby care	2	4	5	2	6	7	7	6	39	27	29	36
21. Child care	1	1	4	1	9	4	3	7	26	8	15	22
26. Child health	0	0	0	0	1	0	0	1	2	1	0	1
13. Other child care												
22. Help with study	—a	0	2	1	2	0	0	2	6	1	2	4
23. Talk to child	1	0	1	1	1	—	5	1	5	0	1	3
24. Indoor play	4	5	10	5	1	0	1	1	4	2	6	4
25. Outdoor play	1	0	1	1	—	0	0	—	1	1	0	0
27. Other, baby-sit	1	2	—	1	4	3	0	3	3	6	4	4
Total Hours per Week	.8 + .2 + .4 = 1.4				2.0 + .2 + .3 = 2.5				7.1 + .7 + .9 = 8.7			
Total Hours per Day of Housework^b	1.3	2.5	2.5	1.6	3.8	5.4	4.1	4.1	8.4	6.9	4.7	7.6
Total Hours per Week of Housework	6.3 + 2.5 + 2.5 = 11.3				18.6 + 5.4 + 4.1 = 28.1				38.9 + 6.4 + 4.5 = 53.2			

aA dash indicates less than .5 minutes per day.

bAdding in all other household duties (that is, activities 5-11 in Table 3.5) and related travel (activities 29 and 39 in Table 3.10).

Source: Compiled by the author from the Study of Americans' Use of Time (1965-66).

perspective, however, half of all child care was play activity for men, while less than a tenth of women's child care was in the form of play.

The figures in the bottom half of Table 3.5 indicate than men did share a more equitable burden of shopping and house repair. Men did roughly 40 percent of all grocery shopping and most of the weekend marketing and shopping for durables. But they still spent less than half as much time as women on garden or pet care, helping other adults, and household management duties, such as paying bills.

The most notable shifts in housework by day of the week did not occur between men and women but between employed women and housewives. Employed women used Saturday and, to a lesser extent, Sunday, to catch up on the basic housework not attended to during the week. However, they spent little more time shopping and even less daily time on child care on weekends than they did during the week. Housewives, on the other hand, reported a decrease of an hour and a half in housework on Saturday and a three-and-a-half-hour decrease on Sunday. Overall, however, the housewife still spent two more hours on housework on the weekend than the employed woman.

The pattern of correlations of other factors, such as education and family structure, showed more differentiation for women than for men, as can be seen in Tables 2.4 to 2.6 of the previous chapter. Among women, higher education was associated with less housework (particularly cooking), as was living further from work. Women with more children did more of the "core" housework of cooking and cleaning, but spent no more on other house-related duties than women with fewer children. Consistent with this picture of the higher priority (or inelasticity) of core housework is the fact that mothers of more demanding younger children spent no less time than average on core housework, apparently giving up errands and pet or garden care instead. Black women reported well below average amounts of time devoted to garden and pet care, errands, and miscellaneous household chores.

The simultaneous impact of many of these factors is examined in more detail in the Multiple Classification Analysis (MCA) of housework in Table 3.7. Multiple Classification Analysis is a multivariate regression program developed at the Survey Research Center by Andrews, Morgan, and Sonquist (1969) to assess the impact of particular variables after control for the effects of other predictor variables. Its capabilities are particularly helpful in the analysis of our time-use data, given the wide variety of predictors that are available and the desire to determine the effects of predictor variables when other factors can be "held constant."

TABLE 3.7

MCA Results for Housework Time
(minutes per day above and below the overall average; 1965-66 national and Jackson data combined)

	(N)	Women	(N)	Men
Total Sample Average		247 min.		52 min.
Standard Deviation		155 min.		81 min.
Personal Factors				
Education				
Grade school	(126)	+14	(129)	−6
Some high school	(216)	+4	(187)	+1
High school graduate	(492)	+2	(304)	0
Some college	(154)	−24	(135)	−6
College graduate	(109)	+6	(141)	+16
Age				
18–29	(307)	−30	(241)	−7
30–39	(251)	−8	(198)	−4
40–49	(264)	+19	(228)	+3
50–59	(67)	+24	(233)	+8
Race				
White	(1013)	0	(835)	0
Black	(79)	−7	(55)	+1
Religion				
Catholic	(299)	−2	(233)	−3
Jewish	(42)	−26	(23)	−23
Established Protestant	(155)	+4	(105)	+11
Traditional Protestant	(503)	+2	(418)	−1
Modern Protestant	(76)	+8	(70)	+3
None, other	(29)	−1	(53)	0
Role Factors				
Employment				
Yes	(534)	−59	(865)	−2
Student	(10)	−100	(18)	+5
No	(558)	+58	(19)	−3
Spouse employment				
Yes	(811)	+8	(248)	+5
No	(30)	+43	(509)	−1
Not married	(251)	−29	(140)	−1
Family composition				
No children	(422)	−32	(323)	−3
At least one child under four years				
One	(60)	−10	(51)	−10
Two	(70)	+10	(71)	+7
Three	(54)	+31	(45)	−6
Four	(74)	+64	(58)	+8

	(N)	Women	(N)	Men
All children over				
four years				
One	(130)	+3	(114)	−2
Two	(137)	+13	(129)	+2
Three	(93)	+26	(68)	+7
Four	(54)	+43	(41)	−10
Environmental Factors				
City size				
Large city	(131)	+25	(98)	+3
Medium city	(156)	−32	(138)	+3
Large suburb	(185)	+16	(134)	−1
Medium suburb	(186)	−3	(139)	−7
Outlying areas	(42)	+42	(32)	+1
Metropolitan area				
New York	(105)	−16	(72)	−16
Los Angeles; Chicago	(86)	−28	(67)	+6
Other large cities	(186)	+9	(138)	+2
Medium cities	(182)	+5	(161)	−6
Smaller cities	(103)	−4	(103)	−2
Jackson, Michigan	(361)	+1	(361)	+2
Day of Week				
Weekday	(775)	0	(651)	−11
Saturday	(155)	+25	(113)	+33
Sunday	(156)	−31	(138)	+25
Season				
Fall	(770)	+4	(611)	+1
Spring	(333)	−10	(291)	−3
Resource Factors				
Income				
Under $4,000	(120)	0	(46)	+4
$4,000–5,999	(200)	+13	(132)	+3
$6,000–9,999	(446)	+4	(382)	+2
$10,000–14,999	(215)	−17	⎰(316)	−5
$15,000 and over	(94)	+13	⎱	
Paid help				
None	(857)	+1		—
Infrequent	(119)	+12		—
Part-time	(215)	−11		—
Full-time	(19)	−33		—

Source: Compiled by the author from the Study of Americans' Use of Time (1965–66).

The housework figures in Table 3.7 are given separately for men and for women. It should be noted that child care (examined separately in Table 3.8), shopping for durables, or taking care of other personal business outside the home are excluded from these figures, as is secondary activity housework. The reader may be assured that their inclusion does not noticeably affect the conclusions reached in Table 3.7. The results are also not affected by including data from the Jackson, Michigan, sample to increase the sample sizes for these estimates.

Of the four personal factors in Table 3.7, only age showed a steady effect on housework. The data, surprisingly, show more devotion to housework as women and men grow older, despite the fact that one would expect household demands on people to decrease steadily with age, particularly with children leaving home. Whether this means older people become more fastidious housekeepers with age, or more inefficient, or simply do more housework because they have more time on their hands is a question obviously deserving further exploration. Only two other personal differences stand out in Table 3.7: (1) the somewhat greater housework burden shared by college graduate men, and (2) the lower housework reported by Jewish women, and more particularly by Jewish men (although the sample sizes are extremely small for Jewish respondents).

Among role factors, family composition was a major determinant of housework, but only for women. Contrary to the case for child care (examined next), it was the number and not the age of the children that increased housework. Also unlike the case for child care, one finds smooth monotonic relations between housework time and number of children, increases of about 10 percent being found for each additional child for households with preschool children and of about 5 percent for each additional child in households where all children are over four years of age.

The effect of labor-force membership on women's housework is somewhat attenuated when other factors are taken into account by the MCA, such as the employed woman's being less likely to be married or to have children. When these factors are considered, the effect of employment on housework is remarkably similar to its effect on child care, that is, after employed MCA adjustments, employed women put in 62 percent of the housework time that housewives did rather than the 54 percent in Table 3.4.

Also similar to what will be shown for child care was the lack of sensitivity of male contribution to housework with the burden of a preschool child in the family. Moreover, the male contribution did not even rise significantly with more children present in the family. While it was higher for men whose wives were in the labor market, the increase was barely over 10 percent. On the other hand, rather than decreasing their housework load, those few wives whose husbands were unemployed reported higher than average housework, perhaps because many of these unemployed men were out of work due to illness or injury. Yet male chauvinists may take great comfort in the finding that even women without husbands did 85 percent as much housework as those who were married, and that roughly the same percentage held true for men without wives. In other words, marriage itself seemed to result in only minor modifications of the housework patterns of both partners.

Among environmental factors, some day-of-the-week differences were found, Saturday being everyone's most popular day for housework. Women in outlying rural areas reported more housework, with women in the New York, Chicago, and Los Angeles areas reporting less housework. Slightly more housework was reported in the fall than in the spring "housecleaning" season.

The resource factor of income was not associated in any systematic way with housework, a surprising finding given the ability of the affluent to afford outside help and the implicitly higher economic value of the time the affluent spend on housework; neither did the presence of outside household help reduce housework, with the exception of that most fortunate, but small, group of women with full-time housekeepers.

The major differences in housework time by other variables then were found among women, who also did the lion's share of the housework. While women's housework time was dramatically related to additional role demands brought on by labor-force participation and number of children, men's housework time was not. We shall examine some consequences of this phenomenon in Chapter 6.

CHILD CARE

Perhaps the clearest example of what economists consider an "investment" of time is that devoted to child care. While parents may not consciously pattern their child-care behavior as such, the time they devote to caring for and interacting with their children represents an investment that does determine how the child will mature and develop. The time-diary data provide a unique opportunity to document clearly how a parent's use of time is affected by the arrival and presence of children in the household.

The 1965-66 time-use data provide three separate estimates of child-care time, as can be seen in Figure 1.1 of Chapter 1. The first, primary activity child care, consisted of about four hours each week in Table 3.6 that adult respondents reported some form of child-care activity, like "feeding the baby," "helping children with their homework," as the main activity in the diary. The second estimate, primary plus secondary activity child care, was the sum of this four-hour figure and the roughly two hours during the week when the respondent reported some child-care activity when asked, "Were you doing anything else?" for each primary activity; here one would include, for example, feeding the baby when it was done while getting supper ready for the rest of the family.* The third, with whom or child-contact time, was calculated from the total time during which respondents reported children as social partners in the activity, that is, when one or more children were mentioned in response to the question "With whom were you doing this [primary] activity?"

Total contact time in the "with whom" entries (18.7 hours per week) exceeded primary and secondary activity time (6.3 hours per week) by a factor of three. Figure 3.2 illustrates the magnitude of these differences and also shows the cumulative nature of the three estimates, such that secondary activities are a subset of primary and secondary activities and both are subsets of total contact time. These figures can be considered "upper bound" and "lower bound" estimates of child care, running the gamut from time when the presence of children is virtually ignored to time when the child's behavior is at the forefront of the parent's consciousness. The "with whom" estimate, or total contact time, does fail to register significant amounts of parental worrying and planning or other times when the child is "out of sight but not out of mind"; but from the other patterns of activities in parents' time diaries, the amount of time included in the total contact time does seem reasonably close to the upper limit of time they would have available for their children.

If the total contact time of about 19 hours per week seems a rather skimpy investment in children, it should be remembered that this figure is artificially low due to the inclusion of that third of the 1965-66 sample who were not parents of children under 18 years of age. Their exclusion thus brings this figure for parents closer to 30 hours a week, which represents over a quarter of their waking time. Moreover, these figures were considerably higher for mothers (36.4 hours) than for fathers (21.0 hours).

Table 2.2 in Chapter 2 identifies sex, employment status, and age and number of children as the major determinants of child-care time with number of children being a less important factor than age

---

*While over two-thirds of primary activity child care in the 1965-66 study was "custodial" (feeding, clothing, chauffering, etc.) rather than "interactional" (reading, playing, etc.) in nature, the bulk of secondary activity child care consisted of interactional activities.

FIGURE 3.2

Relation Between Primary and Secondary
Activity Time for Child Care

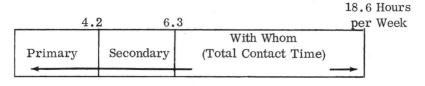

Source: Compiled by the author.

of children. Table 2.2, however, documented that with the exception
of employment, these factors distinguished custodial child-care time
(feeding, dressing, etc.) far better than interactional child care
(playing, helping with homework, etc.). Other major predictors
of child care found in Table 2.2 include, of course, age and marital
status, as well as automobile ownership and having an unusual day.*

Again, a number of these background factors were entered as
predictive factors in MCAs of the low and high estimates of child-
care time, for the purpose of examining which of them survived as
predictors in a multivariate context. These factors, which are the
same as those used in Table 3.7, are on the left side of Table 3.8.
Again, data from the Jackson sample are included to increase sample
sizes.†

Child-care time for each of these factors is analyzed first for
all women, and then separately for employed women and housewives;
the extreme right side of Table 3.8 provides the parallel analyses
for men. The entries are corrected MCA estimates, first for

---

*Owners of more than one automobile reported less primary
activity child care (particularly interactional care); persons reporting
an unusual day, on the other hand, reported more child care (particularly custodial). Whether it is the parents' or the children's use of
the extra automobiles that keeps the family apart, or whether the
additional custodial care is brought on by unusual parental or child
matters is unknown.

†The marital status factor includes consideration of the employment of the spouse as well, and the residents in the Jackson sample
are analyzed separately within the environmental factor of metropolitan size. The limited number of Chicano and other minority
group respondents (N = 10) are excluded from Tables 3.7 and 3.8.

TABLE 3.8

MCA Results for Child-Care Variables
(minutes per day above and below
the average; 1965–66 national and
Jackson data combined)

	(N)	Women		Employed Women		Housewives		(N)	Men	
		Primary Activity	Total Contact	Primary Activity	Total Contact	Primary Activity	Total Contact		Primary Activity	Total Contact
Total Sample		48 min.	199 min.	21 min.	111 min.	75 min.	286 min.		11 min.	115 min.
Standard Deviation		79 min.	216 min.	50 min.	163 min.	91 min.	224 min.		32 min.	153 min.
Personal Factors										
Education										
Grade school	(126)	-7	-17	+5	+2	+5	-10	(129)	-3	0
Some high school	(216)	-3	+2	-6	+5	+1	-1	(187)	-4	-19
High school graduate	(492)	+3	+1	+1	-6	+4	+6	(304)	+3	+9
Some college	(154)	-10	-14	-5	-13	-15	-11	(135)	-1	-10
College graduate	(109)	+22	+25	+2	+25	+23	+10	(141)	+4	+12
Age										
18–29	(307)	+2	-4	+3	-8	+3	-1	(241)	0	-5
30–39	(261)	+2	+20	-7	+17	+8	+17	(198)	+8	+5
40–49	(264)	-7	-1	-5	+9	-11	-19	(228)	-5	-5
50–59	(267)	+1	-16	+4	-12	-2	-4	(233)	0	+2
Race										
White	(1013)	-1	-3	-1	0	-1	-4	(835)	0	+1
Black	(79)	+15	+30	+4	+5	+38	+78	(55)	-4	-20
Religion										
Catholic	(299)	+5	+11	-2	+2	+13	+19	(233)	+3	+5
Jewish	(42)	-5	-35	-6	+2	-8	-64	(23)	-5	-51
Established Protestant	(105)	-1	-8	-2	-7	-1	-13	(105)	+3	+11
Traditional Protestant	(418)	-1	-5	+3	-5	-5	-3	(418)	-1	+2
Modern Protestant	(70)	-8	+12	-6	+20	-4	+7	(70)	-5	-16
None, other	(28)	-5	+23	-6	+72	+1	-10	(53)	-6	-21

							(N)		
Role Factors									
Employment									
Yes	-14	-36	—	—	—	—	(865)	0	-2
Student	-30	-86	—	—	—	—	(18)	+3	+58
No	+13	+36	—	—	—	—	(19)	+3	+26
Spouse employment									
Yes	0	+7	+3	+18	0	0	(248)	-1	+5
No	+6	-11	+7	-19	-16	+25	(509)	0	-14
Not married	0	-22	-5	-19	+13	+10	(140)	-1*	-19*
Family composition									
No children	-36	-161	-18	-97	-57	-253	(323)	-10	-98
At least one child under four years									
One	+55	+123	+42	+64	+56	+127	(51)	+16	+8
Two	+79	+183	+44	+148	+82	+164	(71)	+9	+39
Three	+67	+172	+86	+218	+51	+125	(45)	+6	+29
Four	+84	+213	+89	+232	+72	+179	(58)	+5	+90
All children over four years									
One	-23	-21	-2	+34	-41	-70	(114)	+5	+35
Two	-10	+79	+9	+126	-25	+37	(129)	+3	+66
Three	+8	+97	+7	+135	+1	+59	(68)	+5	+108
Four	+2	+104	+10	+116	-6	+78	(41)	+4	+67
Environmental Factors									
City size									
Large city	+5	+17	-8	+3	+17	+19	(98)	+4	-7
Medium city	-2	-6	+7	+7	-16	-22	(138)	+2	+30
Large suburb	-6	+3	-1	+12	-9	-6	(134)	-4	-26
Medium suburb	+4	-1	+6	+3	+1	-5	(139)	-1	+5
Outlying areas	+4	+26	-6	+45	+17	+15	(32)	-3	+24
Metropolitan area									
New York	+5	-3	+3	-4	+3	+7	(72)	-1	-19
Los Angeles; Chicago	0	-45	+3	-38	-6	-49	(67)	+8	+3

(continued)

Table 3.8 (continued)

	(N)	Women Primary Activity	Women Total Contact	Employed Women Primary Activity	Employed Women Total Contact	Housewives Primary Activity	Housewives Total Contact	(N)	Men Primary Activity	Men Total Contact
Other large cities	(186)	0	−6	+2	−16	0	+7	(138)	0	+8
Medium cities	(182)	+2	−12	+2	−18	0	−11	(161)	−3	−21
Smaller cities	(141)	−2	+11	−5	+2	+8	−4	(103)	+3	−19
Jackson, Michigan	(403)	−2	+16	−2	+24	+1	+9	(361)	0	−1
Day of week										
Weekday	(775)	+3	−9	+1	−18	+7	0	(651)	−2	−27
Saturday	(155)	−9	−1	+1	+19	−18	−15	(113)	−1	+12
Sunday	(156)	−11	+38	−5	+52	−17	+15	(138)	+9	+117
Season										
Fall	(770)	−1	−7	−3	0	+1	+1	(611)	+1	−2
Spring	(333)	+1	+11	+4	−1	+1	−1	(291)	−1	+3
Resource Factors										
Income										
Under $4,000	(120)	+8	+47	+7	+36	−10	+29	(46)	−4	−5
$4,000−5,999	(200)	−5	+12	0	+26	−11	−106	(132)	+5	+12
$6,000−9,999	(446)	0	−4	−5	−7	+5	−1	(382)	+1	−2
$10,000−14,999	(215)	0	−25	} 0	} −31	} +5	} −5	(316)	} −2	} −2
$15,000 and over	(94)	−3	−23							
Paid help										
None	(857)	−1	0	—	—	—	—	—	—	—
Infrequent	(119)	+4	+5	—	—	—	—	—	—	—
Part-time	(215)	−3	−2	—	—	—	—	—	—	—
Full-time	(19)	+17	−29	—	—	—	—	—	—	—

*From separate MCA.

Source: Compiled by the author from the Study of Americans' Use of Time (1965−66).

primary activity time, then for total contact time. As MCA estimates, they reflect the time input for each category of respondents after having been corrected for the presence of the other 12 factors. For example, before this correction, that is, on the basis of the straight-forward diary entries, women over age 50 estimated they spend an average of 51 minutes per day in contact with children (a figure not shown in Table 3.8). However, few women over age 50 have younger children to occupy their time in the household and they differ from the younger women in the sample on other variables as well (employment, education, and so on). When these factors are taken into account, the MCA adjusted figure for this age group increased to 183 minutes (16 minutes below average) which was still lower than that of younger groups, but not much lower than the average of 199 minutes for all women. In this way, then, age becomes a far less significant factor in child care than appears from inspection of the simple diary averages for women over age 50 as a group. The analysis thus suggests that if they had equivalent numbers of children as younger women, they would not spend much less time on child care.

Of all the factors contributing to child care, the role factor of number and age of children, not surprisingly, predominated. As expected, Table 3.8 does show younger children taking up more time than older ones and more children taking more time than fewer children, although the marginal per-child increases in additional children are neither as steep nor as monotonic as one might expect. A more detailed consideration of these family compositional factors will be considered shortly (see Figure 3.3).

A primary personal factor of interest is parental education. The hypothesis that better-educated parents devote more time to children receives only marginal support in the figures of Table 3.8 which are corrected to take into account the smaller families among the better educated. College graduate women and men in the sample did report 10 percent more contact time with children and 20–30 percent more primary activity time after this correction. But while these differences above the average verged on statistical significance, the estimates for men and women with some college experience dipped below the sample mean by almost the same margins. Thus, the lack of a sustained monotonic differential for educational level in Table 3.8 does not constitute strong support for the educational level hypothesis; the below-average child-care time for the college-dropout group held throughout the data in Table 3.8, for men as well as women.*

---

*Two more detailed analyses, not shown in Table 3.7, do provide more support for the importance-of-education argument. Both

The same patterns held true when employed women and housewives were analyzed separately. This separation did tend to sharpen
the educational differentials among housewives, but not among
employed women. Even with this control for employment status,
however, women who did not complete college continued to report
amounts of time with their children that were well below average
and which offset the greater times reported by women who had
completed college.

While the personal factor of age vanished as an important
predictor of child-care time in these MCAs, this was not true for
the personal factors of race and religion. Although based on relatively
small samples, black women did report 15 percent more contact
time and 30 percent more primary activity time than white women;
black men on the other hand reported almost 20 percent less contact
time and 40 percent less primary activity time than white men.
That small group of Jewish women and men, who in Table 3.7
registered among the lowest amounts of housework time, also
reported far below average amounts of child care. Catholics spent
above average time with their children and parents of more higher-
status protestant religions (such as Episcopalian, Presbyterian)
spent more time than parents who were members of more modern
sects (such as Jehovah's Witnesses, Church of God).

Among the role factors outside of family composition, employment status had far greater impact on child care than marital status.
Of the conflicting role pressures that operate on unmarried parents,
it would appear that such additional demands somehow function to
reduce the contact time with children, but do not decrease interaction
in primary activities.* In any event, the effect of employment status
is much clearer, with women who work reporting 30 percent less
than average contact time with their children and almost 45 percent

---

time-use measures may be seen as more reflective of the quality of
care dimension than the measures in Table 3.7. These are: (1)
primary activity care in households where there are children under
five years of age, and (2) that portion of primary activity care which
we have described earlier as interactional (rather than custodial).
College graduate mothers of preschoolers report almost double the
primary activity care that other mothers of preschool children
report and they report 40 percent more interactional primary activity.
Again, however, the inclusion of the some-college group practically
eliminates these gains over the rest of the sample.

*As seen in Table 3.8, the lack of a husband means less time
with children for employed women but more time with children for
women not in the labor force.

less than average primary activity time. In more directly comparative terms, after other factors are taken into account women who
work report about two-thirds as much contact time as women who
do not work, and just over half of the primary activity time reported
by housewives.

A closer examination of the family composition variable in the
two middle columns of Table 3.8 shows employment exerting a
fairly constant effect on child care no matter how many children
in the family.* Roughly the same amount of increased child-care
time is found when the few students or unemployed men in the
sample are compared to those who are employed. It will be remembered again that these figures reflect the differential numbers of
children among employed vs. nonemployed respondents.

Of the four environmental factors in Table 3.8, day of week
proved most significant. Sunday was the primary day for parents
and children to spend time together, although primary activity child-
care time on Sunday increased only for men. Respondents reported
slightly more child contact in the spring than in the fall of the year.
Ecological factors, such as size of city or urban vs. suburban setting,
had little demonstrable effect, with parents in the larger, and presumably more hectic, inner cities reporting more time with children.
The few parents in the outlying, more rural areas of this urban
sample did report more time with children, indicating a possibly
important rural-urban difference.

The major resource factor of income generated results at odds
with those found with its closely related counterpart, education.
Usually in a survey analysis, if one finds differences by educational
levels of respondents, one will find parallel differences by their
income level. While college graduates did tend to report more time
with children, however, those with better incomes reported slightly
less contact time and primary activity time. Presence of paid household help had little effect, except again for that fortunate group of
women who had full-time help. Women with full-time help show an

---

*Moreover, the effect is not much greater if the woman works
full-time rather than part-time. Contact time is unaffected by
women's full-time work, while primary activity time drops less
than an hour per week compared to part-time work. However,
separate analyses reveal that it is the perhaps more important interactional child care that is affected by employment. For employed
mothers of one or two preschoolers, the overall two-to-three ratio
drops to less than one to two, reflecting either that these are older
preschoolers who need less care or that these women receive significant outside child-care help from other family members or from
outside sources.

intensive or compensatory pattern of child care, reporting less
contact time but more primary activity time.

1973 Child-Care Data

Given the considerable interest among economists in the
education–child-care hypotheses (for example, Hill and Stafford,
1974; Leibowitz, 1974; Lindert, forthcoming), it was decided to test
whether the ambiguous results reported in the 1965–66 study could
be clarified with additional and more updated figures. A full-scale
time-use study was too expensive to carry out. Therefore, the following question was inserted in a 1973 national sample and asked only
of mothers with children under 18 years of age:

> We are interested in getting a rough idea of how much
> total time people spend in direct contact with their
> children–doing things with them, talking with them, and
> so forth. We do not include time spent just baby-sitting
> or keeping track of your children. Of the 16 or so hours
> you were awake yesterday, roughly how many hours did
> you spend in direct contact with any of your children?

The question was separately asked for a weekday, Saturday, and
Sunday, to compile a weekly estimate of child-care time.*
 The fact that the average of 45.8 hours was about 25 percent
larger than that contained in the "with whom" diary entries in 1965–66
may be due to increased attention given to children over the eight-year

---

*Since weekend child care is known to exceed weekday child
care, separate estimates were obtained for a weekday (for the day
preceding the interview if the respondent was interviewed on a
Tuesday through a Saturday; for the preceding Friday if the respondent was interviewed on a Sunday or Monday) and for the preceding
Saturday and for the preceding Sunday. As the previous sentence
implies, the specific three days inquired about varied, depending
on the day on which the interview was conducted.
 The total weekly estimate for each respondent was calculated
as follows: the weekday estimate was multiplied by five and the
Saturday and Sunday figures added to it. For example, if the respondent was interviewed on a Thursday and she estimated she had spent
six hours with her children on Wednesday and eight hours on the
preceding Saturday and 12 hours on the preceding Sunday, her weekly
estimate would be 50 hours.

interim between the studies; but it is also in line with the experience of our findings reported in Chapter 1 that respondent estimates exaggerate time spent in various activities in comparison to diary figures. It will also be remembered that respondents in the 1973 study were instructed in the above question not to include perfunctory child-care attention in their estimates, and since such attention was included in the "with whom" diary entries, this is further evidence of the exaggeration of direct estimates. Moreover, much the same conclusion about the generosity of respondent estimates has emerged from data collected from other samples (Robinson, forthcoming).

To control for the effects of other factors, an MCA was also performed on these estimates of total time spent with children. In brief, the results of these analyses ran clearly counter to the central hypothesis. Even after correction for number of children, a strong negative and monotonic relation was found, with grade-school-educated women estimating 52.6 hours a week in contact with their children compared to only 36.3 hours a week for college-graduate mothers. This held true even though it is plausible to expect college-educated women to give inflated estimates because they "know" that spending larger amounts of time with their children is a more socially desirable response.*

As in Table 3.8, the number of children had far less effect on estimated child care than the age of children, and women not in the labor force estimated significantly more child-care time. In this 1973 study, data were also available on two new factors, namely, women's attitudes and the sex ratio of children in the family. As expected, women with more traditional sex-role attitudes (that is, those opposed to the women's liberation movement and those thinking women generally are happier at home) estimated 10 to 20 percent more child-care time than those who disagreed with this point of view. The ratio of boys to girls in the family showed a curious relation to child care, that is, least amount of mother's time with children was spent in families where there were equal numbers of boys and girls. Not surprisingly, these mothers did report slightly more child-care time when there were more girls than boys in the family.

---

*The quality of interaction time with children, however, may be another matter. A question in the 1973 Omnibus Study of the Survey Research Center was designed to reflect the quality of child care; it asked how often and how long the family spent its main meal together. Data for the average number of meals and length of time at meals did show clear, but not large, differences by educational level in the hypothesized direction.

The Impact of Children on Daily Time Use

While parental education may not exert as much influence as is thought, the arrival of children is obviously a crucially important determinant of time use. Table 3.8 has documented the strong relation that exists between child-care time and family composition. These features of time use are examined more extensively in this section, with special attention given to how age and number of children affect time devoted to children, what kinds of long-term time commitments are activated when parents have children to care for, and what activities seem to be given up with the arrival or presence of children in the household.

Figure 3.3 graphically illustrates the conclusion reached in Table 3.8 that the age of the children made more of a difference in women's child-care time than the number of children. The preschool age break used in Table 3.8, namely four years of age, may not be the optimal one, but Figure 3.3 does make it obvious how much more time the preschool child required both in terms of contact time and in primary activity time. Other factors being equal, a child under four years of age received 50 percent more of a mother's contact time and three times as much of her primary activity time than a comparable child beyond the preschool age of four.

While Figure 3.3 makes clear that mothers of large families spent more time with their children than mothers of smaller families, the relation strays markedly from the expected monotonic function once one moves beyond the two-child family. Other things being equal, the addition of a second child added about 50 percent to both contact time and primary activity time if the children were all over four years of age, but only 20 percent if one of the children was under four—again emphasizing the predominance of the child-age variable. While Figure 3.3 does confirm the notion that the first child sets the pattern of a change in life style of the married couple, it is not until the third child that, at least time-wise, children start to become "cheaper by the dozen."

One might ask whether the presence of an older child (that is, over age four) reduces the time expenditures of the mother of a preschool child, since the child can entertain or otherwise baby-sit for the preschooler, or increases these demands, since there are at least two children to care for. A separate MCA designed to answer this question more directly indicates that the former rather than the latter condition prevails, that is, here number of children does become important. In terms of both contact time and primary activity time the mothers of preschool children devoted slightly more attention to children if they also had a school-age child in the family.

FIGURE 3.3

Differences in Child Care by Age and Number of Children

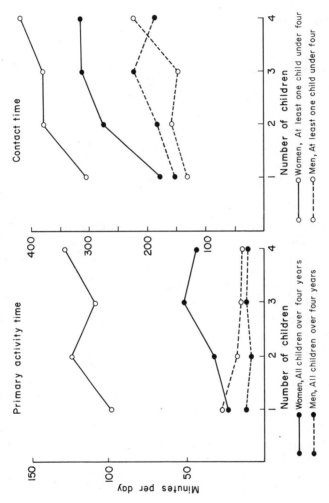

Source: Compiled by the author from the Study of Americans' Use of Time (1965–66; national and Jackson combined).

Undoubtedly, considering the exact age of the school-age child, whether in high school or grade school, can alter this picture, although we have not been able to examine this matter closely.* We have, however, examined in separate analyses the effect of the more detailed ages of the preschool child and find age of the preschooler made practically no difference in total contact time. However, it did make a decided difference in primary activity time. Mothers of infants in their first year of life reported over three hours of primary activity time, compared to less than two hours for mothers of children under two or three years of age.

In contrast to these wide-ranging differentials among women, the data for men in Figure 3.3 are noteworthy for their lack of relation with either the age or the number of children involved. It will be remembered from Table 3.8 that father's child-care time did not increase in response to the wife's employment either. In fact, in terms of contact time, the pattern was quite the reverse of that for women, that is, fathers of older children recorded about 10 percent more child-contact time than did fathers of preschoolers. Only among fathers of older children did contact time approach that for women, namely for those with older children. This can be seen as a further elaboration of men's and women's different parental-role expectation as reflected in the components of the primary activity totals, that is, while 37 percent of men's total child care was custodial in nature (rather than interactional), 75 percent of women's child care was custodial.

The data in Table 3.8 make it possible to form rough estimates of the long-term time demands brought on by children. A woman with only one child will devote 5 percent of her waking life to primary activity child care in the first 3.8 years of that child's life, with 22 percent of her time spent in contact with the child. If the woman has four or more children, these two percentages approach 7 and 30 percent, respectively. In contrast, practically no matter how many children the man has, less than 2 percent of his primary activity time will be devoted to child care, with most of this being interactional; 17 percent of his total time will be spent in contact with his children, however.

What activities did people "trade off" to devote this time to their children? While the data cannot be taken as definitive since they are uncontrolled for other factors (such as age or race), a comparison of the time diaries of fathers of many children and fathers of few children, or fathers and nonfathers (see Table 2.4

---

*Lindert (forthcoming) has examined this matter with the Walker and Woods data set.

in Chapter 2), suggests that with fewer or no children, free-time activities involving out-of-home entertainment (movies, museums, nightclubs, and sports events) were markedly higher.

Among women (see Tables 2.5 and 2.6 in Chapter 2), the changes were more pervasive and cut across both free-time and nonfree-time activities. Mothers not in the labor market found themselves getting up to half an hour less daily sleep, while mothers in the labor market put in a quarter hour less work time than did employed women without children. While mass media activities were also lower, television and reading seemed the activities replaced, rather than movies. Social visiting was apparently another major casualty, falling off over an hour a week among women with children or with larger numbers of children. Women without children or with fewer children also devoted more time to rest and to hobbies.

With the arrival of children, however, another way of spending time is necessarily increased rather than decreased. Women with children reported over two hours of additional weekly housework. Again, the interesting question of how women feel about the seemingly paltry contribution that their husbands make to child care and housework under these circumstances must be deferred until Chapter 6.

As noted earlier, child care provides more opportunity than other activities to examine possible outputs from inputs of time. The straightforward contention that the more time parents devote to their children, the higher will be the child's academic performance and the higher that child's subsequent occupational status and economic earnings, has not been supported by the major analyses we have conducted. However, other analyses, such as of interactional child care or care given preschoolers or time spent at meals with children, provide some support for the notion that children of better-educated, middle-class parents do receive higher-quality child care than the children of the less affluent. This proposition is being explored in a series of studies of preschool children in the Minneapolis area (Natali and Goldberg, forthcoming). The studies have collected data not only on the quantity and "quality" of time invested in children, but the child's subsequent performance in school and on academic achievement tests.

PERSONAL NEEDS

In contrast to work, housework, and child care, Table 3.9 shows virtual constancies in time required for personal needs by sex, employment status, and days of the week, and these are the variables that provide the major discrimination in these activities in Table 2.2 of Chapter 2. Across all days of the week, employed

TABLE 3.9

Time Spent on Personal Care
(minutes per day)

	Employed Men				Employed Women				Housewives			
	M–F	Sat	Sun	Total	M–F	Sat	Sun	Total	M–F	Sat	Sun	Total
14. Personal care												
32. Personal service	1	3	0	1	1	11	0	2	3	0	0	2
33. Medical service	1	4	0	1	1	1	0	1	3	–	1	2
40. Personal hygiene	45	52	42	46	56	64	70	59	51	59	54	52
41. Personal medical	–*	–	1	–	–	0	0	–	1	0	–	1
48. Private, other	9	18	12	11	12	19	24	15	18	15	14	17
15. Eating												
06. Meals at work	21	7	3	16	18	6	2	14	–	0	0	–
43. Meals, snacks	54	59	71	57	46	55	54	48	73	65	64	71
44. Restaurant meals	15	25	12	16	9	17	5	10	6	7	6	6
16. Sleep												
45. Night sleep	439	452	522	453	436	469	533	455	456	475	495	464
46. Day sleep	9	15	18	11	9	9	34	12	9	8	14	9
Total Hours per Day	9.9	10.6	11.3	10.2	9.8	10.8	12.0	10.3	10.3	10.5	10.8	10.4
Total Hours per Week	49.3 + 10.6 + 11.3 = 71.4				49.8 + 10.8 + 12.0 = 72.0				51.6 + 10.5 + 10.8 = 72.9			

*A dash indicates less than .5 minutes per day.

Source: Compiled by the author from the Study of Americans' Use of Time (1965–66).

men averaged 10.2 hours per day; employed women, 10.3 hours; and housewives, 10.4 hours. Women reported more personal care, while men reported more eating, although sex differences were reduced by including eating as a secondary activity. Table 3.9 also shows the increased sleep and personal care that took place on weekends and the changed locus of meal consumption that occurred then as well.*

There are hints of certain "trade-offs" among some activities in Table 3.9 that may be noted. These mainly concern the employed woman, whose dual work and housework burdens did not appear to affect the overall amount of sleep that she obtained across the week. However, this was achieved through an hour and a half more sleep and almost an additional half hour of naps on Sundays. When compared to the housewife, the employed woman also appeared to trade the greater time on personal hygiene for less time eating.

Perhaps the most interesting observation about personal-need activities is the closeness of the average-amount-of-sleep total to the proverbial eight-hour-per-day figure. It is, however, necessary to add naps, resting (treated below as a leisure activity), and the increased sleep achieved on weekends to reach this average figure over the week.

One stereotyped predictor of sleep, however, failed to yield any difference in amount of sleep time, namely age. Older people, if employed, slept no more than younger people. Two other stereotyped predictors were associated with less sleep but only among women, namely, presence of more children and distance to work.

TRAVEL

One of the novel features of the current time-use survey is that it may be the first full inventory of travel behavior in this country. Most transportation statistics focus simply on trips taken by automobile or travel done by mass transit. The travel data in Table 3.9 reflect not only this vehicular movement of adults between locations,

---

*The data in Table 3.9 suggest that while meals eaten at home increased on weekends, total eating time decreased. The figures in this table, however, excluded meals consumed at dinner parties, receptions, etc. (code 76) and addition of these meals could bring the total eating times of housewives up to the level reported by employed men. Employed women still averaged about an hour and a half less eating time than men.

but trips to the neighbors and walks to stores and restaurants.
Overall, transportation by foot is dwarfed by automobile and mass
transit, the modes by which about 85 percent of all travel in our
diaries took place. Nevertheless, the proportion of nonvehicular
travel is an interesting social indicator and it is unfortunate that
reliable comparable figures from earlier time-use surveys are not
available.* The present figure may confirm the worst expectations
of earlier time-diary analysts (Lundberg et al., 1934), who lamented
the decline of pedestrian travel well before the automobile became
as standard a feature of daily life as it is today.†

Table 3.10 considers time required for travel related to each
set of activities.‡ Commutation to work is added up separately at
the bottom of Table 3.10, since it has already been analyzed in
Table 3.1. With its inclusion, employed men emerge as the most
traveled group at 11.0 hours a week, their travel being relatively
constant across all days of the week. With its exclusion, the 6.7
hours of travel time by housewives emerges as the highest travel
figure, not only in connection with obligatory activities (such as
chauffeuring children and shopping) but also in connection with free-

---

*The inclusion of walking and mass transit helped lead us to
quite different conclusions than reached by Lansing and Hendricks
(1967) about the correlation of income with travel behavior. Lansing
and Hendricks found persons with family incomes over $10,000 per
year making 7.7 trips per day compared to only 2.9 when family
income was below $5,000. We also found affluent people, particularly
affluent housewives, spending more time traveling; but after multivariate controls the order of magnitude was more like 30 percent
than the 156 percent differential found by Lansing and Hendricks.
Most pedestrian travel was reported in large cities like New York
and Chicago.

†One interesting social indicator that can be extracted from our
data is time spent in automobiles. This averaged to over an hour
a day, or about 7 percent of adult waking life.

‡Travel times associated with each activity must be approximate
because of our coding conventions. A round trip to a single location
counts as two trips. A trip to the store, dropping the children off
at a neighbor's house along the way, and the return home would count
as three trips—two for shopping, one for child care. Thus, stops
on the way to or from work are excluded from our figures on work
trips. The largest number of trips reported by any respondent on
the diary day was ten, the smallest, zero. While less than 3 percent
of employed men reported no travel on their diary day, 8 percent of
employed women and 19 percent of housewives reported no travel.

TABLE 3.10

Travel Time
(minutes and hours per day)

	Employed Men				Employed Women				Housewives			
	M–F	Sat	Sun	Total	M–F	Sat	Sun	Total	M–F	Sat	Sun	Total
17. Personal												
29. Child	3	3	8	3	4	4	1	3	8	6	4	7
39. Shop	14	28	16	16	18	27	11	18	25	22	6	22
49. Personal	7	18	9	9	6	16	3	7	6	10	12	7
18. Leisure												
59. Study	1	0	—a	1	1	0	0	—	1	0	0	1
69. Organizational	2	7	10	4	1	5	12	3	3	2	15	5
79. Social	9	20	20	12	6	20	21	10	10	21	21	13
89. Active leisure	1	3	5	2	1	3	5	2	1	3	5	2
99. Passive leisure	—	—	—	—	—	—	—	—	—	—	—	—
Total Nonwork Travel Hours per Day	.6	1.3	1.1	.8	.6	1.2	.9	.7	.9	1.1	1.1	1.0
Total Nonwork Travel Hours per Week	3.0 + 1.3 + 1.1 = 5.4				3.1 + 1.2 + .9 = 5.2				4.5 + 1.1 + 1.1 = 6.7			
Total Travel Hoursb per Day	1.6	1.8	1.4	1.6	1.3	1.4	.9	1.3	.9	1.1	1.1	1.0
Total Travel Hoursb per Week	7.8 + 1.8 + 1.4 = 11.0				6.5 + 1.4 + .9 = 8.8				4.5 + 1.1 + 1.1 = 6.7			

aA dash indicates less than .5 minutes per day.

bIncluding work–related travel (09).

Source: Compiled by the author from the Study of Americans' Use of Time (1965–66).

time activities. Table 3.10 also shows the extent of predictable day-of-the-week differences in travel, that is, shopping trips showed a 50 percent spurt on Saturdays and trips to church an even larger spurt on Sundays; trips for social activities or for leisure activities more than doubled on both Saturdays and Sundays.

Again, several factors that we expected would predict the amount of nonwork travel time failed to produce much discrimination. Car owners did not spend consistently less time traveling than those without cars.* Moreover, while the environmental factors of city size, urbanicity, distance to city, distance to work, region, season, and weather generally emerged as rather poor predictors of most activities in Table 2.2 of Chapter 2, their lack of correlation with nonwork travel was perhaps most surprising. Occasionally these factors did perform as expected in individual entries in Tables 2.4 to 2.6 of Chapter 2, as when housewives' nonwork travel is lower in poor weather in Table 2.6. However, the only consistent differences were found for the greater nonwork travel for people in more densely settled urban areas and for people who lived further away from the center of the city. Even these somewhat paradoxical results suggest the need for a much larger data base and an analysis program sensitive to interactions among these environmental factors, such as Morgan et al. (1966) have carried out for the trip to work.

Nor is this picture clarified when an MCA is performed on all nonwork travel as a dependent variable. After control for other factors, we find lower-than-average travel times in outlying areas for women, but within the city limits for men. The patterns noted earlier for automobile ownership all but disappear when multivariate controls are applied, as do educational differences.

Two predictors do emerge from the analysis, however, namely, presence of only older children in the household, and income. Older children appear to require more chauffeuring and shopping travel than younger children, while the affluent use their automobiles more for both obligatory and leisure activities.

———

*The picture is a complicated one as Tables 2.4-2.6 in Chapter 2 indicate. First of all, automobile owners did not spend more time in such travel than nonowners, but slightly less, as a result of less leisure-related travel. With the addition of second (or third) cars, however, such travel increased but only for women and here in connection with obligatory activities rather than for leisure activities. In other words, the presence of an automobile was associated with less nonwork travel, except apparently for the wife who has access to a second car in the family, a vehicle she mainly uses to carry out her family obligations.

4

Of the 168 hours available to them weekly, respondents in our 1965–66 national sample devoted about 80 percent to the obligatory activities of work, housework, personal needs, and related travel considered in Chapter 3.* For employed men, about 135 weekly hours were consumed by these activities, compared to 140 hours for employed women and 128 for housewives.

The figures on obligatory activities discussed in Chapter 3 are depicted graphically by day of the week in Figure 4.1. Time required for personal needs clearly dominates each of the nine bar graphs and its relatively small variation can be clearly seen. While work and housework declined markedly on the weekend, they still required over six hours of collective attention on Saturdays and up to five hours on Sundays. Even though employed women devoted less time than housewives to housework on the weekends, additional work time that some of them put in on Saturdays and Sundays raised their total "work" to a slightly higher figure than that of housewives even on the traditional "days off" from work.

What remained was far less "free time" than we anticipated before the survey, only 40 hours per week for housewives, 28 hours for employed women, and 33 hours for employed men. Combining the data for housewives and employed women produced almost exactly the same amounts of free time available to women as men.

------

*The travel figures here and in Figure 4.1 include commutation to work but do not include travel associated with leisure-time activities (noted in Table 3.9 of Chapter 3). Leisure travel is included in the block of other free-time activities in Figure 4.1, and is noted by a dotted line in that block.

FIGURE 4.1

Hours per Day Devoted to Various Types of Activities

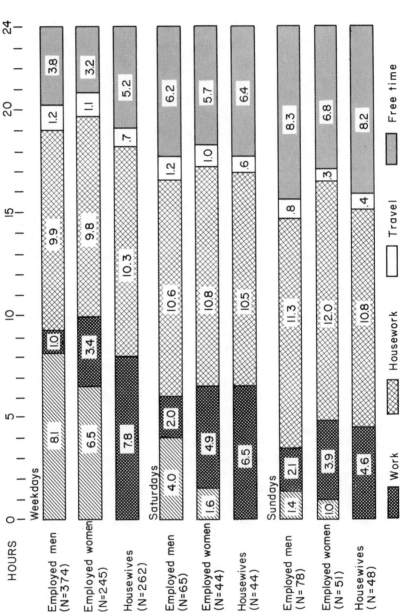

Source: Compiled by the author from the Study of Americans' Use of Time (1965–66).

In other words, the combined work and housework of women in 1965 balanced almost exactly the figures for men, and while men spent slightly more time in travel, women used slightly more for physical care and rest. The overall result was practically no difference in free time by sex.

While housewives had 40 percent more free time available to them than employed women (4 percent of employed women reported no free-time activity during the diary day), on a proportional basis they distributed this time in remarkably similar fashion across activities. The data in Table 4.1 do show some possible "trade-offs," although many of these were attributable to employed women being more likely to be unmarried and younger than housewives. Thus, while housewives spent proportionately more time on organizational activity, employed women spent more on adult education. While housewives spent slightly more time watching television or on hobbies at home, employed women spent more time going out to movies, sports or cultural events, and places of entertainment.

There were, of course, more differences in percentage allocations of free time between men and women in Table 4.1, but even these differences were not as large as might have been expected. Men were heavier consumers of the mass media and adult education and spent more time in sports and other outdoor activities. Women, on the other hand, devoted proportionately more time to such home-based activities as entertaining, conversation, resting, and needlework; they were also more involved in religious activities. Few of these differences are greater, however, or even approach the four-to-one ratio for housework and child care found in Chapter 3. Nor, as we shall see, were weekday-weekend differences in leisure activities as dominant as might be expected, given the larger blocks of uninterrupted free time on weekends. Proportionately somewhat less free time was spent with the mass media on weekends, and proportionately more to active leisure, particularly socializing and outdoor recreation.

The rest of this chapter contains, first, an overall analysis of differences in available free time and then an analysis of each free-time activity in the three major components of free time we have identified.

THE PREDICTORS OF FREE TIME

The coding of time-use data into discrete categories naturally involves arbitrary definitions and procedures. The definition of free time utilized here, consisting of activity categories 18-37 in Table 2.2 of Chapter 2, could be said to be "culture free." It was

TABLE 4.1

Differences in Free-Time Use by Sex and
Employment Status

	Percent of Free Time		
	Employed Men (N = 520)	Employed Women (N = 342)	Housewives (N = 355)
18. Leisure travel	7	6	6
19. Study	4	3	1
20. Religion	3	4	4
21. Organizations	2	1	3
22. Radio	2	2	1
23. TV (home)	35	26	28
24. TV (away)	—[a]	1	—
25. Read paper	9	6	6
26. Read magazines	2	3	2
27. Read books	1	2	2
28. Movies	1	1	1
29. Social (home)	7	12	10
30. Social (away)	12	12	12
31. Conversation	4	7	8
32. Active sports	3	2	1
33. Outdoors	1	—	1
34. Entertainment	2	3	1
35. Cultural events	—	—	—
36. Rest	2	4	4
37. Other leisure	3	7	10
Total Free Time	100[b]	100[b]	100[b]

[a]A dash indicates less than .5 percent.

[b]Totals do not add to exactly 100 percent due to rounding.

Source: Compiled by the author from the Study of Americans'
Use of Time (1965–66).

established from the non-Western and noncapitalist perspective of
the Eastern European partners in the multination project. The
definition drew heavily on the considerable policy experiences of
these researchers in the analysis of time-use data.

This definition does exclude from free time any leisure that
may be obtained during work or housework, or during personal care
activities (such as eating) that can have a strong discretionary
component. Moreover, it includes education and organizational

activity, along with social entertaining and other leisure activities all of which often have a work orientation. Nevertheless, it is objectively defined on the basis of activities themselves, rather than some additional subjective judgment that would have to be imposed by respondents or researchers onto time-diary entries. Some empirical support for this division of free time and obligatory activities will be found in the next chapter.

To recapitulate, the definition consists of the three main classes of activities considered in this chapter:

1. Organizational activity, including time spent in adult education, religious activities, and more straightforward participation in formal organizations such as PTA, Boy Scouts, or union activities.

2. Mass media, including both broadcast media of radio and television, attendance at movies, and reading of the printed media.

3. Socializing and recreation, including mainly visiting and conversations, but also sports and hobbies, relaxation, and organized forms of social entertainment.

We have seen that these activities average out to just under five hours per day across all days of the week, a figure short of the proverbial "eight hours for play" because of time needed for household demands and personal care. Table 4.2 contains the adjusted MCA figures for the 298 minutes of free time that both men and women had, using the same sets of predictor variables employed in Chapter 3 and including the Jackson sample data.

Among the personal variables in Table 4.2, only age produced systematic variation, people under age 30 recording about 45 minutes more free time than groups of older people.* Free time declined steadily with age, and the most dramatic age break occurred between those under age 30 and those over 30. Among the other personal variables, slightly more free time was found among the better educated and among black and Jewish women.

All three role factors of employment, marriage, and parenthood related to free time in the expected directions. Marriage, however, was associated with only about 20 minutes less free time for men and 30 minutes for women. In contrast, free time practically doubled

---

*The difference cannot be attributed to longer sleeping times among the elderly, since we have already seen that such expected differences in sleeping time were all but nonexistent. There was a tendency for older people to spend more time eating, but it was the greater housework and shopping time recorded by older people that accounted for their having less free time.

TABLE 4.2

MCA Results for Free Time
(minutes per day above and below average;
national and Jackson data combined)

	(N)	Women	(N)	Men
Total Sample Average		298 min.		298 min.
Standard Deviation		170 min.		194 min.
Personal Factors				
Education				
Grade school	(126)	−16	(129)	−17
Some high school	(215)	+2	(187)	−2
High school graduate	(492)	−8	(304)	+1
Some college	(153)	+32	(134)	0
College graduate	(109)	+4	(141)	+11
Age				
18–29	(306)	+23	(240)	+31
30–39	(261)	0	(198)	−6
40–49	(264)	−11	(228)	−4
50–59	(266)	−16	(233)	−23
Race				
White	(1011)	−3	(835)	0
Black	(79)	+38	(54)	+1
Religion				
Catholic	(299)	−12	(233)	+15
Jewish	(42)	+28	(23)	−27
Established protestant	(154)	+14	(105)	−26
Traditional protestant	(502)	0	(418)	+5
Modern protestant	(76)	+7	(70)	−7
None, other	(28)	−14	(52)	−6
Role Factors				
Employment				
Yes	(532)	−66	(883)	−8
No	(560)	+62	(27)	+267
Spouse employment				
Yes	(810)	−7	(248)	+8
No	(30)	−28	(509)	−8
Not married	(250)	+25	(139)	+10
Family composition				
No children	(420)	+37	(322)	+13
At least one child under four years				
One	(60)	−25	(51)	−61
Two	(70)	−35	(61)	−13
Three	(54)	−41	(45)	−7
Four	(74)	−71	(58)	+11

	(N)	Women	(N)	Men
All children over four years				
One	(130)	+5	(114)	−25
Two	(137)	−16	(124)	+6
Three	(93)	−21	(68)	+22
Four	(54)	−17	(41)	+9
Environmental Factors				
City size				
Large city	(131)	−26	(97)	+8
Medium city	(155)	+10	(138)	−13
Large suburb	(185)	0	(134)	+9
Medium suburb	(186)	−9	(139)	−16
Outlying areas	(42)	−42	(32)	+39
Metropolitan area				
New York	(105)	−7	(71)	−44
Los Angeles; Chicago	(86)	−5	(67)	−47
Other large cities	(186)	+11	(138)	−8
Medium cities	(182)	−5	(161)	+14
Smaller cities	(140)	−2	(103)	+26
Jackson, Michigan	(402)	0	(361)	+6
Day of week				
Weekday	(790)	−37	(650)	−56
Saturday	(154)	+38	(113)	+58
Sunday	(156)	+152	(138)	+224
Season				
Fall	(769)	+3	(610)	+3
Spring	(332)	−7	(291)	−7
Weather				
Beautiful	(252)	−7	(206)	+1
Fairly good	(307)	0	(233)	−8
Average	(205)	−10	(193)	0
Somewhat poor	(186)	+8	(174)	−3
Extremely poor	(114)	+17	(84)	+6
Mixed	(17)	+15	(3)	+173
Region				
Northeast	(156)	+4	(107)	−13
Midwest	(198)	−7	(172)	+3
South	(214)	+14	(158)	−6
West	(131)	+3	(103)	+6
Resource Factors				
Income				
Under $5,000	(191)	−13	(97)	+11
$5,000–5,999	(118)	+22	(78)	−4
$6,000–7,499	(194)	+2	(154)	−14
$7,500–9,999	(252)	−11	(238)	−3
$10,000–14,999	(215)	+12	(213)	+1
$15,000 and over	(94)	+11	(102)	+17

Source: Compiled by the author from the Study of Americans'
Use of Time (1965–66).

for the unemployed and for students. Least free time in Table 4.2, less than four hours daily, was found within a very substantial and familiar segment of the sample, namely, employed women.

Parenthood was also another important role variable. Consistent with our observations about child care in Chapter 3, age of children had more effect on women's free time than the number of children. Having children in the family meant about a half an hour less free time for men, compared to over an hour for women. Nor did men's free time vary systematically as a function of age or number of children as it did for women; some entries in Table 4.2 show fathers of larger families having substantially more free time.

Day of the week, of course, predominated among the environmental variables, free time rising by 50 percent on Saturday and by almost 100 percent on Sunday over the weekday. Slightly more free time was reported in the fall and by respondents living in the West. Among men, one can see some tendency for free time to be more scarce in the larger metropolitan areas of New York, Los Angeles, and Chicago than in smaller metropolitan areas.

Again, we find little systematic or important variation in free time by the resource variable of income, outside of the slightly higher free time reported by the most affluent group (over $15,000) in the sample.

In summary, employment-related factors predominated as predictors of available free time. While presence of children reduced available free time, lower free time was also found among older people largely freed of the burdens of child care. The more affluent and better-educated segments tended to report more free time, but the differences were neither large enough nor systematic enough to warrant extended speculation about the "harried leisure class" or leisure-deprived lower classes. However, social class differences will become apparent as we examine the types of activities people chose to participate in during their free time.

ORGANIZATIONAL ACTIVITY AND
ADULT EDUCATION

Adult education and organizational participation are perhaps the least leisurely of the activities analyzed in this chapter. Indeed, Productive Americans (Morgan et al., 1966) included both of them as clearly productive activities. Adult education activity is motivated more by future occupational gain than by self-fulfillment or the pursuit of knowledge for its own sake (Morgan et al., 1966). Likewise, organizational activity can be more a social obligation imposed by one's social status than a freely volunteered contribution of leisure time to organizational goals. Furthermore, for the deeply religious person, religious practice can be considered an obligatory exercise of their beliefs. Nonetheless, for most people, participation in these activities still involves a considerable degree of discretion.

Such dilemmas of definition may be resolved with the finding of less than 10 percent of one's free time being spent on such formalized activity in the 1965-66 study. Its inclusion then does not grossly inflate figures on free time. As shown in Table 4.3, the average time across the week totaled only 2.0 hours for employed women, 2.5 hours for employed men, and 3.4 hours for housewives.

Religious practice comprised about half of women's time in these activities in Table 4.3, and about a third of men's time. It is practically the only organizational activity reported on Sundays, when a participation rate of 42 percent was found. During the rest of the week, the participation rate dropped to 6 percent, although respondents were not likely to have reported short daily prayers in their diaries, as witnessed by the fact that average length per participant in weekly religious practice was over 40 minutes. Moreover, a good deal of weekday religious observance consisted of reading the Bible, which was coded under reading books (see Table 4.4).

The lower religious activity of the employed woman compared to the housewife suggests that religious observance was adversely affected by her dual burdens of work and housework. On the other hand, their differential participation in other organizational activities puts things in a different perspective. While housewives spent 30 percent more time in religious devotion than employed women, they were over 300 percent more active in other formal organizational activity. Housewives even spent twice as much time as employed men on organizations. Their higher participation during the week and the nature of the meetings themselves (such as scouts, civic hearings) further suggests their "obligatory" character.* Employed men and women either made up this time on organizational matters on Saturdays or belonged to organizations in which Saturday participation was more feasible.

----

*That these activities were performed by housewives from high-income households who have a higher stake in the social system further reinforces this view of the character of these activities (see also Morgan et al., 1966).

The coding of organizational activities into the various categories of Table 4.3 certainly involved the most difficult and arbitrary decisions in the diary-coding process. These European codes did not translate well into the American organizational context. Thus,

TABLE 4.3

Time Spent on Organizational and Educational Activities
(minutes per day)

	Employed Men				Employed Women				Housewives			
	M-F	Sat	Sun	Total	M-F	Sat	Sun	Total	M-F	Sat	Sun	Total
19. Education												
50. Classes (full-time student)	1	0	0	1	1	0	0	1	—*	0	0	—
51. Classes (part-time student)	2	0	0	3	1	0	0	1	2	0	0	2
52. Special lecture	0	0	0	0	—	0	0	—	1	0	0	1
53. Political class	1	0	0	1	0	0	0	0	0	3	0	0
54. Homework	4	2	5	4	4	3	1	3	1	3	0	1
55. Scientific reading	1	0	0	1	0	0	0	0	0	0	0	0
56. Other study	—	0	1	—	—	0	0	—	1	0	0	1
20. Religion												
64. Religious organization	1	—	0	1	1	1	0	1	3	3	3	3
65. Religious practice	2	4	29	6	1	9	39	8	4	7	52	11
21. Organizations												
60. Member participation	—	0	1	—	0	0	0	0	—	0	0	—
61. Participation as officer	—	0	0	—	0	1	0	—	0	0	0	0
62. Other participation	1	2	0	1	—	0	0	—	2	0	2	2
63. Volunteer work	1	2	0	1	—	0	4	1	3	0	0	2
66. Factory council	0	0	0	0	0	0	0	0	0	0	0	0
67. Other associations	2	3	—	2	—	0	0	—	3	0	0	2
68. Other organizations	1	1	2	1	1	6	2	2	5	0	1	3
Total study and organizations												
Hours per day	.3	.3	.7	.4	.2	.3	.7	.3	.4	.2	1.0	.5
Hours per week	1.5 +	.3 +	.7 =	2.5	1.0 +	.3 +	.7 =	2.0	2.2 +	.2 +	1.0 =	3.4

*A dash indicates less than .5 minutes per day.

Source: Compiled by the author from the Study of Americans' Use of Time (1965–66).

Note that across the entire sample, the average 5 percent daily participation in formal organization translated to less than one hour a week in terms of time, and only a small fraction of that involved organizational activity in which the individual, or members of his or her immediate family, was not the sole beneficiary. Little of it, in other words, was "philanthropic" in terms of the larger society. Far more "helping behavior" was accomplished through informal channels (code 42), as when individuals in their diaries reported shopping for a sick neighbor or helping a friend move.

More time was reported for adult education than participation in formal organizations, although the number of participants on any given day was about the same (about 5 percent). Since full-time students who were either unmarried or whose spouses were not employed were excluded from the sample, our estimate of adult education time must vastly underestimate actual participation.

Men spent twice as much time in adult education as either employed women or housewives, even with the exclusion of those few full-time students in the sample; these students' educational activity totaled over four hours a day. As much of this total was spent doing homework and reading as in attending classes themselves, which may be a lower ratio of homework to class time than their instructors expected. While attending classes took place during the week, homework was spread across the week.

Adult education was more prevalent among those with higher incomes and those already having greater education, another example of the "rich getting richer" phenomenon or the selective tendency for people to engage in activities in which they are already proficient.*

---

the three entries we made under code 60 consisted of two union meetings and a meeting for a charity square dance. The only entry under code 61 was for a woman paying bills for her club. Code 62 contained ten diary entries, including attendance at meetings of the Future Nurses Club, the YMCA, the AAUW, and a teachers' group. Code 63 contained nine instances of volunteer work at hospitals and volunteer agencies, the most "philanthropic" of the organizational activities recorded. No activity was recorded under code 66. Codes 67 and 68 included the most participants, 24 and 28 respectively, the usual activities being coded under "other organizations" being parental participation in scouting activities; miscellaneous organizations included a discussion group of the neighborhood elderly, a hearing at city hall, jury duty, and attendance at an organizational Christmas show, among many others.

*Morgan et al. (1966) also reported this finding with their more representative national sample.

Table 2.2 of Chapter 2 also reveals that the better educated reported greater organizational participation. Presence of young children, on the other hand, appears to have had adverse effects not only on organizational participation, but on religious devotion and adult education as well. As expected, older people reported more religious devotion and less adult education and organizational activity. The same pattern was found among blacks with their participation in formal organizations being particularly low. On the other hand, shift workers reported notably less religious activity than average.

MASS MEDIA

Data from commercial rating services, such as Nielsen and Simmons, might lead one to believe that the American public does little else with its free time than attend to the mass media. On the other hand, media use is often neglected in discussions and writings on the topic of leisure. In fact, our data show about half of all free time is given to the media.

Mass media were also a most important locus of secondary activities, which by their nature are thought to "deepen" or expand the time we have available. If secondary attention to the media while performing other activities is included, then time with the media practically doubled. In other words, the additional accompaniment to other activities of an hour's radio listening, over a half hour's television, and close to 20 minutes of reading translates to at least a quarter of our waking lives being spent in contact with one of the mass media. Less than 5 percent of our sample had no contact with the media on their diary day.

Most of this secondary media use accompanied obligatory activities, rather than leisure, such as work (in the case of radio), housework (in the case of radio and television), and eating (in the case of reading).* Hence, the "time-deepening" effect of the media

---

*Separate analyses indicate that 83 percent of secondary radio time, 57 percent of television time, and 42 percent of reading time were associated with obligatory rather than free-time activities. Radio usage was most frequently accompanied by work, housework, eating, and travel; television usage with visiting, housework, child care, and eating; and reading with television and eating. Compared to other countries, radio listening in the United States was more often associated with work and travel and less with reading; television more with housework, child care, and reading, but less with meals and visiting. The data are given in Szalai et al. (1972, pp. 707-709).

introduced more leisure into these obligatory activities than would otherwise have been the case. Including secondary usage, television and newspapers reached the widest audiences on the diary day (about 80 percent), radio being close behind with about 70 percent usage. In contrast, about a quarter of our sample said they had read a magazine and 17 percent a book; less than 2 percent went to a movie.

Table 4.4 documents television's role as America's major medium, consuming twice as much primary activity time as all other media combined. Still, the figures fall well short of the figure of three hours or more per day estimated in Roper's (1971) surveys of the television-viewing public or the six hours per day usually recorded on Nielsen devices. The latter figure is an inappropriate basis of comparison, of course, because it refers to households and not individuals, but the figures of over three hours of individual viewing per day have been regularly reported in other surveys (for example, Steiner, 1963; Bower, 1973) and are widely accepted. In contrast, the data in Table 4.4 show half this much viewing.

What is the source of this wide difference in results? To some extent, the gap is bridged by including secondary activity viewing and by including unemployed and retired people who were not part of our sampling frame. There are other methodological reasons, however, and these are explored in detail in Chapter 6.

For the television viewing that was reported as a primary activity in our diaries, Table 4.4 does show significant differences by sex, employment status, and day of the week. Men reported more viewing than women, and considerably more than employed women; housewives watched more television than employed women. More viewing was reported on Saturdays than weekdays, and even more on Sundays. However, on a percentage-of-free-time basis, only the male-female differences held up. Housewives spent about the same proportion of free time viewing as employed women. Moreover, television viewing actually declined as a function of available free time not only for employed men but also for employed women and housewives.

Men also reported more time reading the newspaper than women; the greater newspaper reading by housewives than employed women in Table 4.4 does not hold up as a function of available free time. Sex and employment status differences in reading books, magazines, and other printed matter were minimal, however. While all reading did increase on the weekends, it was lower as a function of available free time, even with twice as much time being devoted to the Sunday newspaper.

Men also reported more radio listening and movie going in Table 4.4, although women reported more radio listening as a secondary activity. Both radio use and movie attendance were higher

TABLE 4.4

Mass Media Usage
(minutes per day)

	Employed Men				Employed Women				Housewives			
	M-F	Sat	Sun	Total	M-F	Sat	Sun	Total	M-F	Sat	Sun	Total
22. Radio	4	7	4	5	5	4	3	4	2	1	3	2
23. Television	85	92	179	99	57	72	78	62	89	102	121	96
24. Reading, unspecified	3	2	2	3	2	1	1	2	4	6	3	4
25. Reading newspapers	21	23	44	25	14	11	30	16	18	18	38	21
26. Reading magazines	6	11	3	6	3	6	6	4	6	7	3	6
27. Reading books	5	4	4	5	5	0	6	4	7	6	6	7
28. Movies	1	12	10	4	1	11	3	3	1	4	3	2
Total Mass Media												
Hours per day	2.1	2.5	4.1	2.5	1.5	1.8	2.1	1.6	2.1	2.4	3.0	2.3
Hours per week	10.4 +	2.5 +	4.1 =	17.0	7.3 +	1.8 +	2.1 =	11.2	10.6 +	2.4 +	3.0 =	16.0

Source: Compiled by the author from the Study of Americans' Use of Time (1965-66).

among employed women than housewives. While radio use varied
unsystematically by day of the week, movie attendance was dramatically higher on Saturdays.

Table 2.2 identifies education as a predictor of media use
equally as powerful as any of the three variables in Table 4.4.
It will be remembered that this cannot be attributed to better-educated
people having more (or less) free time available than less-educated
people. Better-educated people spent more time reading magazines
and books, listening to the radio, and going to the movies than the
less educated.* The major educational difference, however, occurred
for television.

The simultaneous effects of education, and several other predictors of television viewing in Table 2.2 of Chapter 2, are estimated
in the MCA outlined in Table 4.5. The predominance of education
as a predictor is clear, with significant and monotonic decreases
at progressive steps of education. Its presence also decreases
significantly the viewing differentials noted by the related factors
of income and race.

Employment continues to be the other major factor associated
with lower television viewing in the multivariate context of Table 4.5.
Lower than average viewing was also reported by people aged 18-29,
married people, respondents living in the West and in New York City,
people experiencing better weather, and women with three or more
children.†

––––––

*Follow-up questions on respondents' diary media usage revealed
that the better educated particularly read more news and commentary
magazines, scientific nonfiction and "serious" fiction books, and
editorial-page material in the newspaper. The less educated read
more fiction and general women's magazines, more religious and
light fiction books, and general news stories in the newspaper.
About half the magazine reading reported was accounted for by
general news and interest magazines (such as Look, Reader's Digest,
and Time); women's magazines accounted for another quarter, with
men's magazines, science, business, travel, fiction, and religious
magazines comprising the other quarter. Most books read were
nonfiction, with religious and business books being first; fiction
accounted for only about a quarter of all reading.

Better-educated respondents also listened to more background
and classical music on the radio, while the less educated listened
more to top-40 stations. The better educated watched less fictional-
ized entertainment programs on television, but just as much news
and sports as the less educated.

†Two other factors associated with less viewing, noted in Table
2.2 of Chapter 2 but not included in the MCA of Table 4.5, are adult

TABLE 4.5

MCA Results for Television Viewing
(minutes per day above and below the average;
national and Jackson data combined)

	(N)	Women	(N)	Men
Total Sample Average		80 min.		107 min.
Standard Deviation		89 min.		112 min.
Personal Factors				
Education				
Grade school	(126)	+32	(129)	+5
Some high school	(215)	+17	(187)	+14
High school graduate	(492)	−4	(304)	+8
Some college	(153)	−17	(134)	−20
College graduate	(109)	−25	(141)	−24
Age				
18–29	(306)	+11	(240)	+12
30–39	(261)	0	(198)	−10
40–49	(264)	−4	(228)	+2
50–59	(266)	−8	(233)	−5
Race				
White	(1011)	−1	(835)	+1
Black	(79)	+17	(54)	−14
Religion				
Catholic	(299)	−1	(233)	−2
Jewish	(42)	+6	(23)	−40
Established protestant	(154)	+3	(105)	+8
Traditional protestant	(502)	−2	(418)	−2
Modern protestant	(76)	0	(70)	+15
None, other	(28)	+17	(52)	+5
Role Factors				
Employment				
Yes	(532)	−18	(883)	−2
No	(560)	+16	(27)	+41
Spouse Employment				
Yes	(810)	+2	(248)	+12
No	(30)	−6	(509)	+2
Not married	(250)	−6	(139)	−29
Family Composition				
No children	(420)	+10	(322)	+7
At least one child under four years				
One	(60)	+4	(51)	−22
Two	(70)	−23	(61)	−8
Three	(54)	−17	(45)	−15
Four	(74)	−13	(58)	+4

	(N)	Women	(N)	Men
All children over four years				
One	(130)	−4	(114)	−17
Two	(137)	+14	(124)	+7
Three	(93)	−23	(68)	−1
Four	(54)	−16	(41)	+23
Environmental Factors				
City Size				
Large city	(131)	+7	(97)	+4
Medium city	(155)	−2	(138)	+7
Large suburb	(185)	−4	(134)	−2
Medium suburb	(186)	−6	(139)	+6
Outlying areas	(42)	−12	(32)	+31
Metropolitan Area				
New York	(105)	−28	(71)	−35
Los Angeles; Chicago	(86)	+5	(67)	+15
Other large cities	(186)	0	(138)	−13
Medium cities	(182)	+6	(161)	−8
Smaller cities	(140)	+10	(103)	+13
Jackson, Michigan	(402)	0	(361)	+9
Day of Week				
Weekday	(790)	−3	(650)	−15
Saturday	(154)	0	(113)	+2
Sunday	(156)	+19	(138)	+70
Season				
Fall	(769)	0	(610)	−1
Spring	(332)	0	(291)	+2
Weather				
Beautiful	(252)	−6	(206)	−2
Fairly good	(307)	−1	(233)	0
Average	(205)	−12	(193)	+8
Somewhat poor	(186)	+4	(174)	−13
Extremely poor	(114)	+24	(84)	+5
Region				
Northeast	(156)	+11	(107)	−26
Midwest	(198)	−6	(172)	+7
South	(214)	+15	(158)	+7
West	(131)	−10	(103)	−23
Resource Factors				
Income				
Under $5,000	(191)	+12	(97)	+26
$5,000–5,999	(118)	+7	(78)	−2
$6,000–7,499	(194)	−4	(154)	−13
$7,500–9,999	(252)	−2	(238)	−4
$10,000–14,999	(215)	−4	(213)	−3
$15,000 and over	(94)	−9	(102)	−1

Source: Compiled by the author from the Study of Americans' Use of Time (1965–66).

Of the other variables predicting usage of the other media in Table 2.2 of Chapter 2, age was the most important. Younger adults spent less time reading the newspaper but more time attending movies; the same held true for the related factors of being unmarried, a student, and not owning an automobile.

Note also that a comparison is made in that table parallel to the one made for length of the workweek in the previous chapter, of the activities engaged in less often by people who watched more television on the diary day. Note first that television viewers did not have more free time available. Those free-time activities most consistently associated with less participation by heavier television viewers were visiting, entertainment, adult education, and organizational activity.

SOCIALIZING AND RECREATION

The remaining leisure activities tend to be more "active" than media usage and they consumed just about the same amount of primary activity time as the media did. Of the three general types of activities in this category, over two-thirds were represented by socializing, which consists of entertaining in one's own home or visiting at someone else's home. It also includes conversations, parties, receptions, and games that may be part of the socializing, as well as the socializing that occurs in bars and coffee shops.

The other two types of activities fall into the broad categories of recreation away from home (including sports participation and being a spectator at places of entertainment, sports, and culture) and home-centered leisure, such as hobbies and resting. The full list of such activities is presented in Table 4.6, along with variations in these activities by the basic predictors of sex, employment status, and day of the week.

Socializing, of course, increased greatly on weekends and was higher for women not in the labor force. Overall, women reported more visiting than men; they also reported twice as much conversation as a primary activity.* Sex and day-of-the-week differences

---

education courses and experiencing an unusual day; the latter are seen to arise because of heavier-than-average socializing (as in the case of a family reunion), organizational activity, child care or household management duties, which constitute plausible explanations for decreased viewing.

*Men reported more conversation as a secondary activity, however, and over 90 percent of the daily conversation reported in

TABLE 4.6

Socializing and Recreation (Other Leisure)
(minutes per day)

	Employed Men				Employed Women				Housewives			
	M-F	Sat	Sun	Total	M-F	Sat	Sun	Total	M-F	Sat	Sun	Total
28. Social activities												
75. Visiting	16	62	81	32	17	86	97	39	39	63	82	49
76. Parties (with meals)	6	27	27	12	9	26	30	14	15	33	56	23
77. Cafes, bars, etc.	6	9	2	6	1	0	1	1	—	2	0	—
78. Other social	—*	1	0	—	2	1	1	1	1	0	1	1
87. Parlor games	3	8	9	5	3	5	7	4	6	3	3	5
29. Conversation	12	10	16	12	16	20	22	17	30	17	24	28
30. Active sports	9	3	8	8	4	3	4	4	3	8	0	3
31. Outdoor activities												
81. Fishing, hiking, etc.	1	8	9	3	0	0	0	0	0	3	3	1
82. Taking a walk	—	3	3	1	—	1	5	1	1	1	0	1
32. Entertainment												
70. Sports events	1	4	2	2	0	0	0	0	1	3	0	1
71. Nightclub, circus, etc.	3	13	4	4	5	23	4	8	2	8	3	3
33. Cultural events												
73. Theatre, concert, etc.	1	2	0	1	0	2	0	—	—	0	0	—
74. Museum, exhibit, etc.	0	3	0	—	0	0	1	—	0	0	1	—
34. Resting												
47. Resting	2	3	1	2	5	3	12	6	4	20	15	8
98. Relaxing, thinking	1	6	4	2	4	4	5	4	5	12	5	6
35. Other leisure												
83. Hobbies, collections	3	—	6	3	—	—	1	—	1	0	0	—
84. Ladies' hobbies	0	0	0	0	10	5	4	8	18	13	5	15
85. Art work	—	1	0	—	0	1	0	—	—	1	2	1
86. Making music	1	1	0	1	1	—	0	—	3	0	0	2
88. Other pastimes	2	3	4	2	1	3	1	1	1	3	1	1
92. Playing records	1	1	1	1	1	1	3	1	—	0	1	1
97. Correspondence	2	5	2	3	6	4	8	6	9	10	17	10
Total Leisure												
Hours per day	1.2	2.9	3.0	1.7	1.4	3.1	3.4	1.9	2.3	3.4	3.6	2.7
Hours per week	5.8 +	2.9 +	3.0 =	11.7	7.1 +	3.1 +	3.4 =	13.6	11.7 +	3.4 +	3.6 =	18.7

*A dash indicates less than .5 minutes per day.

Source: Compiled by the author from the Study of Americans' Use of Time (1965-66).

continue to hold on a percentage-of-free-time basis, but not employ-ment-status.

These factors continue to predict to increased visiting in the multivariate context of the MCA in Table 4.7. One different factor that emerges from the analysis in Table 4.7 is age of children, visiting among parents of only older children being notably lower than average; presence of one preschool child, on the other hand, was associated with more visiting, suggesting either the increased social interest generated by the birth of the first child or the need for new parents to seek the company of other adults. Overall, however, socializing was higher among people with no children. It was also more prevalent among younger men and women. Unmar-ried people, black men, suburban residents, and people in the West also reported above average amounts of socializing; Jewish men and women reported below average amounts.

In contrast to socializing, it was men who dominated participation in the four types of away-from-home recreation activities in Table 4.6. Saturdays were the most popular days for these diverse activi-ties; participation did not appear constrained by a woman's employ-ment. In addition to these variables, Table 2.2 of Chapter 2 shows that better-educated and higher-income respondents were more frequent spectators at both places of mass entertainment (such as nightclubs and sports arenas) and of higher culture (like theatres and museums).*

----

the diaries was as a secondary activity. A fuller analysis of conver-sation as a function of the opportunities for conversation during the day reveals that women do make greater use of these opportunities (Robinson and Converse, 1972). Better-educated and younger respondents reported considerably more conversation as a secondary activity than average, but this may be a simple function of the more detailed activity reporting of these two groups. That not all conver-sation was captured in our diaries is reflected by the 15 percent of diaries that contained no conversation even as a secondary activity. In our Jackson sample, where tighter interviewing controls were possible, 50 percent more conversation as a secondary activity was reported and only about 5 percent of diaries listed no conversation.

*The various sports activities and events reported in respondent diaries were of a rather mundane sort. First of all, over half of sports activity consisted of bowling, which explains the lack of a clear relation between sports participation and age; another quarter of "active sports" consisted of exercises. In all but two instances, the "sports events" attended were local high school games or bowling matches.

TABLE 4.7

MCA Results for Visiting Time
(minutes per day above and below the average;
national and Jackson data combined)

	(N)	Women	(N)	Men
Total Sample Average		68 min.		55 min.
Standard Deviation		93 min.		91 min.
Personal Factors				
Education				
Grade school	(126)	−21	(129)	+10
Some high school	(215)	+7	(187)	−6
High school graduate	(492)	−1	(304)	+4
Some college	(153)	+8	(134)	−10
College graduate	(109)	+3	(141)	+2
Age				
18–29	(306)	+10	(240)	+12
30–39	(261)	+6	(198)	−2
40–49	(264)	−9	(228)	−3
50–59	(266)	−9	(233)	−9
Race				
White	(1011)	−3	(835)	−2
Black	(79)	0	(54)	+23
Religion				
Catholic	(299)	−4	(233)	−3
Jewish	(42)	−13	(23)	−10
Established Protestant	(154)	+7	(105)	−1?
Traditional Protestant	(502)	+3	(418)	+5
Modern Protestant	(76)	−13	(70)	−1
None, other	(28)	−4	(52)	0
Role Factors				
Employment				
Yes	(532)	−14	(883)	0
No	(560)	+12	(27)	−6
Spouse Employment				
Yes	(810)	0	(248)	+5
No	(30)	−6	(509)	−4
Not married	(250)	+4	(139)	+8
Family Composition				
No children	(420)	+12	(322)	+7
At least one child under four years				
One	(60)	+24	(51)	+7
Two	(70)	+3	(61)	−1
Three	(54)	−16	(45)	+16
Four	(74)	−13	(58)	−12

(continued)

(Table 4.7 continued)

	(N)	Women	(N)	Men
All children over four years				
One	(130)	−14	(114)	−7
Two	(137)	−7	(124)	−2
Three	(93)	−9	(68)	−11
Four	(54)	−22	(41)	−20
Environmental Factors				
City Size				
Large city	(131)	−20	(97)	−1
Medium city	(155)	+15	(138)	−15
Large suburb	(185)	+1	(134)	+11
Medium suburb	(186)	+8	(139)	+7
Outlying areas	(42)	−36	(32)	+1
Metropolitan Area				
New York	(105)	+4	(71)	+16
Los Angeles; Chicago	(86)	+25	(67)	−28
Other large cities	(186)	+5	(138)	−2
Medium cities	(182)	−9	(161)	+5
Smaller cities	(140)	−8	(103)	−1
Jackson, Michigan	(402)	−2	(361)	+1
Day of Week				
Weekday	(790)	−18	(650)	−20
Saturday	(154)	+33	(113)	+41
Sunday	(156)	+58	(138)	+61
Season				
Fall	(769)	−2	(610)	0
Spring	(332)	+5	(291)	0
Weather				
Beautiful	(252)	−3	(206)	0
Fairly good	(307)	0	(233)	−1
Average	(205)	+4	(193)	+3
Somewhat poor	(186)	+8	(174)	−3
Extremely poor	(114)	−13	(84)	0
Mixed	(17)	+4	(3)	−44
Region				
Northeast	(156)	−1	(107)	+5
Midwest	(198)	−3	(172)	0
South	(214)	+9	(158)	−15
West	(131)	+2	(103)	+15
Resource Factors				
Income				
Under $5,000	(191)	−6	(97)	+7
$5,000-5,999	(118)	+20	(78)	−2
$6,000-7,499	(194)	−5	(154)	+11
$7,500-9,999	(252)	−3	(238)	−4
$10,000-14,999	(215)	+4	(213)	−9
$15,000 and over	(94)	−2	(102)	+10

Source: Compiled by the author from the Study of Americans' Use of Time (1965–66).

Women generally spent more time than men on the various at-home activities reported at the bottom of Table 4.6. They spent considerably more time in rest and contemplation, on women's hobbies (mainly needlework and canning), and on correspondence; men spent more time on other hobbies and pastimes. No sex differences were found for artistic work (painting or making music) or playing records.* With the exception of resting, this diverse collection of activities did not increase on the weekends. While housewives reported over 50 percent more such activity than employed women, this was not much above what one would expect given their greater free time.

In Table 2.2 of Chapter 2, it can be seen that better-educated respondents reported less resting but more hobbies than less-educated respondents. Presence of preschool children produced the opposite pattern, that is, more resting and fewer hobbies; the same pattern was also found among blacks. On the other hand, older women reported more rest and more hobbies.

In general, then, the three role factors of employment, parenthood, and marriage which dominated as predictors of amount of free time did not loom as large in the prediction of the particular free-time activities chosen. Here personal factors become more important, particularly the factor of education which is not only associated with widely varying patterns of mass media usage, but with participation in more active forms of leisure (mass entertainment, organizations, adult education) as well.

The topic of free time is a central one in the following two chapters, Chapter 5 dealing generally with activity characteristics of distinguishing work from leisure and Chapter 6 dealing with some possible conclusions from the application of these "meaning" dimensions of time to the 1965-66 data.

----

*Note that the amount of time spent playing records and tapes was considerably less than that spent listening to the radio. The difference between the two media activities increased by a factor of two when their usage as a secondary activity was included. This suggests that people may prefer to have their music packaged by someone else rather than select it themselves. This may have considerable implications for the acceptance of cassette television in the home, since it too involves far more decision making than turning a dial or selecting among three or four programs. Although not shown in Table 4.6, there was an interesting switch in secondary activity use of radio and records on Sunday when record listening rose dramatically (by a factor of three) while radio listening dropped by half. Perhaps on Sunday people feel they have more opportunity to make decisions about what music to play.

INTERPRETATIONS
AND MEANINGS
OF TIME-USE DATA

5

MEANINGS ATTACHED
TO EVERYDAY ACTIVITIES

The virtue of time being a "neutral" social indicator is also a major liability. It is very difficult to interpret unusually high or low time-budget figures as desirable or undesirable for the people affected. For example, can decreases in the length of the workweek, or time devoted to housework, be seen as increasing the overall quality of life? Should American parents be devoting more time to their children? How much real discretion is involved in "free-time" activities that may involve visiting with business acquaintances or working for a voluntary organization? How much of their "potential" viewing time do Americans spend watching television? What daily activities are most "inelastic," that is, least able to be given up if time pressures arise?

This chapter reviews several experimental attempts to provide preliminary answers to these questions. Most of the data collected have been concerned with the affective meanings attached to daily activities—how people feel about various activities. How much satisfaction does participation in various activities provide? What activities do people isolate as being the "highlights" or the "low points" of their day? These are reviewed first in the general context of all activities, and then with respect to the distinction between obligatory activities and discretionary time.

The second section of this chapter deals with various aspects of the time-scarcity problem, with special attention to the degree of choice involved in various activities. To what extent are various activities seen as obligations or as expressions of inner motivations? What daily activities are most elastic or could be most easily given up in case of emergency? What activities are seen as simple routine, rather than as the result of earlier planning or an unexpected opportunity or bit of free time?

Finally, some further data on information processing during the day are described. What of the respondent's everyday mental life— the conversations or the problems that were found most significant or provocative?

GENERAL AFFECTIVE MEASURES

Three sources of data on affective assessments of daily life are reviewed here: the original 1965-66 national study, and two very small cross-section samples, one in Jackson, Michigan, in 1973, and the other the Interim Survey of the Survey Research Center in summer 1975.

The 1965-66 Time-Use Study

A major portion of this pioneering study of time use was devoted to ascertaining how people felt about various uses of time. The most systematic attempt involved having respondents rate 18 facets of their everyday life on a five-point satisfaction scale; the scale ran between "great" satisfaction at the top of the scale and "no" satisfaction at the bottom. Of these 18 facets, 14 dealt fairly directly with activities (such as, watching television, being with friends), two with possessions central to everyday life (housing and automobiles) and two with basic family structure (children and marriage). As can be seen in Table 5.1, these latter four nonactivity facets were rated as highly potent sources of satisfaction. Children and marriage rated at the top of the list, over 75 percent of respondents saying these provided "great" satisfaction. Housing and automobiles also were placed well above average, being rated as "great" satisfaction by 40 and 25 percent of the sample, respectively.

Among the more satisfying activities rated by respondents, being with friends, helping others, religion, and reading were rated highest. At the other end of the scale, clubs, politics, shopping, sports, and cooking were most frequently cited as providing "little" or "no" satisfaction.

These overall percentages, of course, conceal important variations by social background factors, the most important of which is sex. For example, men rated sports and games near the top of their list, while women put it near the bottom along with politics and clubs. On the other hand, women rated preparing food and shopping near the top half of their list of activities bringing satisfaction, while men rated them even lower than politics and clubs. Women also rated religion as one of their major sources

TABLE 5.1

Activity Satisfaction Items and Responses in the 1965-66 Study
(percent expressing satisfaction on a five-point scale)

	5. Great	4. Much	3. Some	2. Little	1. None	Total	Average Score Men	Average Score Women
Watching TV	17	24	46	11	2	100	3.5	3.4
Sports or games	26	22	22	13	17	100	4.0	2.8
Your house (or apartment)	40	38	15	6	1	100	4.1	4.1
Shopping, except for groceries	17	25	26	20	12	100	2.5	3.7
Religion	34	28	24	9	5	100	3.5	4.0
Reading	32	30	23	10	5	100	3.6	3.8
Following politics or voting	9	16	33	26	16	100	3.0	2.7
Your (house)work	25	35	25	9	6	100	3.7	3.6
Preparing or cooking food	23	26	21	13	17	100	2.5	3.7
Making or fixing things	27	31	23	13	6	100	3.5	3.7
Your children[a]	79	16	3	–[b]	2	100	4.6	4.8
Your car[a]	25	29	27	12	7	100	3.6	3.5
Relaxing, sitting around	24	29	27	14	6	100	3.7	3.4
Helping others	33	44	21	2	–	100	3.9	4.2
Being with relatives	27	37	27	7	2	100	3.6	4.0
Being with friends	33	46	18	2	1	100	4.0	4.2
Clubs you belong to	13	21	21	10	35	100	2.7	2.6
Your marriage	75	18	4	1	2	100	4.7	4.6

[a] if respondent has.
[b] A dash indicates less than .5 percent.

Note: The following question was asked: "Some ways of spending spare time are very satisfying to one person, while another may not enjoy them at all. I'd like to ask how much satisfaction you get out of some of these different things (hand card). Take watching TV, for example. All in all would you say you get great satisfaction, much satisfaction, some satisfaction, little satisfaction, or no satisfaction from watching TV?"

Source: Compiled by the author from the Study of Americans' Use of Time (1965-66).

of satisfaction, while men put it more toward the middle of the list. Women also rated social activities (being with friends, with relatives, or helping others) higher than men. Sex differences were minimal for television watching, reading, making and fixing things, and relaxing; and men and women did not differ dramatically in the satisfaction derived from politics, clubs, and the four nonactivity items (marriage, children, house, and car).

The various satisfaction items intercorrelated differently for men and women as well. Among men, there was some clustering across 11 of the items (such as house, shopping, marriage) around a "home-centered" factor; still only three of the 153 interitem correlations exceeded a value of .30. Among women such a home-centered factor was also found; but it was defined by fewer and different items; for example, food preparation was not among them but religion was. In general, the tendency for a general "satisfaction syndrome" was also more pronounced for men; in other words, if women derived more or less satisfaction from one activity, there was less likelihood that they would derive satisfaction from some other activity.

Other background factors were associated with differential sources of satisfaction as well. The most prominent of these correlates was social status, respondents with higher education, income, and occupational status claiming to derive greater satisfaction from "cultural" items, such as reading, politics, and clubs, but less satisfaction from television and relaxing. In addition, higher education (but not occupation or income) was related to greater satisfaction with sports and being with friends; less-educated people derived more satisfaction from being with relatives.

The other background factors, such as age, marital status, number of children, and race, correlated only sporadically with satisfaction. Older respondents tended to express more satisfaction generally than younger respondents, but only significantly more so for housework, work, religion, and housing. Married people were more satisfied with religion and being with relatives, while single people derived greater satisfaction from watching television. Parents of larger families derived more satisfaction from their children than parents with fewer children in the household, and greater satisfaction from their automobiles—perhaps as a means of escape. Blacks derived greater satisfaction from religion, television, and relaxation.

For many of these correlations, the reader may have detected a correspondence with the results in Chapters 3 and 4 regarding time expenditures for the same activities, that is, greater socializing among women, more sports activities among men, more reading among the higher status coupled with greater aversion to television, more housework and religion among the elderly, and so forth. This correspondence between satisfaction and time expenditures is examined in closer detail in Table 5.2 in which adjusted averages on the various satisfaction scales from an MCA on the relation are presented. This MCA controls for the outside effects on each satisfaction scale of employment status, marital status, number of and age of children, sex, and day of the week; controls are also introduced for the tendency of respondents to report large numbers of "great" satisfactions. Respondents for whom the item was irrelevant (those without automobiles for "car" satisfaction; those not belonging to organizations for "club" satisfaction) are excluded from the calculations, as are those 10 percent of respondents who were not asked this question sequence because they fell into the methodological portion of the sample (see Chapter 1).

The correspondence is indeed a striking one for 10 of the 17 activities for which comparisons can be reasonably made: watching television, playing sports or games, shopping, religion, reading, housework, preparing food, making and fixing things, children, and club activities. For five other activities in Table 5.2, the differences tend to be in the right direction, but are either somewhat inconsistent or nonmonotonic; these activities include work, relaxing, helping others, being with friends, and being with one's spouse. Usually these departures from consistency occur in the bottom two satisfaction categories, which tend to have very low sample sizes and are more likely to generate unstable estimates.

For only two activities (housing and being with relatives), therefore, is any trace of a positive correspondence between satisfaction and time expenditure totally absent. Moreover, these are two of the factors on the list for which an appropriate match-up between satisfaction and daily time use was most difficult to find, housing being linked with total time at home and being with relatives with total time spent on social gatherings (since no distinction in the diary coding was made between socializing done with friends and with relatives).*

The dramatic correspondence between satisfaction and time use in Table 5.2 tempts one to speculate about the direction of causality

---

*A more direct indicator of the "gregariousness" relation may be afforded by comparing how respondents felt generally about meeting new people and making new friends and how much time they spent alone on the diary day. The relation is again a strong one: those "very" interested in expanding their social networks spent 30 minutes less time alone on the diary day than those "somewhat" interested and 113 minutes less time alone than those "not very" interested in making new acquaintances.

TABLE 5.2

Correspondence Between Derived Satisfaction
and Associated Diary-Time Expenditures
(minutes per day[a]; national
and Jackson data combined)

	Great	Much	Some	Little	None
a. Watching TV	131	100	86	55	17
b. Sports or games	15	14	6	2	3
c. Your house	988[b]	962[b]	965[b]	971[b]	1018[b]
d. Shopping	16	12	14	11	9
e. Religion	21	8	3	2	3
f. Reading	51	36	25	14	9
g. Politics	NA[c]	NA	NA	NA	NA
h. Work	228	247	NA	211	136
Housework	248	224	NA	216	202
i. Cooking	53	44	45	39	33
j. Making things	27	11	12	6	7
k. Children	8	6	4	1	5
l. Car	NA	NA	NA	NA	NA
m. Relaxing	11	8	11	7	6
n. Helping others	9	6	3	12	3
o. Relatives	53[d]	55[d]	54[d]	40[d]	60[d]
p. Friends	64[d]	54[d]	37[d]	32[d]	48[d]
q. Clubs	22	14	13	5	4
r. Marriage	178[e]	175[e]	124[e]	133[e]	152[e]

[a]Data are corrected by MCA for employment status, marital
status, number and age of children, sex, and day of the week.

[b]Time spent at home.

[c]NA = No activity.

[d]Total time visiting and at parties (NA whether with friends or
relatives).

[e]Total time spent with spouse.

Source: Compiled by the author from the Study of Americans'
Use of Time (1965-66).

between the two. Do people arrange their daily lives in such a way as
to spend maximum time on those activities that bring them greatest
satisfaction? The fact that most activities in Table 5.2 fall into
the "discretionary" category offers powerful evidence in this regard
(for example, time spent watching television or socializing clearly
can be regulated by individual preferences and values. On the other

hand, the relation also holds for "obligatory" activities, like work
and housework, and it fails to hold well for such highly discretionary
activities as relaxing and helping other people, raising the possibility
of the reverse flow of causality—people deriving greatest satisfactions
from the activities on which they have to spend most time. The
latter outcome would also be predicted on the basis of the social-
psychological literature supporting the theory of cognitive dissonance
(for example, Festinger, 1957; Sears and Abeles 1969). In either
case, the data in Table 5.2 offer dramatic support for the contro-
versial and usually empirically unsupportable view that people's
attitudes and their behavior are strongly interdependent.

A second approach to understanding how people relate affectively
to the various activities that make up their daily lives is to ask them
to isolate the highlights and the low points of a particular day. After
completing the diary in the 1965-66 study, respondents were asked
to think back over the day and to point out the "things you enjoyed
most in the day or the parts that you were most interested in."
Replies were coded into one of the 19 categories in Table 5.3,
which are of three types:
1. Related directly to diary activities (categories 1-10).
2. Related to the general context of activities or qualitative
    aspects of activities; for example, "Seeing a friend again,"
    "Having done the morally right thing" (categories 11-15).
3. Related to the larger social environment, including news
    events reported in the media which the respondent felt
    positive about (categories 16-18).
Other answers and vague replies (for example, "a dog") were coded
into the miscellaneous category. Because of multiple mentions,
the figures in Table 5.3 total to over 100 percent.

It is hardly surprising to find the most frequently mentioned
sources of enjoyment and interest during the day, as listed in
Table 5.3, to be those activities that consumed most time, including
work, housework, child care, personal needs, socializing, and
television.* In addition, however, general interpersonal conditions

---

*Readers interested in comparing these figures to the daily
participation rates on which they are based can find some relevant
data in Table 2.3 of Chapter 2. On a per-participant basis, it would
appear that hobbies, adult education, conversations, and socializing
were more likely to be associated with the most enjoyable parts of
the day and housework, shopping, and organizational activity with
fewest enjoyable daily occasions. With regard to least enjoyable
parts of the day (Table 5.4), socializing, conversation, television,
child care, and organizational participation were mentioned most

TABLE 5.3

Distribution of Parts of the Day Enjoyed Most by Educational Level, Sex, and Employment Status
(percent giving each response)*

	Men			Women					
				Employed			Housewives		
	Less than high school	High school graduate	Some college or more	Less than high school	High school graduate	Some college or more	Less than high school	High school graduate	Some college or more
N =	(153)	(130)	(167)	(83)	(119)	(85)	(96)	(125)	(74)
Part Enjoyed Most									
Activity Related									
1. Work	24	21	30	19	18	36	2	0	0
2. Housework	2	0	1	10	8	2	24	18	11
3. Child care	3	4	5	4	9	4	14	13	15
4. Shopping	4	4	5	10	8	4	8	10	8
5. Personal needs	17	18	18	12	16	4	10	12	8
6. Adult education	0	1	7	1	0	7	0	1	9
7. Organizations	2	2	2	1	1	0	1	2	5
8. Social life	6	14	16	16	17	24	18	22	24
9. Active leisure	9	9	12	9	9	6	8	16	23
10. Passive leisure	31	24	28	22	25	22	30	26	33
(TV)	17	13	10	12	9	3	16	10	4
Contextual									
11. Financial	1	1	1	0	0	0	0	0	0
12. Activities of others	1	1	0	0	1	1	1	1	0
13. Interpersonal	12	13	17	10	11	12	3	12	13
14. Religious, moral	3	6	1	3	4	3	7	2	3
15. Property	4	5	4	1	1	2	6	1	1
General									
16. Societal concerns	0	0	0	0	0	0	0	0	0
17. National	1	0	1	0	0	0	0	0	1
18. International	0	0	0	0	0	0	0	0	0
19. Miscellaneous	0	1	1	0	1	2	2	1	0
No Part Enjoyed Most	9	13	4	12	9	4	8	3	4

*Percentages add to more than 100 because some respondents gave more than one reply.

<u>Source</u>: Compiled by the author from the Study of Americans' Use of Time (1965–66).

("being with the family"; "seeing an old friend") were mentioned with
some frequency.

Table 5.3 provides a breakdown of these responses by our basic
tripartite division using sex and employment status simultaneously
with the factor of education. In Table 5.3, women can be seen as
more likely to mention household-related activities and socializing
as a highlight of their day, while men listed television and general
interpersonal relations ("being with my family") with somewhat
greater frequency. Housewives were more likely than employed
women to mention household-related matters and leisure activities
as highlights; some work activity constituted the most enjoyable or
interesting part of the day for employed women.

The day's highlights varied by educational level as well.
College-educated respondents were more likely to mention work,
adult education, and reading, as well as socializing, conversations,
and general interpersonal situations, than were respondents with
less education. On the other hand, respondents who had not finished
high school were more likely to mention housework and television as
highlights of the day.

Table 5.4 presents the parallel analysis for the least enjoyable
parts of the day. Again the more time-consuming obligatory activities were mentioned most often as low points during the day. In
contrast to Table 5.3, however, this did not hold for socializing
and other leisure activities.

Housework in particular stood out as a least enjoyable part of
the day in Table 5.4. Housewives mentioned it more often than all
other activities combined. Employed women mentioned some facet
of housework as the least enjoyable part of the day more often than
they did work-related activities.

This evaluation of housework offsets a major sex difference
between enjoyable and unenjoyable parts of the day. Employed men
can be seen to be far more likely than employed women to mention
work as a least enjoyable part of the day, even though both mentioned
it with about equal frequency as a highlight of the day. By combining
housework with work, however, employed women as well as house-

---

infrequently on a per-participant basis while work, housework, and
adult education were mentioned relatively most often as low points
during the day. Thus, socializing and child care are seldom noted
as negative activities, housework seldom as a positive activity.
Interestingly, television evokes an average number of positive
reactions per participant but lower than average negative reactions,
consistent with the proposition that audiences choose television
programs on the basis of "least objectionable" programming.

TABLE 5.4

Distribution of Parts of the Day Enjoyed Least by Educational Level, Sex, and Employment Status
(percent giving each response)*

	Men			Women Employed			Women Housewives		
	Less than high school	High school graduate	Some college or more	Less than high school	High school graduate	Some college or more	Less than high school	High school graduate	Some college or more
N =	(153)	(140)	(168)	(83)	(119)	(85)	(97)	(125)	(74)
Part Enjoyed Least									
Activity Related									
1. Work	36	36	33	16	26	21	0	0	1
2. Housework	3	4	4	25	32	31	55	53	46
3. Child care	0	1	3	1	2	1	3	10	4
4. Shopping	3	1	8	5	5	7	5	5	15
5. Personal needs	12	15	17	10	14	17	9	13	12
6. Adult education	0	0	3	0	0	3	0	0	1
7. Organizations	1	1	0	0	0	1	0	0	1
8. Social life	2	0	1	0	2	2	0	1	4
9. Active leisure	4	3	5	1	2	2	3	2	6
10. Passive leisure	2	4	5	2	1	1	4	3	5
Contextual									
11. Financial	3	1	1	1	0	1	0	0	1
12. Activities of others	0	0	0	1	1	0	0	1	0
13. Interpersonal	3	4	3	1	2	5	4	2	4
14. Religious, moral	0	0	1	0	0	1	0	0	0
15. Property	2	6	3	3	1	0	3	1	6
General									
16. Societal concerns	0	0	0	0	1	0	1	0	0
17. National	3	1	1	2	2	1	0	0	0
18. International	0	0	0	0	0	0	0	0	0
19. Miscellaneous	2	4	2	1	0	1	1	3	1
No Part Enjoyed Least	29	27	19	37	18	14	23	12	11

*Percentages add to more than 100 because some respondents gave more than one reply.
Source: Compiled by the author from the Study of Americans' Use of Time (1965–66).

124

wives become considerably more likely to find the "work" portions of their day least enjoyable.

One additional comment is in order about the frequency with which work is mentioned as the least enjoyable daily activity. Note that it is brought up in the negative context of a least enjoyable part of the day more often than in the positive context as the highlight of the day. This stands in marked contrast to the traditional survey finding that workers overwhelmingly rate themselves as satisfied with their jobs (see Quinn and Shepard, 1974; Robinson et al., 1969).* The relation between satisfaction as rated generally and in the context of a single day is examined again in the next study we shall review; the results here show more agreement (see Table 5.5).

The bottom line in Table 5.4 offers an interesting contrast to the bottom line in Table 5.3 in the context of the positivity bias just discussed. Far more respondents could list a most enjoyable part of the day (92 percent) than could name a least enjoyable part (78 percent). Women were more likely to identify both enjoyable and unenjoyable day parts than men, and housewives were more likely to identify both good and bad parts than employed women.

If this ratio can be taken as an index of the richer variety of everyday experiences of housewives, it also describes the everyday experience of better-educated people, who were far more likely than less-educated people to report both high or low points of their day. Perhaps this was also a reflection of the more limited verbal or self-observation skills of the less educated. Table 5.4 suggests that shopping, adult education, and personal-care activities were more likely to be sources of unenjoyable episodes in the daily lives of better-educated people than among the less educated.

Despite the different focus of the two questions in the 1965-66 study, there are certain convergences in Tables 5.3 and 5.4 and Table 5.2. Social life, particularly with members of one's immediate family, clearly stands out as a prime provider of enjoyment and satisfaction. Shopping—and to a lesser extent other housework-related activities—are associated with lower than average satisfaction. The aversion of college-educated people to television is apparent in replies to both questions, as is their stronger preference for educational activities (like reading), conversations with friends, and other active leisure.

———

*The same comment applies to survey questions that dealt with satisfaction with housework, which also tend to be highly positive in contrast to Table 5.4. Note also that national news is more likely to be mentioned as a negative feature of daily life than as a positive feature.

On the other hand, there are numerous inconsistencies. For example, work is rated in the upper half of the objective satisfaction scale for men (Table 5.2), and yet is associated far more with least enjoyable than most enjoyable parts of the day. Television is rated lower than work on the objective scale and yet is mentioned far more often as a high point during the day than as a least enjoyable part. Religion and helping others rate quite high on the objective scale, but both activities occur too infrequently on an average day to constitute distinguishing features of that day.

The data described next were collected to help clarify some of these inconsistencies and to elaborate the general relations between affective measures by examining satisfaction derived from general and specific daily activities in a more systematic manner.

The 1973 Jackson Data

As part of a special methodological study conducted in the spring of 1973, a small cross-section of 140 respondents in the Jackson, Michigan, area, taken from a subset of addresses from the 1965-66 study, took part in a different approach to evaluating the components of their daily lives. They reported their feelings for each activity in the daily diary that they kept on the following five-point scale:

1. Delighted or pleased
2. Mostly satisfied
3. Mixed or neutral
4. Mostly dissatisfied
5. Terrible or unhappy

The scale was derived from the basic research of Andrews and Withey (forthcoming) into the perceived quality of life. Note that on the scale, the lower the score the more positive the feelings toward that activity.

Average ratings attached to the activities in women's and men's diaries using this scale are presented in the left-hand columns of Table 5.5. The overall average scale ratings of 2.0 (for women) and 1.9 (for men) mean that typically activities recorded in the diaries were associated with a "mostly satisfied" response.

The right-hand columns in Table 5.5 contain the ratings on the same scale when respondents were asked to rate how they felt about each of these activities in general; if respondents said they never or almost never participated in the activity, no scale ratings were obtained. The average scale ratings of 1.6 (for women) and 1.9 (for men) mean that the average activity was rated between "delighted or pleased" and "mostly satisfied" for women, but closer to the "mostly satisfied" point on the scale for men. That this average

TABLE 5.5

Average Satisfaction Scores Associated with
Various Activities Generally and as
Recorded in Daily Diaries
(Jackson 1973)[a]

Activity	Women (N = 96)		(Men (N = 44)	
	Diary	General	Diary	General
Obligatory				
Work	2.1	1.8	2.1	1.9
Trip to work	2.1	2.0	2.3	1.9
All other travel	2.2	1.7	2.1	1.9
House chores	2.2	2.0	2.1	2.0
Household maintenance	2.2	2.2	1.9	2.0
Grocery shopping	2.2	2.2	1.8	2.5
Other shopping	2.5	1.7	2.1[b]	2.3
Basic child care	2.0	1.4	1.7[b]	2.5
Child interaction	1.8	1.2	1.4[b]	1.7
Sleeping	1.8	1.6	1.8	1.3
Eating	1.8	1.7	1.7	1.4
Personal care	2.1	1.5	2.1	1.9
Leisure				
Church and religion	1.7	1.3	2.0[b]	1.8
Social organizations	1.9	1.6	2.1	2.1
Education	2.4	1.6	1.7	1.8
TV	1.9	2.1	1.7	1.9
Reading paper	2.0	2.1	1.9	2.2
Reading books/ magazines	1.8	1.5	2.4[b]	1.7
Visiting	1.6	1.2	1.5	1.4
Taking a night out	1.7	1.3	1.3	1.3
Hobbies and sports	1.5	1.3	1.9	1.4
Resting	2.1	1.5	1.7	1.5
Average for all activities	2.0	1.6	1.9	1.9
Average standard deviation	2.2	1.0	2.2	1.0

[a]Scores on a scale running from 1 = delighted or pleased to 5 =
terrible or unhappy.
[b]Less than 10 entries
Source: Compiled by the author from the Jackson Methodological
Study (1973).

general scale response for women was more positive than that recorded in their diaries raises the interesting possibility that responses to activities in general elicit a more positive feeling than as they are actually experienced in everyday life. In this way, the finding is reminiscent of the Table 5.4 finding about the frequency with which work and housework were cited as least enjoyable parts of the particular day, despite the overwhelmingly positive response they elicited when general satisfaction questions were asked.

The data in Table 5.5 however, indicate that the differences between diary and general ratings do vary for different activities. At the same time, these differences were not systematic by activity type. For example, among women, work, travel, and child care were rated more highly in general than in diaries, while housework and grocery shopping were rated at the same level in diaries and in general. In fact, the most interesting difference is opposite to the general trend for both women and men, namely, television viewing was rated more positively in the context of the actual day than in general. This would be in line with the hypothesis that people feel some social pressure to evaluate television as a less enjoyable activity overall than it is as generally experienced. In contrast, the media activity of reading books and magazines was rated more positively in general than it was in diaries, indicating the opposite problem for this behavior, namely, one of social desirability.

Despite these variations, however, there was considerable agreement between the general ratings and diary ratings concerning activities that are associated with most and least enjoyment. Visiting, going out for an evening's entertainment, and hobbies and sports rated at the top of both lists for both men and women. Shopping and housework, on the other hand, fell near the bottom. In addition, religious activities rated high on both lists as positively evaluated activities among women, while among men, child-interaction activities rated high on both lists and commuting and reading rated rather low.*

------

*The collapsing of activities in Table 5.5 did conceal certain interesting variations within activities in the diaries, since diverse activities were often included together in the general categories of Table 5.5. For example, cooking (average score 1.9) was a more satisfying activity than other house chores, and playing with children (average score 1.5) was far more satisfying than other interaction with children. Both of these activities were distinguished in subsequent data collection. More fascinating, however, was the situation concerning travel activities in the diary. Felt satisfaction during travel depended on the purpose of the trip, indicating considerable anticipation or lingering moods associated with its objective. Thus,

Contrary to the satisfaction data obtained in the 1965-66 study, however, the overriding impression from Table 5.5 is the limited variation that exists in activity satisfaction. The range was quite restricted even for these small samples. Among women, average scores varied between 1.5 and 2.5 on the scale for the diaries and between 1.2 and 2.2 for general ratings; averages for most activities were within 0.2 scale units of the overall average, which would be short of statistical significance given the standard deviations and sample sizes.

This was particularly true for the fundamental distinction between "obligatory" and "leisure" activities made so often in discussion about time. To be sure, leisure activities were rated higher on both the general and the diary satisfaction scales than were obligatory activities. However, the differences were not large, being less than at 0.3 scale units overall.

One reason for this, as Table 5.5 makes clear, is that there can be as much variation between obligatory activities as between obligatory and leisure activities. Both child- and personal-care activities often obtained considerably higher satisfaction ratings than many leisure activities. One might even consider child and personal care to be leisure activities if associated satisfaction was the criterion of defining leisure time. Moreover, differences in satisfaction associated with the remaining obligatory activities and leisure activities were not that large.*

The findings from this Jackson sample in Table 5.5 do generally reinforce the findings from the national sample data in Tables 5.1-5.4 about the relative attractiveness of social life and active leisure as daily activities. This was true even though the questions analyzed in Table 5.5 differ significantly in context and in structure from

---

average satisfaction with travel to and from social activities (1.8) was far greater than that associated with all other activities (2.4), including the trip to work (2.2).

*This matter was pursued more directly in the male portion of the Jackson sample. These men were asked whether they enjoyed themselves more at work or more in their spare time. Most of them could not make a clear choice between the two. And while spare time was rated as more enjoyable twice as frequently as work for the remaining third, it is clear that on the basis of this small body of evidence, work and leisure can hardly be said to define polar opposites in terms of satisfaction or enjoyment. Additional questions about difficulties involving degree of effort at work and work schedules, asked of this Jackson sample, further illustrated the ambivalence people have about work (see Chapter 7).

those in Tables 5.3 and 5.5. There are also significant differences in question format from the satisfaction ratings in Table 5.1, since an activity like reading or helping others can provide great satisfaction to people in retrospect, while they may not particularly enjoy doing them as activities as they happen. They also verify the unattractive character of housework and shopping. Nonetheless, one would like to have a wider sampling base on which to place reliance on some of the more provocative findings emerging from the discussion centering on Table 5.5. We turn now to some more recent data from a national sample for corroborating evidence.

1975 National Sample

The methodological focus in this data collection was on evaluation of activities generally rather than for specific instances or days. In addition to verifying the earlier results, there was some experimentation with a scale thought to provide more sensitivity to affective differences between activities than the "delighted to terrible" scale employed in Table 5.5. Toward this end, one cross-section of respondents was asked to rate 28 daily activities in general on this direct scale and another cross-section was asked to rate the same activities on the "delighted to terrible" scale.

The "direct" scale simply ran between +3 and -3, +3 being assigned to activities respondents said they liked doing "a great deal," and -3 to activities respondents said they disliked doing "a great deal." Perhaps the most important feature of this scale is that the use of negative and positive scale numbers makes it possible to define a convenient and perhaps more natural neutral point, namely, zero. In order to make the ratings comparable, the "delighted to terrible" scale ratings were also obtained on a seven-point scale, with four being the neutral point. For comparison with the "like to dislike" scale in Table 5.6, however, four points have been added to the average ratings on the "like to dislike" scale in order to make the value four the common neutral or middle point for both scales.

The total sample consisted of a random subset of 133 respondents from the 1975 Summer Interim Study, a national survey done by the Survey Research Center. Despite the small samples, the results in Table 5.6 show basic consistency not only across the two scales used but with the results in Table 5.5. Both the "delighted to terrible" and the zero-based "like to dislike" scale show child-care interaction, visiting, hobbies, and work to rate near the top of the list and grocery and other shopping, social organizations, household maintenance, and record keeping to rate at the bottom of the list of favorite activities.

TABLE 5.6

Average Ratings of General Activities on Seven-Point Scales[a]

Obligatory Activities	D-T (N=69)	+3 to -3 (N=64)	Free-Time Activities	D-T (N=69)	+3 to -3 (N=64)
1. House chores, cleaning, and laundry	4.6	4.5	15. Church and religious devotion	5.5	4.9
2. Cooking	4.8	5.5	16. Clubs and social organizations (scouts, union)	4.4	4.2
3. House maintenance, repairs, upkeep	4.2	4.8	17. Adult education (classes, homework, reading for class)	5.1	4.9
4. Working around the house or garden	5.2	5.0			
5. Keeping track of household records and expenses	4.1	4.2	18. Watching TV	4.8	5.3
6. Your job[b]	6.0	5.7	19. Reading the paper	5.2	6.0
7. The trip to work[b]	4.8	4.8	20. Reading books and magazines	5.3	6.0
8. Grocery shopping	4.0	4.1	21. Visiting friends or neighbors	5.4	5.7
9. Other shopping—clothes, furniture, appliances	4.4	4.3	22. Entertaining people in your own home	5.6	5.4
10. Basic child care (feeding and clothing your children)[c]	5.4	5.4	23. Going out to a movie, restaurant, or sporting event	5.4	5.6
11. Other activities with your children (playing, reading, teaching)[c]	6.2	6.4	24. Hobbies	5.6	6.0
12. Sleeping	5.7	5.6	25. Playing sports and games	5.0	5.1
13. Eating	5.7	5.8	26. Resting or relaxing	5.5	5.6
14. Personal care (washing, dressing)	5.7	6.2	27. Planning or thinking	5.5	5.8
			28. All your daily travel, except to work	4.7	5.0

[a]D-T scale runs from 1 = delighted to 7 = terrible; +3 to -3 scale runs from 1 = -3, dislike a lot, to 7 = +3, like a lot.

[b]If respondent works.

[c]If respondent has children under 18 in household.

Source: Compiled by the author from the Summer Interim Survey (1975).

There are some differences from the ratings in Table 5.5.
Religious activity in this sample was not rated as highly as it was
in the Jackson sample, and personal hygiene was rated more positively
than in Table 5.5. The wisdom of separating cooking, general work
around the house, and garden from other household work is shown
by their much higher satisfaction ratings in Table 5.6.

In general, however, the results in Table 5.5 line up quite well
with those reported from the two other surveys we have examined.
Activities involving interpersonal interaction, child care, and socializing, again clearly emerged as the most enjoyable parts of everyday
life reported by respondents. While people also derived above-
average enjoyment from going out for an evening's entertainment,
they also enjoyed resting, contemplation, eating, and sleeping. While
it often generated the most frustrating problems of daily life, work
was also judged to provide above-average enjoyment.

Shopping and routine housework, on the other hand, define the
bottom "anchor points" of daily satisfaction. Nor do household
maintenance and paperwork generate much joy. Organizational
participation, television viewing, and the travel associated with
leisure activities are discretionary activities that appear to arouse
less than average positive reactions as well. Evidently, one must
identify free-time activities before interpreting more free time as
leading to a higher perceived quality of life.

TIME PRESSURE

A fairly commonly heard complaint about time in daily life in
the United States is the "pressure" of time, the feeling ultimately
arising from Linder's (1970) key concept of time scarcity. We have
examined this aspect of time from three analytical perspectives.

The most elaborate approach was employed in the 1965-66 study.
It involved asking respondents to make judgments about which daily
activities they would forego given an unexpected pressing demand on
their time from an outside source. More specifically, after completing their diaries, respondents were asked to examine their log
of previous day's activities and then to:

> Suppose that early on (Diary Day) you discovered that
> something had come up suddenly. You could tend to it
> any part of the day or night, but somehow you simply
> had to find one hour to take care of it before you went
> to bed again. In a day like the one you had on (Diary
> Day), what things would you have given up to make room
> for that hour?

The question was then repeated for three-hour periods of time and six-hour periods of time to identify the less "elastic" of these replaceable activities.

Without question, the most "elastic" of daily activities, that is the one most quickly volunteered for replacement, was television. The casual attachment of people to the programs on their television sets could not be more persuasively demonstrated than by the frequency with which it was chosen to be foregone in the event that anything important arose. This was true whether measured in terms of total numbers of hours replaced or in terms of the proportion of time available to be given up (Robinson and Converse, 1972).

The great elasticity of television was also apparent from a second approach to measuring time pressure that we employed in the survey, which involved a single, but more direct, question. Respondents were asked how often they felt rushed to complete their day's activities, with the following percentage responses:

Always feel rushed (even to do the things
  you have to do)   25 percent
Only sometimes feel rushed   53 percent
Almost never feel rushed   22 percent

Those who only almost never felt rushed then were asked how often "you have time on your hands that you don't know what to do with." About half of this last group said they almost never experienced the feeling of unwanted time; a third said they now and then experienced unwanted time; and only a sixth said they experienced it quite often. All together, then, 10 percent of this urban employed sample felt significant problems with excessive free time.*

General confidence in the validity of responses to the question is enhanced by its strong correlation with available free time; thus on a population-group basis, we find employed women most likely to complain about being always rushed, employed men next most likely, and housewives least likely to complain about being rushed. As was the case with free time, then, overall sex differences were minimal after employment status was taken into account.

Of all the daily activities people engaged in, responses to the question correlated most vividly with television viewing. Television

---

*In a full national survey in 1971, responses were not very different from those found in this 1965-66 urban employed sample. For example, 26 percent in the 1971 sample said that they always felt rushed even to do the things that had to be done compared to the 25 percent figure in 1965-66.

had little appeal for the person who felt rushed. In the multivariate context of predicting amount of television viewing in Table 4.7 in Chapter 4, people who almost always felt rushed watched over 20 minutes less television than average, while those who seldom felt rushed watched over 20 minutes more television than average. Note that this difference held up after education and other powerful predictors of viewing had been taken into account, including those which related directly to time availability, such as employment status, day of the week, and age.

Television was not as clearly singled out as an unusual activity, using a third approach we took to measuring perceptions of time pressure. This approach was in effect a basic definitional exercise concerning the attributes of the entity that we and others have variously referred to as leisure, "free time," or discretionary time. At several points in earlier discussion, we have lamented the a priori and somewhat arbitrary way in which our operational definition of this important concept was derived.

It is a concept with multidimensional attributes. One of them, enjoyment or pleasure, has already been examined in this chapter. Another attribute of free time is its discretionary nature, that is, people engage in the activity out of personal choice, and not because it is dictated or expected by others or because it is something "that has to be done." Spontaneity is often noted as a third attribute, that is, free-time activities are those that are not part of a daily routine; they should not involve the same degree of planning and anticipation as obligatory activities.

We attempted a tentative operational exercise examining these latter two attributes with a small subset of 134 respondents in the 1975 Summer Interim Survey. These respondents, who were a separate group from the national sample described in Table 5.6, were asked to complete a diary of their previous day's activities. After describing each activity for which it was applicable, the respondent was asked first "Was that something you feel you had to do, or something you wanted to do, or what?" and then "Was that something that was planned ahead, was just routine, or came up unexpectedly yesterday, or what?" The first question, then, attempted to identify the discretionary component of the activity, and the second, its routine or spontaneous character. While the sample of respondents may be small, the sample of activities is again in the thousands.

First of all, it is clear from the responses of this sample that these are not matters that people think about extensively, or if they do, not in the terms reflected in our questions. In fact, we experienced unusual difficulty in designing this question sequence, and the above questions reflect the optimal strategy suggested from several pilot tests. One major problem arose concerning the time frame of the questions, since, for example, a particular piece of housecleaning may not have to be done at a particular moment or on a particular day, while it does have to be done eventually.

One decision that emerged before these pilot tests was to omit the questions for obviously nondiscretionary activities, since respondents would find answers to the questions obvious and insulting. For example, how meaningful is it to ask whether sleep or work was "planned in advance" or "came up unexpectedly" or "something you had to do?" The same is true of travel tied to the activity itself. Thus, interviewers were given instructions not to ask the questions about travel, work, or personal-care activities in the diaries, and to ask the questions only when there was some uncertainty about the activity or when it would not be likely to offend the respondent. The results from this definitional exercise "in real time" are outlined in Table 5.7. For simplicity of exposition, Table 5.7 contains only the entries for the "wanted to do" and "came up" responses, that is, those of most central definitional interest to us.

That respondents may not have responded to these questions in the frame of reference we intended is reflected in the surprising frequency with which obligatory activities were listed as something the respondent "wanted to do." Again, respondents' intention in such answers may have been to draw attention to something they "wanted to get out of the way," but noteworthy differentials are evident in this response across activities. Meal cleanup and laundry, for example, were described as something one wanted to do much less often than cooking, cleaning, shopping, and care to animals and plants. Child-related activities were distinguished in the same way, child interaction being much more likely to be described as something one "wanted to do" than custodial child care.

The same distinctive pattern is found for the questions about the routine or spontaneous character of the activity. Again, meal cleanup and laundry were less likely than other housework to be seen as something that unexpectedly came up, and child care less likely than child interaction. Among the more discretionary or nonroutine of the "obligatory" activities are the help given to adult family members and friends and shopping; note, surprisingly, that no difference is found between shopping for groceries and shopping for durables and other goods in this respect.

In contrast, the free-time activities in Table 5.7 are usually described as something one wanted to do. Free-time activities lowest in this regard were those in Chapter 4 that we expressed most concern about being nondiscretionary, namely, adult education, religion, and other organizational activity. Interestingly, on several occasions hobbies and conversations were not described as something

TABLE 5.7

Occasions when Daily Activities are Described
as Discretionary or Spontaneous
(percent)

	Wanted To	Came Up
Obligatory Activities, Occasions		
Cooking (131)	38	11
Meal cleanup (55)	13	7
Cleaning (69)	33	15
Laundry (35)	13	5
Animal and plant care (37)	34	33
Other (24)	45	33
Child care (72)	26	15
Child interaction (20)	65	35
Grocery shopping (33)	39	50
Other shopping (48)	42	46
Help other adults (24)	42	50
Free-Time Activities, Occasions		
Classes (6)	50	15
Organizations (11)	72	22
Religion (10)	67	0
Entertainment (7)	100	0
Socializing (76)	86	58
Outdoor recreation (28)	86	32
Hobbies (16)	77	50
Games (14)	100	31
TV, radio (167)	98	30
Reading (76)	95	26
Conversation (63)	78	52
Relaxing, thinking, resting (49)	88	40

Source: Compiled by the author from the Summer Interim Survey
(1975).

one wanted to do; in contrast, the proportion of socializing that one wanted to do was higher than we expected, given the frequent references to the socializing expected as part of work or other social obligation.

Education and organizational activity were also "free-time" activities most often described as routine or planned in advance. Going to places of entertainment also required considerable advance preparation. Social interaction and hobbies were the most spontaneous free-time activities, although they were not that much more likely to come up unexpectedly during the day than shopping.

Television, on the other hand, was less likely to be described simply as something that came up. In that respect, it is remarkably similar to the media activity of reading, which we saw in Chapter 4 had almost the opposite audience profile to television. Note that both media activities were also close to each other in terms of choice, both being nearly always described as something one wanted to do.

The data in Table 5.7 suffer from too many shortcomings to be more than suggestive of the proper classification of activities as obligatory or free. The results do provide general support for the definition of free time employed in our analyses, although much of the activity we have considered as obligatory child care is seen as discretionary by parents, who also consider it one of the most enjoyable of daily activities as well. Our concern about including adult education and organizational activity is seen to be well founded, and the description of these activities as "semi-leisure" seems most appropriate. The concern that socializing is largely imposed on people seems misplaced, hobbies and conversations being more likely to be seen as obligatory.

There is some correspondence between the discretionary nature of an activity and its spontaneous or enjoyable character, but it is far from complete. The activity that most clearly manifests all three characteristics of free time is socializing, and respondents describe it as more discretionary, more spontaneous, and more enjoyable than other free-time activities. The mass media activities of television and reading may be freely chosen, but they usually involve more routine or planning than socializing and are significantly lower on the enjoyment factor. Recreation and entertainment away from home are freely chosen and well above average in enjoyment; but they require a fair amount of advance preparation. The same may be said to characterize religion, organizational participation, and interaction with one's children. Fewer respondents than expected reported rest and relaxation as spontaneous.

It is hoped that these results will stimulate further research into operational definitions of free time. The definition of free time

is too central a topic of societal concern to be left to arbitrary or
a priori definitions. Clearly, the need for improving operational
definitions of the concept precedes any public-policy decisions aimed
at improving the quality of Americans' leisure time.

INFORMATION PROCESSING

In Chapter 4, we examined in broad outline the extent of mass
media information to which individuals were exposed on a particular
day. Exposure to the mass media was found to be practically
universal, and while it can be argued that the information presented
by and gained from the media was far less than it might have been,
media attention does involve a noteworthy degree of information
processing on the part of the public.

Two other sources of information processing are examined here.
These are interpersonal and intrapersonal communication. Interpersonal communication is perhaps the most important source of
information people have and it can be argued that the information to
which people are exposed in the mass media is likely to be absorbed
only to the extent that media information stimulates subsequent
interpersonal conversation and interpretation. Intrapersonal communication refers to the mental communication individuals undertake
with their "selves"; in particular, we will examine the plans and
problems respondents pondered while completing their daily routine.

As was the case with media exposure, we saw in Chapter 4 that
a complete picture of conversational activity required examination
of secondary activities in people's diaries. Less than 20 minutes of
daily conversation was reported as a primary activity. Even with
the inclusion of secondary activities, a good deal of conversation
was left unreported in the diaries, as witnessed by the estimate
from these diaries that 15 percent of respondents did not enter into
a conversation with another person during the entire day; furthermore,
the amount of conversation reported varied as a function of how
complete the diary recording process was.

We expected a fuller reporting of conversational activity from
another portion of the diary, namely, that concerned with the social
partners whom the respondent reported as present during the activity.
Time spent in the company of children was examined in Chapter 3.
The full set of "with whom" data is listed in Table 5.8 by sex,
employment status, and day of the week. It defines the broad
dimensions of the social networks in which individuals find themselves
during the day.

Table 5.8 describes certain unique features of these social
networks; for example, the large amounts of time the housewife

TABLE 5.8

Hours per Day Spent in Different Company
(hours per day)

	Employed Men			Employed Women			Housewives		
	M-F	Sat	Sun	M-F	Sat	Sun	M-F	Sat	Sun
All alone[a]	14.0	12.5	13.5	14.0	13.5	15.1	14.6	14.6	13.6
Family									
Spouse only	1.5	2.0	2.4	1.1	2.0	1.7	1.8	2.0	2.2
Children and spouse	.9	1.5	2.4	.5	.3	1.0	1.2	2.0	2.7
Children only	.5	.6	1.3	1.0	1.8	1.2	3.4	1.8	2.1
Total Family	2.9	4.1	6.1	2.6	4.1	3.9	6.4	5.8	7.0
Other household adults	.2	.3	.2	.9	1.6	.6	.4	1.0	.2
Other friends and relatives	.8	2.9	2.7	1.1	3.5	3.7	1.5	2.3	2.8
Work colleagues	4.2	1.9	.9	3.4	.8	.7	.3	.0	.0
Organization members	.2	.2	.4	.1	.2	.5	.2	.1	.4
Neighbors and their children	.3	.6	.3	.8	.6	.6	.5	.5	.6
Officials, professionals, etc.	—[b]	.0	.0	—	.0	.0	—	.0	.0
Others, unidentified	1.2	1.4	.4	1.1	1.3	.8	.7	.5	.4
Not ascertained	1.5	1.8	.6	1.7	1.1	.3	.7	.4	.2
Total[c]	25.3	25.7	25.1	25.7	26.7	26.4	25.3	25.2	25.2

[a]Includes sleeping.

[b]A dash indicates less than 3 minutes per day.

[c]Because of double entries, times do not add to 24 hours.

Source: Compiled by the author from the Study of Americans' Use of Time (1965–66).

spends solely with her children compared to the employed man; or
the large blocs of time employed people spent with co-workers and
"others" (such as clients, casual contacts); or the time women
spend with other adults in the household.* While most differences
in Table 5.8 arise from rather obvious sources, such as going to
church on Sundays or visiting on the weekends, these data do provide
a useful backdrop against which to consider the interesting conversations respondents reported on the diary day.

Perhaps the most striking figures in Table 5.8 concerning conversations, or the lack of them, however, concern time spent alone.
It needs to be noted, first of all, that sleep was by definition coded
as time spent alone, so that an average of eight hours needs to be
deducted from the totals in the first row of these figures to achieve
the more realistic base of waking time spent alone. Still, the amount
of waking time Americans spent alone was quite high (over five hours
per day) and was a unique characteristic of American daily life in
the multinational context (Robinson, Converse, and Szalai, 1972).
This was true even after the time Americans spent alone in commuting
to work and at the workplace were taken into account.†

The five hours per day of time spent alone as measured from
our diaries, however, only point to the times when conversations
were least likely to occur. We would also expect conversations to
be minimal during other large blocs of primary activity time when
the person was not completely in solitude, such as religious devotion
or mass media usage.

Of the conversations that did occur during the other periods of
the day, we attempted to determine the priorities of information
that was exchanged. How many and what types of conversations
were of sufficient interest or importance that respondents could
recall them to an interviewer on the following day? Replies to a

---

*Time spent with other adults in the household is unusually
high for employed women because more of them are single and
share living quarters with another adult.

†Our figures on percentage of time spent alone for employed
men (30 percent) represent twice as much of their waking life as
that found in the more intensive time-diary study by Reiss (1959)
of social contacts done ten years previously in a single urban setting.
This study, which probed into the solitude of the work place far
more extensively than our study, did find more time being spent
alone in rural settings (not examinable in our study). The major
demographic factor in our study affecting time spent alone was
absence of children, which was associated with up to two hours
more time spent alone among some groups of women.

question series on these topics are provided in Table 5.9, which
lists the topics of interesting conversations arranged by sex, employment, and education. These responses provide unique insight into
the topics that create greatest interest in the extensive social networks
that tie our society together.

One particularly noteworthy set of entries appears at the bottom
of Table 5.9, namely, those pertaining to respondents who failed to
recall an interesting conversation. Almost half of the sample could
not recall an interesting conversation to the interviewer, with
employed and less-educated respondents being less likely to recall
engaging in such a conversation. However, the degree of respondent
involvement in the conversations that were reported was significant.
Respondents estimated that these conversations consumed over 20
minutes of time on the average.

Better-educated people were not only more likely to mention an
interesting conversation, but more than a single topic of conversation
as well. This finding is consistent with expectations of the greater
information-processing skills of people with more education, but it
may also arise from the better rapport our middle-class interviewers
had with better-educated respondents. In Table 5.9, however, it
can be seen once their greater recall is taken into account, better-
educated respondents generally discussed the same sorts of topics
as less-educated respondents. Exceptions to this did occur, as in
the greater frequency of conversations about work among better-
educated employed women, but the major differences appeared
among housewives. Better-educated housewives were more likely
to discuss topics external to the family, such as news events, social
problems, and religion, while less-educated housewives (and employed
women) talked more about child care, shopping, and the health
problems of other people. Generally, however, clear and systematic
educational differences in topics chosen for conversation are quite
difficult to locate in Table 5.9.

Sex differences are more apparent and follow a traditional
"internal-external" distinction. Thus, women talked more than
men about such home-centered topics as child care, personal needs
(such as food, particularly meals for upcoming holidays), health
concerns, and other concerns about other people (such as family or
friends). On the other hand, men tended to talk more about topics
external to the home, such as work and news events.

The topics of most interesting or enjoyable conversations,
then, centered on the relatively immediate milieux of everyday life
such as work and family. Social relations with relations and friends
and events in their lives received somewhat less attention in the
most engaging of conversations. Lower in this hierarchy were
more abstract concerns about personal welfare, such as the state

TABLE 5.9

Topics of Conversations of Particular Interest to Respondents on the Diary Day
by Educational Level, Sex, and Employment Status
(percent)

	Men			Employed Women			Housewives		
Topic N =	Less than high school	High school graduate	Some college or more	Less than high school	High school graduate	Some college or more	Less than high school	High school graduate	Some college or more
	(153)	(130)	(167)	(83)	(129)	(85)	(96)	(125)	(74)
Activity Related									
1. Work	25	25	32	4	11	26	0	1	1
2. Housework	0	0	0	0	0	1	1	0	0
3. Child care	8	5	5	10	11	8	21	14	8
4. Shopping	2	1	2	2	3	2	8	6	1
5. Personal needs	4	8	2	6	7	12	10	6	9
6. Adult education	0	5	4	2	1	6	0	2	4
7. Organizations	4	0	1	2	1	0	0	4	6
8. Social life	4	5	6	6	3	4	5	8	1
9. Active leisure	4	12	4	4	5	2	4	1	6
10. Passive leisure	2	5	3	2	8	1	2	1	4
Contextual									
11. Money, finances	8	1	5	4	0	2	5	2	5
12. Health, accidents	4	5	4	17	11	2	13	17	8
13. Others' concerns	8	8	10	15	19	16	20	13	21
14. Religion	4	5	2	6	3	2	0	10	11
15. Property	4	7	4	12	1	5	6	2	8
General									
16. Social problems	2	0	2	2	1	1	0	4	6
17. News events	13	5	8	4	9	5	0	1	9
18. International	4	1	3	0	4	2	4	2	1
19. Miscellaneous	2	1	3	2	1	3	1	3	0
Total	100	100	100	100	100	100	100	100	100
No Interesting Conversation	58	50	39	60	45	34	45	41	31

Source: Compiled by the author from the Study of Americans' Use of Time (1965–66).

of finances, possessions, and neighborhood, and news events and
world conditions. Fewer than 10 percent of engaging conversations,
then, concerned topics discussed in the news media. This has
important implications for models of media information processing
in the public, such as the two-step flow of communication of Katz
and Lazarsfeld (1955). Such models tend to overstate the ease with
which news information diffuses through the public, particularly in
light of the startlingly low awareness levels of items in the news
found in public opinion polls (for example, Robinson, 1972a). The
relatively low frequency with which items in the news are mentioned
by our sample in Table 5.9 makes these low awareness levels more
understandable.

    With whom do these engaging conversations occur? To some
extent, differences in conversational partners parallel what one
would expect on the basis of the time spent with each of these groups,
as reported in Table 5.8. Work colleagues are mentioned most
frequently by employed people, and friends, neighbors, and relatives
by housewives. However, the rate at which friends and neighbors
were chosen as conversational partners for interesting conversations
far exceeded the proportion of time spent with them. Thus, the
crucial role of friendship networks in information transmission and
diffusion becomes quite apparent. This is particularly true with
respect to the adult with whom most time is spent in Table 5.7,
namely, one's spouse. While married people may spend twice as
much time with their spouses as with relatives, friends, and neighbors, they were the partners for only a third as many interesting
conversations. In this sense, then, the most engaging information
was exchanged outside of one's immediate family.

    Among women, in fact, children were mentioned as partners
of interesting conversations as often as husbands; among less-
educated women, children were actually mentioned more often. A
more striking educational difference for both men and women, however, was the more frequent mention of relatives as conversational
partners among the less educated and the more frequent mention of
friends and neighbors among the better educated. Education, and
social class generally, appear to involve more transmission of
information outside the network of one's extended family.

    In Table 5.9, relatively little interpersonal conversation was
reported about international affairs or world events. On an intrapersonal basis, however, such topics were noted with much greater
frequency in response to a question asking about the daily incidence
of "important plans or problems—about work, family, or things
going on in the world—that stayed on your mind even while you were
doing other things." The international problem noted by these
respondents was, of course, Vietnam; and most respondents' concern
was how it would personally affect themselves or their loved ones.

At first glance, problems and plans discussed in private fall
into roughly the same areas as those noted in Table 5.8, that is,
main concern was with family and work. However, the specific
content referent was usually different. In contrast to the concrete
events and situations that were brought up in interpersonal discussion,
private problems and plans were more affective and speculative in
character. On the topic of work, for example, conversations tended
toward things that had to be done at work; topics that were thought
about in private more, and talked about less, were longer-range
speculations and dissatisfactions. While conversations about children
centered on current school performance, private mental activity
focused on how well children would eventually do in school. While
conversations often centered on health and other personal problems
of friends and co-workers, far more private thought was devoted to
family members faced with such problems. And far less mental
concern was devoted to general relational problems of an interpersonal
nature (with friends, family, or merchants) than would be expected
from the proportion of interesting conversations devoted to the topic.
Relational problems apparently are things that must be unburdened
with other people, or are most appropriately brought up in the interpersonal context. The same seems to be true of news events reported
in the media; outside of situations with the personal implications of
a Vietnam, they are grist for the conversational mill but evoke
minimal consideration when one is alone with one's thoughts.

Topic differences in problems or plans for different sex, employment, and educational groups are shown in Table 5.10. As was the
case with conversations in Table 5.9, about half of the sample did
not mention any problem or plan. Again the mention of such mental
activity was more likely among the better than the less educated and
among housewives rather than employed women or men.

As was also the case in Table 5.9, sex differences predominated
over educational differences. Sex differences again followed the
"internal-external" pattern, women worrying more about family-
related matters such as housework, child care, personal needs, and
the needs and problems of other people. In addition to work and
world problems, men also were more likely to think about financial
problems. Better-educated people tended to report more contemplation about free-time activities than less-educated people, and among
women, the better educated were more likely to mention Vietnam,
the less educated, the health problems of other people.

Tables 5.9 and 5.10, then, do provide supplemental support to
the mass media exposure data that better-educated people are more
active processors of information during a typical day than less-
educated people. Education, however, has much less to do with the
topics that arise in conversation or are in the forefront of thought

TABLE 5.10

Topics of Problems or Plans Thought About on the Diary Day by Educational Level, Sex, and Employment Status (percent)

Topic	Men			Employed Women			Housewives		
	Less than high school	High school graduate	Some college or more	Less than high school	High school graduate	Some college or more	Less than high school	High school graduate	Some college or more
N =	(156)	(130)	(167)	(90)	(129)	(86)	(101)	(135)	(80)
Activity Related									
1. Work	25	33	27	3	19	18	2	2	2
2. Housework	0	0	0	8	1	3	2	2	5
3. Child care	11	7	2	8	16	8	26	18	26
4. Shopping	4	7	6	6	10	7	9	8	7
5. Personal needs	5	8	5	12	12	11	13	10	9
6. Adult education	0	0	1	0	0	3	0	0	2
7. Organizations	0	0	5	0	0	3	0	4	2
8. Social life	0	0	4	3	3	0	0	4	5
9. Active leisure	0	2	4	0	4	2	0	3	2
10. Passive leisure	0	2	2	0	0	0	0	3	0
Contextual									
11. Money, finances	16	8	11	9	3	3	4	5	4
12. Health, accidents	11	5	10	27	12	15	23	16	7
13. Others' concerns	4	7	4	18	10	16	9	9	9
14. Religion	4	2	1	3	0	0	0	0	2
15. Property	4	8	7	3	7	2	4	9	5
General									
16. Social problems	0	3	1	0	0	0	4	0	0
17. News events	0	3	4	0	0	3	0	2	4
18. International	14	5	7	0	3	3	4	5	10
19. Miscellaneous	2	2	0	0	0	2	0	0	0
Total*	100	100	100	100	100	100	100	100	100
No Plans or Problems	61	54	49	59	47	33	50	44	31

*Percentages based on those reporting thinking about a problem or plan. Percentages do not add to exactly 100 percent because of rounding.

Source: Compiled by the author from the Study of Americans' Use of Time (1965-66).

during one's reflective moments. Sex roles appear to be far more important determinants of the differential topics that are processed in personal conversations. Again, these provocative findings warrant further exploration with alternative questions and methodologies.

6

**FREE TIME
AND LIFE STYLE**

In Chapter 4 we examined multivariate analyses of the determinants of available free time and how various social groups used
their free time. In Chapter 5 we examined several bodies of data
that attempted to provide more insight into the human meaning of
these time-use figures. In this chapter, we will attempt some
integrative and synthetic analyses across these various data bases.
In addition to rearranging some of our 1965-66 time-use data, we
have considerable recourse to empirical data from other survey
evidence.

Each of the four sections in this chapter deals mostly with the
matter of free-time. In the first section, we examine the free
time patterns of men and women in closer detail and attempt to
draw some conclusions about the psychological consequences of the
remarkably small amounts of free time available to employed
women. In the second section, we employ the annual participation
estimates of the respondents in the 1965-66 data set to help delineate
longer-range "life styles" with regard to leisure, particularly with
reference to those that require more free time. In the third section,
we attempt to define those features of free-time use that lead to more
satisfying life styles for their participants. The fourth section deals
with more general observations on the activity that consumes more
free time than any other, namely television.

SEX ROLES AND FREE TIME

Time spent on care for home and family, and its accompanying
constraints on the lives of women, is a focal point of the current
social debate on changing life styles of men and women. Time can

function as a useful objective indicator of changing sex roles in this debate, time being one of the few societal resources equally divided between men and women. We have seen evidence in Chapters 3 and 4 that time-use patterns do demarcate a strong and persistent sexual division of labor and leisure in our society.

Of all the ways people spend their time, the figures from people's time diaries show that the greatest sex-role difference in ways of spending time was for housework and child care. Women recorded over four times as much time in both activities (about 36 hours a week) as did men (about 8 hours) in their 1965-66 diaries. The only activities that men came close to dominating so disproportionately were sports and other outdoor recreation, and to a lesser degree, their paid work. Perhaps none of this is surprising, except that the ratios for male domination of these activities were closer to two to one than to the four-to-one share of house and family obligations taken on by females.

In examining the satisfaction people claim to derive from activities in their diaries in Chapter 5, we found most activities associated with housework (like meal cleanup and laundry) to have been judged the least satisfying and least enjoyable of all daily activities by both men and women. The male-dominated activities of outdoor recreation and work, on the other hand, if anything, provided above average satisfaction. That women spent so much more of their available time in such an unsatisfying set of activities as housework clearly means that something other than time is inequitable.

We have seen that the situation becomes particularly inequitable for women who also have jobs outside the home. While an employed woman may have reduced both housework and child-care time by 50 percent when taking on an outside job, these savings in time came nowhere close to the 30 or 40 hours she had to devote to that job. The overall result in Chapter 4 was that employed women had over 10 hours less free time per week to enjoy than women not in the paid labor force.

Nor was this "lost" time made up by the husbands of employed women. While these husbands did record 10 percent more housework than husbands whose wives were not in the paid labor force, these incremental male contributions made up only a minute fraction of the "lost" housework time of employed women. Furthermore, husbands of employed women did not spend more time on child care than men whose wives were not in the labor market. (It will be remembered that these calculations do take into account other factors that discriminate the two groups of men, such as the smaller families of men whose wives were in the labor force.)

Nor did the male contribution to housework appear to be affected by the arrival of children. While the housework time of both employed women and full-time housewives increased between 5 and 10 percent for each additional child in the household, fathers with more children often were found to do less housework than those with fewer children or no children.

Much the same conclusion held for child care. While each additional child may have meant between a 20 and 50 percent increase (depending on the number and age of the children) in direct child-care activities for wives, in many instances husbands showed reduced time on direct child-care activities as family size grew larger. This was particularly true for large families when at least one of the children was of preschool age.

Not only was the male contribution to household and child-care duties unaffected by the burdens imposed by children and by the wife's outside employment; it was barely affected by marriage itself. Thus, we find that men who were not married spent about 85 percent of the time on housework that their married counterparts did, and the same proportion held true for single women. Furthermore, even if these single women had children, the time devoted to care for these children was practically the same whether a husband was present in the household or not.

The social expectations of women that compel them to spend much more time than men on household and child-related activities are thus so culturally ingrained that they hold whether or not marital obligations are present. Perhaps single men spend less time on domestic duties than single women because they are also better able to afford outside cleaning, laundry, and food-preparation costs. In any event, it seems unfair simply to lay the blame for this inequity in housework on husbands when these differences largely exist whether or not women are married.

A crucial part of the findings from these time-use surveys that may hold the key to understanding the meager male contributions to housework thus deals with women's attitudes and expectations about sharing housework. Housewives do rate the overall satisfaction derived from doing housework—rather than specific household tasks which we saw earlier comprised a highly unsatisfying way of spending time—at about the same level as men rate their paid work.* However,

---

*Using the same response scale, 32 percent of employed men said they were completely satisfied with their jobs, 57 percent quite satisfied, and 11 percent not very or not at all satisfied. Among all women, employed or not, the corresponding percentages for

not even this pattern of attitudes prepared us for the responses of
women in the 1965-66 study to the following direct question:

Do you wish your husband would give you more help
with the daily household chores?

Only 19 percent of our national sample of married women answered
affirmatively, that is, that they wanted more help from their husbands
in doing household chores.

Several reasons for this surprisingly low percentage are possible
although we were empirically able to examine and reject the following
plausible explanations:

1. Women were intimidated by their husbands being present.
Yet, most women in our survey were interviewed alone. In fact,
women interviewed with their husbands present were slightly more
likely to express the wish for more help.

2. Women were completely "unliberated" in 1965. Things
certainly have changed in the sex-role arena since 1965. We repeated
our question in the 1973 Fall Omnibus survey described in Chapter 3,
a national survey that also included specific questions about the
women's liberation movement. While agreement did rise, and was
significantly related to positive feelings about women's liberation,
it had increased only four percentage points, to 23 percent, over
the eight-year interval.

3. Women overestimated the amount of help their husbands
gave. In 1965-66, women's estimates of their husbands' weekly
help with the household chores matched almost exactly with what
was recorded in the men's diaries.*

4. Men were helping more with household chores in 1973.
However, wives' estimates of household help on the previous week

_____

housework were 25 percent, 54 percent, and 21 percent, with
employed women being much more dissatisfied than housewives.
Campbell et al. (1976, p. 309) found 83 percent of housewives to be
on the satisfied end of the housework scale (compared to 67 percent
of employed women). Job satisfaction was at about 80 percent for
both employed men and employed women (ibid., pp. 63, 301).

*This was one of the few instances in which people's estimates
of time expenditures matched the more reliable figures on time use
that appear in diaries. It will be remembered that only one person
per household was interviewed, so the women's estimates come
from a different set of households than the entries in the male
diaries. Nonetheless, both sets of data should be nationally project-
able to a common aggregate.

were no higher in 1973 than they were in 1965. About one wife in
three in 1965-66 and in 1973 reported receiving no help in the previous
week, while one in ten reported receiving more than ten hours help.
Consistent with these figures, then, 35 percent of the women
receiving no help in the 1973 study (and 24 percent in 1965) wanted
more help from their husbands, compared to less than 5 percent of
the women receiving more than ten hours help (and 12 percent in
1965), indicating that lack of help was indeed an important explanatory
factor in women's attitudes.

Table 6.1 examines the effects of five other predictors of desire
for more housework help that were included in both the 1965-66 and
1973 surveys, as gauged by MCA. In both surveys, desire for more
husband help is concentrated among younger, employed, and black
wives. Table 6.1 indicates more significant changes in support
over the eight-year interim within these groups, however. On the
one hand, it can be seen that these shifts are most pronounced among
groups that should be most open to change: namely, younger women
(particularly those in the most hectic period from age 30-39),
college graduates, blacks, and those receiving no help at all from
their husbands.* Somewhat surprisingly, on the other hand, desire
for more help increased more among housewives than employed
women and among mothers with one or two children rather than
three or four. This provides even further evidence of the difficulty
of making overly sweeping and simplified assumptions about basic
sex-role attitudes and behaviors and their historical changes.

These important variables then fail to provide much help in
explaining why most women basically resist expressing a preference
for more male help. Is there a trade-off in maintaining separate
role territories for men and women that keeps women doing the

---

*Black women were also the only group in the 1973 study among
whom majority support was found for having more husband help in
caring for children. The overall proportion of married women saying
they wished they had more child-care help from their husbands was
29 percent, somewhat higher than the 23-percent figure for household chores. Support again was higher among employed women,
younger women, and women more adamant about women's liberation.
Unlike the case with household chores, desire for more child-care
help was found among mothers of larger families and mothers of
preschool children. Desire for more child-care help did not relate
to the mother's education (better-educated men did report above
average child care in the analyses in Chapter 3, which could account
for the finding. However, better-educated men also reported more
housework as well and better-educated women in Table 6.1 did express above average desire for more help with housework).

TABLE 6.1

Mothers Expressing More Interest in Having Their Husbands Help with the Housework[a]
(percent)

	1965–66		1973		1965–1973 Change in Adjusted Averages
	(N)	Adjusted Average	(N)	Adjusted Average	
Total	(765)	19	(300)	23	+4
Age					
18–29	(207)	25	(100)	26	+1
30–39	(200)	20	(99)	32	+12
40–49	(182)	15	(72)	18	+3
50+	(165)	15	(28)	22	+7
Education					
Grade school	(73)	22	(28)	24	+2
Some high school	(149)	27	(58)	22	−5
High school graduate	(346)	18	(153)	26	+8
Some college	(114)	20	(39)	25	+5
College graduate	(70)	10	(22)	30	+20
Employment					
Yes	(265)	32	(120)	29	−3
No	(488)	13	(180)	23	+10
Children					
None	(235)	19	(0)	−b	—
One	(135)	14	(96)	30	+16
Two	(167)	18	(116)	27	+9
Three	(122)	21	(55)	18	−3
Four or more	(96)	29	(34)	21	−8
Race					
White	(713)	18	(275)	23	+5
Black	(35)	35	(17)	58	+23
Husband's Help Last Week					
None	(373)	24	(72)	35	+11
1–4 hours	(94)	25	(41)	20	−5
5 hours	(126)	16	(46)	12	−4
Above 5 hours	(152)	8	(100)	5	−3

[a]After adjustment by MCA.

[b]A dash indicates no data collected.

Source: Compiled by the author from the Study of Americans' Use of Time (1965–66).

major portion of the unsatisfying parts of house and child care? Perhaps in return for a traditional sexual division of labor, women reap highly satisfying and compensating benefits and rewards, such as feelings of competence and self-esteem from clearly defined responsibilities and obligations, control over when and how activities are done, and freedom from the major financial responsibility of providing for the family. The benefits to women of such defined male and female roles can motivate a certain protection of their territory. Men too may give, or receive, subtle messages to stay within certain boundaries. Husbands who resent being asked to enter the province of household chores may turn in such a poor performance that women find themselves redoing the work. On the other hand, the wife's fastidiousness about the cleanliness of the house may be such that she will never be satisfied with what her husband does. While men cannot figure out how properly to dust a living room or clean a bathroom, women are helpless to operate a lawnmower or change a tire. In the presence of such underlying capabilities and attitudes, it is safer for both sexes to remain in their perceived area of competence and avoid any invitations to participate in the other's domain.

In evaluating the small statistical change in women's expressed desire for help from 1965-66 to 1973, we should also consider the effect on a relationship where roles are unclear or changing. For example, the woman who takes on an important financial responsibility through outside employment (male territory) may want her husband to help more with household and child-care needs (female territory), but she and her husband may still be uncomfortable with the blurring or exchanging of traditional roles. She may respond by trying to be a superwoman able to manage both home and job spheres rather than give up part of her "femininity." While the employed woman struggles with this conflict in sex roles, the wife not in the labor market may be sufficiently satisfied with the husband's financial support for her and her children so that to confront her husband with demands for more household help would be inappropriate. Hence, desire for help may be present but unacknowledged by women in and out of the labor market for different reasons.

Whatever the system of trade-offs between men and women, our time-budget data make it clear that employment causes a much greater imbalance in the sexual division of labor and leisure than the demands of either marriage or children. It will be remembered from Chapter 4 that the largest gap in free time occurred between the housewife and the employed woman.

Tables 6.2 and 6.3 restructure the time-use data in Chapters 3 and 4 in order to review the comparative effects of three central determinants of time-use patterns, as well as their possible conse-

TABLE 6.2

Differences in Time Use and Perceptions by Marriage, Parenthood, and Wife's Employment, for Women

	1965-66 Time-Use Data		1971 Quality-of-Life Data		
Life Situation	Obligatory time (min/day)	Free time (min/day)	Rushed (1-7)	Spare time satisfaction (1-7)	Life satisfaction (1-7)
01. Not married, no kids, not employed	310	432	3.0	2.4	3.0
02. Not married, no kids, employed	464	265	5.1	2.7	2.9
03. Not married, kids, employed	480	264	5.1	2.1	3.2
04. Married, no kids, not employed	370	384	3.8	2.3	2.3
05. Married, no kids, employed	484	254	4.6	2.2	1.9
06. Married, 1-2 kids over 4, not employed	393	366	4.2	2.2	2.2
07. Married, 1-2 kids over 4, employed	537	207	4.9	2.2	2.2
08. Married, 1-2 kids under 4, not employed	461	323	4.6	2.5	2.2
09. Married, 1-2 kids under 4, employed	560	221	4.9	2.7	2.2
10. Married, 3 or more kids over 4, not employed	444	342	4.3	2.1	2.1
11. Married, 3 or more kids over 4, employed	559	193	5.3	2.7	2.6
12. Married, 3 or more kids under 4, not employed	506	296	4.8	2.6	2.5
13. Married, 3 or more kids under 4, employed	652	172	5.8	2.8	2.6
Summary of Differences*					
Marriage	+54	-37	-.03	+.01	-.93
1-2 kids	+61	-40	+.45	+.15	+.10
3-4 kids	+52	-28	+.40	+.40	+.25
Kids under 4	+62	-24	+.35	+.35	-.10
Wife employed	+129	-139	-.98	+.20	+.02

*Differences calculated as follows:

Marriage: Group 01 vs. 04; 02 vs. 05; 03 vs. 07; 03 vs. 09.

1-2 kids: 04 vs. 06; 04 vs. 08; 05 vs. 07; 05 vs. 09.

3-4 kids: 06 vs. 10; 07 vs. 11; 08 vs. 12; 09 vs. 13.

Kids under 4: 06 vs. 08; 07 vs. 09; 10 vs. 11; 12 vs. 13.

Employment: 01 vs. 02; 04 vs. 05; 06 vs. 07; 08 vs. 09; 10 vs. 11; 12 vs. 13.

Source: Compiled by the author from the Study of Americans' Use of Time (1965-66) and the Quality of Life study (Campbell, Converse, and Rodgers, 1976).

TABLE 6.3

Differences in Time Use and Perceptions by Marriage, Parenthood, and Wife's Employment, for Men

	1965–66 Time–Use Data		1971 Quality-of-Life Data		
Life Situation	Obligatory time (min/day)	Free time (min/day)	Rushed (1–7)	Spare time satisfaction (1–7)	Life satisfaction (1–7)
01. Not applicable	—a	—	—	—	—
02. Not married, no kids	392	350	3.4	2.3	2.7
03. Not married, kids	360	352	4.3	2.4	2.9
04. Married, no kids, not employed	410	288	4.1	2.2	2.0
05. Married, no kids, employed	396	344	4.7	2.4	2.3
06. Married, 1–2 kids over four, not employed	456	272	4.7	2.0	2.3
07. Married, 1–2 kids over four, employed	443	257	4.3	2.3	2.2
08. Married, 1–2 kids under four, not employed	467	266	4.6	2.6	2.4
09. Married, 1–2 kids under four, employed	400	339	4.5	2.6	2.1
10. Married, 3 or more kids over four, not employed	455	281	4.5	2.2	2.2
11. Married, 3 or more kids over four, employed	389	362	4.9	2.4	2.5
12. Married, 3 or more kids under four, not employed	457	280	4.9	2.5	2.8
13. Married, 3 or more kids under four, employed	444	314	4.2	2.6	2.6
Summary of Differencesb					
Marriage	+56	−57	+.48	−.02	−.61
1–2 kids	+39	−32	+.13	+.03	+.10
3–4 kids	−5	+28	+.10	+.05	+.28
Kids under 4	+6	+7	+.05	+.35	−.17
Wife employed	−35	+46	−.04	+.18	.00

aA dash indicates an inapplicable life-situation category.

bDifferences calculated as follows:

Marriage: Group 02 vs. 04; 02 vs. 05; 03 vs. 06; 03 vs. 07; 03 vs. 08; 03 vs. 09.

1–2 kids: 04 vs. 06; 04 vs. 08; 05 vs. 08; 05 vs. 09.

3–4 kids: 06 vs. 10; 07 vs. 11; 08 vs. 12; 09 vs. 13.

Kids under four: 06 vs. 08; 07 vs. 09; 10 vs. 12; 11 vs. 13.

Employment: 04 vs. 05; 06 vs. 07; 08 vs. 09; 10 vs. 11; 12 vs. 13.

Source: Compiled by the author from the Study of Americans' Use of Time (1965–66) and the Quality of Life study (Campbell, Converse, and Rodgers, 1976).

quences. The first two columns in these tables contain data on time
use from the 1965–66 study; the last three columns contain data on
attitudinal and perceptual differences for the same demographic
groups in the Quality of Life Survey conducted by the Survey Research
Center six years later (Campbell et al., 1976). These perceptual
data from the 1971 Quality of Life study in the final three columns
of Table 6.2 were collected on seven-point rating scales. The "feel
rushed" scale runs from "1 = always feel rushed" to "7 = quite often
have time on one's hands," while the satisfaction scale runs from
"1 = completely satisfied" to "7 = totally dissatisfied." Thus, the
higher the number, the less satisfied the response.

The life situations of men and women are arranged in Tables
6.2 and 6.3 to show how time-use patterns and possibly resultant
attitudes vary as the burdens of three role responsibilities are added
to each marital partner:

1. Marriage itself.
2. The arrival of children (as well as their numbers and ages).
3. The entry of the wife into the labor force.*

The data are arranged in a way that allows the detection of interaction
effects across the three role burdens, although our interests will
focus on differences in average expenditures of time and average
scores on the perceptual and satisfaction scales. The methods of
calculating each of these effects are described at the bottom of each
table.

Employment's role as the major thief of women's free time is
confirmed, the loss of 139 minutes per day on the average being
greater than the combined effects of marriage (37 minutes), arrival
of children (40 minutes), additional children (28 minutes), and even
preschool children (24 minutes). There is a more direct translation
of the greater demands of employment into lower free time than any
of these other factors as well. In other words, not all obligatory
time "required" by marriage and children meant lost free time.
However, all time spent for work was associated with lost free time.

Parallel perceptual data, in the three right-hand columns of
Table 6.2, show employment to be the major factor affecting women's

---

*Thus, in the first column in Table 6.2, the "effect" of wife's
employment on obligatory time (defined as the sum of paid work,
housework, child care, and shopping) is estimated by the average
of six differences between women in and out of the labor force (that
is, between groups 1 and 2; groups 4 and 5; groups 6 and 7; groups 8
and 9; groups 10 and 11; and groups 12 and 13). The total average
difference for these six group comparisons is 129 more minutes per
day of obligatory activities for employed women than for women not in
the labor force.

feelings of "being rushed." Children, particularly if more numerous
and younger, add considerably to those feelings of being rushed.
Marriage, per se, was not associated with greater feelings of being
rushed, despite the fact that the roughly half an hour less free time
reported by married women in the 1965-66 time study was equivalent
to that associated with each of the three child-related conditions (that
is, presence, numbers, and being of preschool age).

Nor was marriage associated with a decrease in woman's
reported satisfaction with free-time activities. The only factor
associated with notably lower free-time satisfaction was the presence
of a preschool child in the household, as indicated by the +.35 entry
for this group in this column of Table 6.2; while employment and
larger numbers of children were associated with lower free-time
satisfaction, there is no indication that either factor made the
presence of a preschool child harder on mothers than otherwise
would have been the case.

When it comes to overall satisfaction with life, however, marriage was the factor that related most dramatically to greater
satisfaction. In contrast, children seemed to have marginally
negative effects on life satisfaction. Most importantly at the bottom
of Table 6.2, however, employment was not associated with less
life satisfaction for women, despite its tremendous intrusion on
their free time.

Table 6.3 arrays these identical sets of data for men in the
1965-66 and 1971 studies. Again we find marriage and the arrival
of first children being associated with less available free time.
However, as we saw in Chapter 3, men's obligatory and free time
were particularly insensitive to the presence of younger and more
children, both of which had such a strong effect on women's use of
time.

The most dramatic figures in Table 6.3, however, appear at
the bottom of the first two columns. The wife's employment not
only was associated with less obligatory time for her husband, but
with greater free time for him as well. In other words, a major
impact of a wife's employment could be to increase her husband's
free time. Much the same conclusion emerges from a parallel
analysis of this type conducted on time-diary data from a sample
340 couples in Vancouver, Canada by Meissner et al (1975). Moreover the finding is also corroborated by the shorter workweek
reported by husbands of employed wives in the 1971 Quality of Life
study, unfortunately the only time-use data collected in this study.

Interestingly, the greater free-time hours made possible by
their wives' employment does not decrease these husbands' feelings
of being rushed, however. Actually, the patterns of perceptions
of feeling rushed were exactly the opposite for men and women.

While married women felt no more rushed than unmarried women, married men did feel more rushed (remember that both married men and women had less free time available.)

Furthermore, this wifely contribution to their leisure was not reflected in increased feelings of satisfaction among husbands of women in the labor force. In fact, the pattern of satisfactions in Tables 6.2 and 6.3 are remarkably similar for men and women in parallel life situations.*

As was the case for women, marriage was the major contributor to increased life satisfaction among men; and again presence of younger children was the major factor associated with decreased satisfaction with spare time activities.

Moreover, we found in Chapter 4 that whatever inequities were found in the free time available, the proportional allocation of free time across activities of women who entered the labor force and those who stayed at home did not appear to be that different. There was no evidence that having less free time forced them to abandon any free-time activities, although certain trade-offs between activities with a similar function were noted. These trade-offs centered around the locus of the activity, housewives, as the name implies, being more wedded to the home. While the employed woman was able to escape the confines of the home for 60 hours each week, the house-wife got away for just over 20 hours.

Perhaps it is being so tied to the home that leads housewives to express no more satisfaction with their lives than their more harried counterparts in the labor force, despite their 50 percent greater free time. A basic dilemma facing the woman considering outside employment is whether to exchange the extra free time that must be spent in or near the house for the challenge and stimulation of the wider employment environment.

LONG-RANGE PATTERNS OF LEISURE
LIFE STYLES

It was obvious at the outset of the project that the single-day diaries were not going to provide much insight into or appreciation of the "life styles" of individual respondents in our sample. Ulti-mately we hoped to be able to link basic time-use data to such larger life styles as separating the outdoors man from the collector, the gardener from the sports enthusiast, the homebody from the

---

*Again, in both surveys, wives and husbands are sampled separately, that is, only one person per household was interviewed.

culture consumer, or the gourmet cook from the "social butterfly."
This was the main rationale, therefore, behind asking respondents
about their yearly participation in the list of 18 activities examined
in Chapter 1.

Only four of the 18 activities were not strictly free-time activities,
and even these four had a strong leisure component, such as gardening,
making and fixing things, shopping, and helping others. Because of
the large sex differences in yearly participation in most of these
activities, intercorrelations between reported participation in the
18 activities were calculated separately for men and women. Nonetheless, the patterns of intercorrelations were quite similar for both.

In general, there was far less structure in these yearly participation data than we had expected. This meant that we were not able to
differentiate larger life styles with much precision using this approach.
The activities, however, did tend to group into the following four
clusters:

1. Home-centered: Activities include gardening, making and
fixing things, nongrocery shopping, helping others, visiting, playing
cards and other games, and hobbies. The average interitem correlation across this cluster of activities was $r = .18$. The first two
items in this list, gardening and home improvements, were distinct
from the latter five activities in that they were likely to be engaged
in by men rather than by women, and by older people rather than
younger people. In contrast, the more social of the activities in
this group (visiting, card playing, etc.) were more popular among
women and younger people. There were virtually no relations
between social class and participation in any of the seven home-
centered activities.

2. Recreation: The items which clustered most closely here
(average $r = .16$) were attending and participating in sports events,
outdoor activities (fishing, hiking, etc.), water-based activities,
excursions, and frequenting nightclubs and bars. This was pre-
dominately a "male" cluster of activities, a common feature of all
but the water-based activities being their greater popularity among
men. An additional common feature was the heavier participation
of younger people in recreation, the outdoor activities being the
exception here. Again virtually no relation was found with social
class.

3. Culture: The four items in this cluster (average $r = .14$)
were movies, adult education, concert- and theatre-going, and
attendance at fairs, museums, etc. Here, reported participation
was highly related to social class. With the exception of the heavier
movie and class attendance of younger people, participation in these
cultural activities was unrelated to age or to sex.

4. Organizations: The final two items in the list, church and club activity, were significantly correlated with each other (r = .19). Both women and older people participated more in these activities than men and younger people. While reported church attendance was unrelated to social class, far more participation in other organizational activity was reported by the better educated and more affluent.

It needs to be emphasized that the correlations are disappointingly low and that the 18 activities tended to fall into these clusters. There are several significant correlations between activities in different clusters; for example, a .18 correlation is found between movie attendance and going to nightclubs and bars, a .17 correlation between organizational participation and helping others, and an average .15 correlation between water-based activities (which also include picnicking) and each of the items in the home-centered cluster.

A more revealing exercise with these annual participation data consisted of relating them to the extent of free time recorded in respondents' diaries. The intent of this exercise was to note whether there was a systematic enough connection between reported participation and free time to suggest types of activities that may motivate people to have more free time available, or types of activities that attract people who have more free time already available. Greater free time in diaries, in fact, was found to be recorded by people who reported they were more active in the 18 various activities.

Respondents, then, were internally consistent in estimates of annual participation in free-time vs. obligatory activities. Rough comparisons with specific activities indicated free time to be most responsive to reported participation in the active outdoor cluster of activities (that is, sports, fishing, and boating). Free time was also linked significantly to participation in organizations and in certain home-centered activities (playing cards, hobbies, and to a lesser extent, visiting). On the whole, available free time related least clearly to the cultural activities, and another spectator activity, going to sports events.*

----

*Parallel analysis of this type applied to television viewing rather than total free time yielded a much weaker pattern of relationship. Not surprisingly, television viewing related most consistently and negatively with social activities and with spectator activities of a cultural sort (such as movies and concerts). This indicates a trade-off function with television, in which people who are more active socially and who prefer spectatorship away from home watch less television and vice versa. In other words, television emerges as a competitor both for socializing and for other cultural activities,

Making strong assumptions about the motivational nature of these annual activity responses, the following hypothesis is suggested: The greatest push for (or availability of) more free time comes from people who make use of free time for outdoor recreation and non-religious organizational activity rather than spectator-type activities or home improvement. Spectator activities and home improvement appear to be more attractive outlets to people with least free time.

THE SATISFACTORY USE OF FREE TIME

One goal of a "modern society is the creation of greater amounts of free time, free time being considered that time period during which people can express their values, interests, and talents, presumably to enjoy life at its fullest. Thus, the freeing of leisure by the reduction of the workweek to five days is considered a major accomplishment of Western capitalist societies in this century. The shorter workweek, and its usual concomitant of more free time, was in fact a major distinguishing feature of daily life in Western vs. Eastern European countries in the multinational time-budget study.*

Since free time implies periods which allow individuals maximum choice over their activities, it has by definition been valued positively.

---

and perhaps interferes with time spent on such activities. Such a conclusion is reinforced by examination of the differences in daily activities reported by television set owners and nonowners in the multinational study.

On the other hand, television is seen as complementary to out-door recreation activities. Respondents who claimed to participate more in active sports, fishing, and water-based activity spent more time watching television; home-centered people who frequently played cards and other games were particularly heavy television viewers. These results, while interesting, are not controlled for other factors, and may in fact be due to sex differences, since men are not only heavier viewers but more frequent participants in outdoor recreation.

*The more free time available in the United States compared to Western European societies in this study adds further corroboration to this contention. At the same time, amounts of free time equivalent to those found in the United States were reported in the two sites in the multinational study that were at the earliest stages of technological and economic development. This finding suggests a curvilinear relation between modernity and availability of free time, with minimal free time in developing societies, and most free time in societies in either pre- or postindustrial phases. While in large

Yet, as more free time becomes available, concern increases that individuals may not be using this valuable resource wisely. These concerns often arise from larger societal considerations, such as whether people's use of free time represents a threat to the environment or to the supply of nonrenewable natural resources. But they also arise from considerations for the individual, such as whether people are aware of possibly more satisfying ways of spending their free time. Helping professions, such as social work, reportedly encounter a clientele increasingly saddled with the burdens of "overchoice," including an overabundance of free time to spend productively or meaningfully; best-selling books and articles in leading magazines increasingly address this issue of how to spend free time more enjoyably.

Data from the time-use study and the Quality of Life study provide intriguing insights into some often-raised questions about American patterns of leisure. We found in Chapter 5 that, while free-time activities were generally valued more positively than activities with a work orientation, the differences are not as large as one would expect. In this section we examine more generally the relation between ways of spending free time and the satisfaction that people seem to derive from them in the context of several other factors that affect the perceived quality of people's lives.

We begin by examining the basic relation between amount of free time and satisfaction with life in the 1965-66 study. Table 6.4 shows that, contrary to the positive value placed on free time in our society, greater life satisfaction generally was associated with less rather than more available free time. Employed men who claimed to be "completely satisfied" with life recorded much less time per day (268 minutes) in free-time activities than employed men who claimed to be "not very satisfied" with life (328 minutes). The same relation was found for housewives, but interestingly not among employed women.

We have already seen that employed women somehow function with minimal amounts of available free time, and under such circumstances free time apparently becomes a highly valued commodity. Completely satisfied employed women reported more available free time than less satisfied employed women, which indicates that when scarce, free time can provide the expected source of positive satis-

———

part these differences were due to high rates of employment among women in these countries (over 65 percent), this conclusion held when the free time of employed men, employed women, and housewives was examined separately (Szalai et al., 1972, pp. 681-695).

TABLE 6.4

Relation Between Daily Free Time and Life
Satisfaction in 1965-66 National Sample
(minutes per day corrected for
day-of-the-week differences)

	General Life Satisfaction		
	Complete	Fairly	Not very
Employed men	268	279	328
(N = 476)	(97)	(332)	(47)
Employed women	272	230	234
(N = 310)	(71)	(194)	(45)
Housewives	333	329	371
(N = 322)	(95)	(196)	(31)

Source: Compiled by the author from the Study of Americans'
Use of Time (1965-66).

faction. Overall, however, Table 6.4 does suggest a basically
negative relation between available free time and life satisfaction
(although the requisite sample sizes are barely large enough to
support a claim of statistical significance).

Social critics usually express more alarm, however, at what
Americans do with their leisure time rather than how much they
have. Particular concern is voiced about the inadequate portion of
free time people give to participation in organizations, active sports,
walking and outdoor recreation, and general cultural enrichment.
The extent to which such alarm is justified or exaggerated may be
ascertained by examining data from the 1971 study by Campbell
et al. (1976) of the perceived quality of American life, described
in the previous section. It will be remembered that in this study
a national probability sample of about 2,200 respondents was asked
directly about their overall satisfaction with life and about the
satisfaction they derived from several of the various "components"
of their lives, namely, work, marriage, housing, and nonwork-time
activities. In one section of this interview, respondents were also
asked about the kinds of activities they enjoyed doing in their spare
time, and these activities were coded into one of the six categories
described in Table 6.5. The categories proceed generally on the
basis of their degree of mental involvement and energy, from educational and productive at the top to less energetic and passive at the
bottom, the latter two receiving more frequent mention or participa-

TABLE 6.5

Spare-Time and Life Satisfaction as a Function of Participation in Various Activities[a]

	Satisfaction with			
	Spare-Time Activities[b]		Life[b]	
	Women (N = 1245)	Men (N = 901)	Women (N = 1249)	Men (N = 885)
Total Sample	2.43	2.39	2.47	2.44
Participate in				
Educational (taking courses, study, learning new things, etc.)				
No	(1232) 2.47	(886) 2.37	2.48c	2.44
Yes	(12) 2.20d	(11) 2.30	2.63	2.45
Productive (needlecrafts; home improvement, repair, upkeep; working on car; volunteer work)				
No	(631) 2.53	(603) 2.49	2.51	2.46
Yes	(613) 2.30d	(290) 2.20d	2.41e	2.41
Hobbies (creative, such as painting, playing music, writing, etc.; noncreative, such as collections and photography)				
No	(1088) 2.41c	(805) 2.43	2.47	2.46
Yes	(159) 2.55	(92) 2.11d	2.47	2.30c
Energetic (sports and outdoor activities, including bowling, dancing, and snowmobiling)				
No	(912) 2.45	(442) 2.54	2.46	2.48
Yes	(326) 2.37	(448) 2.26d	2.49	2.40e
Less energetic (pleasure driving, reading, visiting, fishing, shopping, mass entertainment, etc.)				
No	(447) 2.52	(286) 2.56	2.51	2.52
Yes	(798) 2.36c	(608) 2.29d	2.45	2.41c
Passive (watch TV, listen to radio or records; loafing, resting, sleeping)				
No	(1025) 2.41	(735) 2.41	2.47	2.46
Yes	(220) 2.43	(162) 2.31c	2.47	2.34c

[a] After correction by MCA for various factors in Tables 6.6-6.8.
[b] Rating scales run between 1 = completely satisfied and 7 = completely dissatisfied.
[c] Greater satisfaction at .01 level.
[d] Greater satisfaction at .001 level.
[e] Greater satisfaction at .05 level.

Source: Compiled by the author from the Quality of Life study (Campbell, Converse, and Rodgers, 1976).

tion than the former. Men were more likely to list activities in the energetic category (mainly sports), while far more women mentioned productive-type activities (such as needlecrafts and home repairs). Sex differences for the remaining activity categories were minimal.

The distinction of greatest interest here is between the four more active activities (educational, productive, hobbies, and energetic) listed at the top of Table 6.5 and the two less active (less energetic and passive) listed at the bottom, in terms of whether participants in more active leisure pursuits claim to derive more satisfaction in their patterns of nonwork activities than participants in less active leisure pursuits; we shall also examine the relation between participation and perceived satisfaction with life. The relations between participation and both life satisfaction and spare-time satisfaction will be examined in a multivariate context in which such factors as amount of participation, constraints (due to time, money, or health), satisfactions from job and marriage, and traditional demographics are also introduced.

The entries in the two left-hand columns of Table 6.5 show the variations between people who did and who did not report participation in the six types of leisure activities in average perceived satisfaction with use of spare time, which respondents in the study rated on a scale running from 1 (meaning completely satisfied) through 7 (meaning completely dissatisfied). These figures are corrected by MCA for differences in satisfaction due to education, marital status, marital satisfaction, employment status, employment satisfaction, and life-cycle stage of respondents; in other words, for each of the important predictors of satisfaction examined in Tables 6.6-6.8.

The data in Table 6.5 show that while participation itself was associated with increased spare-time satisfaction (noted by lower average numbers on the scale), there was little evidence that the specific types of activities made much of a difference in providing that spare-time satisfaction. We find, for example, almost no difference between participants in sports and participants in passive activities for either men or women, or between participants in productive activities and less energetic activities. Even participants in educational activities, which are usually cited by social critics as the highest form of leisure, were not much more satisfied compared to participants in other activities.

It needs to be noted that the relation between participation and satisfaction was much stronger for men than for women, particularly for hobbies and for sports activities. It appears that men need to identify some specific nonwork activity to feel more satisfied with the use of their spare time. Women, on the other hand, were more likely to be satisfied with spare-time activities, whether they could specify them to an interviewer or not.

TABLE 6.6

Spare-Time Satisfaction and Life Satisfaction by Various Participation Factors*

| | Satisfaction with | | | |
| | Spare Time | | Life | |
	Women (N = 1245)	Men (N = 901)	Women (N = 1249)	Men (N = 885)
Total Sample	2.43	2.39	2.47	2.44
Number of spare-time activities listed				
None	(82) 2.78	(50) 2.79	2.53	2.56
One	(573) 2.39	(350) 2.43	2.47	2.47
Two	(459) 2.43	(387) 2.33	2.44	2.40
Three or more	(131) 2.43	(96) 2.28	2.55	2.41
Total organizational associations and memberships				
None	(214) 2.57	(156) 2.43	2.45	2.59
One	(325) 2.45	(192) 2.40	2.44	2.47
Two	(297) 2.37	(233) 2.36	2.41	2.37
Three	(171) 2.41	(117) 2.47	2.64	2.49
Four or more	(238) 2.40	(185) 2.44	2.46	2.33
Frequency of church attendance				
Once a week	(494) 2.34	(256) 2.29	2.38	2.38
Once a month	(274) 2.34	(159) 2.22	2.43	2.29
Less often	(245) 2.52	(201) 2.41	2.63	2.53
Never	(231) 2.40	(263) 2.55	2.38	2.54
Number of friends				
Good many	(476) 2.27	(343) 2.19	2.22	2.25
Average	(540) 2.44	(382) 2.39	2.54	2.46
Not too many	(225) 2.77	(172) 2.79	2.82	2.76
Number of children				
None	(667) 2.33	(475) 2.22	2.51	2.46
One	(187) 2.43	(138) 2.64	2.32	2.36
Two	(174) 2.60	(131) 2.54	2.49	2.35
Three	(119) 2.62	(76) 2.31	2.49	2.55
Four or more	(98) 2.62	(65) 2.83	2.47	2.60

*On rating scale from 1 = completely satisfied to 7 = completely dissatisfied.

Source: Compiled by the author from the Quality of Life study (Campbell, Converse, and Rodgers, 1976).

TABLE 6.7

Spare-Time and Life Satisfaction by Perceived and Actual Constraints*

| | Satisfaction with | | | |
| | Spare Time | | Life | |
	Women (N = 1245)	Men (N = 901)	Women (N = 1249)	Men (N = 885)
Total Sample	2.43	2.39	2.47	2.44
Constraints on spare-time activities				
Yes	(675) 2.64	(505) 2.88	2.58	2.67
No	(570) 2.07	(376) 1.90	2.23	2.23
Time on hands				
Quite often	(283) 3.26	(90) 2.93	2.89	2.78
Now and then	(131) 2.46	(289) 2.35	2.48	2.40
Almost never	(363) 2.15	(313) 2.11	2.31	2.34
Always rushed	(466) 2.47	(185) 2.67	2.52	2.57
Health problems				
None	(875) 2.34	(648) 2.36	2.39	2.39
Minor	(122) 2.39	(96) 2.40	2.59	2.54
Moderate	(113) 2.67	(65) 2.08	2.54	2.24
Major	(135) 2.84	(73) 2.77	2.84	2.86
Financial worry				
All the time	(109) 3.31	(64) 2.57	3.17	2.66
Most of the time	(132) 2.58	(81) 2.60	2.73	2.84
Some of the time	(214) 2.43	(163) 2.65	2.59	2.57
Now and then	(158) 2.27	(104) 2.52	2.35	2.49
None	(630) 2.29	(469) 2.21	2.28	2.29
Income				
Under $5,000	(197) 2.41	(88) 2.15	2.31	2.28
$5,000-9,999	(336) 2.47	(214) 2.34	2.54	2.46
$10,000-13,999	(338) 2.46	(292) 2.52	2.52	2.52
$14,000-19,999	(168) 2.31	(149) 2.39	2.53	2.43
Over $20,000	(142) 2.40	(120) 2.33	2.29	2.40

*On rating scale from 1 = completely satisfied to 7 = completely dissatisfied.

Source: Compiled by the author from the Quality of Life study (Campbell, Converse, and Rodgers, 1976).

TABLE 6.8

Spare-Time and Life Satisfaction by Other Background Factors and Satisfactions*

| | Satisfaction with | | | |
| | Spare Time | | Life | |
	Women (N = 1245)	Men (N = 901)	Women (N = 1249)	Men (N = 885)
Total Sample	2.43	2.39	2.47	2.44
Life cycle				
1. Never married, under 30 years	(82) 3.02	(79) 2.83	2.64	2.83
2. Never married, 30 years or older	(53) 2.10	(39) 2.62	2.64	2.86
3. Widowed	(215) 2.27	(34) 2.42	2.58	2.64
4. Divorced or separated	(128) 2.52	(52) 2.59	3.02	2.79
5. Married, child under six	(227) 2.51	(207) 2.25	2.34	2.36
6. Married, children six or older	(225) 2.36	(185) 2.30	2.37	2.43
7. Married, no children under 18	(215) 2.45	(180) 2.23	2.36	2.31
8. Married, under 30 years, childless	(45) 2.26	(50) 2.57	1.65	2.30
9. Married, 30 or more years, childless	(49) 2.30	(55) 2.49	2.31	2.06
Education				
1. Grade school only	(255) 2.31	(211) 2.17	2.49	2.30
2. Some high school	(249) 2.30	(148) 2.19	2.44	2.30
3. High school graduate	(453) 2.42	(253) 2.42	2.47	2.54
4. Some college	(185) 2.55	(149) 2.59	2.53	2.67
5. College graduate	(100) 2.85	(138) 2.66	2.54	2.41
Marital satisfaction				
1. Complete	(422) 2.25	(407) 2.18	2.19	2.23
2-3. In-between	(240) 2.80	(225) 2.60	2.80	2.69
4-7. Neutral or dissatisfied	(100) 3.01	(50) 3.25	3.22	3.27
Job satisfaction				
1. Complete	(215) 2.30	(232) 1.92	2.22	2.14
2-3. In-between	(196) 2.70	(331) 2.51	2.62	2.44
4-7. Neutral or dissatisfied	(108) 2.78	(145) 2.82	3.00	2.95
9. Not working	(727) 2.34	(192) 2.43	2.43	2.44

*On rating scale from 1 = completely satisfied to 7 = completely dissatisfied.

Source: Compiled by the author from the Quality of Life study (Campbell, Converse, and Rodgers, 1976).

The entries on the right-hand side of Table 6.5 show differences by participation in perceived overall life satisfaction, rated on the same one-to-seven scale as spare-time activities. The differences in life satisfaction by participation tended to be less pronounced than for spare-time satisfaction, a result that is not surprising, considering that leisure is but one component of life; we would expect factors such as marriage, children, and work to be given much higher priority in people's value hierarchies.

There was, however, a significant correlation between satisfaction with spare-time activities and satisfaction with life as a whole ($r = .35$), made particularly striking by the fact that it was higher than the correlation between life satisfaction and satisfaction with job or family. While this relation may be a methodological artifact, as Campbell et al. (1976) suggest, it is intriguing to contemplate how seriously the lives of people may be adversely affected to the extent that they have difficulty in satisfactorily organizing their time away from the workplace. In addition, there is an empirical implication, that is, if certain nonwork activities increase spare-time satisfaction, it is likely life satisfaction also will be increased.

The data in the right side of Table 6.5 do indicate higher life satisfaction for participants in the six leisure activities than non-participants, but again mainly for men. Participation in more active leisure pursuits (hobbies and sports) was related to higher differentials in life satisfaction for men than participation in less energetic and passive activities. Among both men and women, however, neither participation in educational nor productive activities was associated with significantly higher life satisfaction.*

However, when the six activities described in Table 6.5 are summarized in an index of total amount of participation, the expected relation between participation and satisfaction with spare-time activities emerges more clearly. The MCA data are shown as the top entry in Table 6.6 and here the overall relation holds for both men and women. There was one interesting sex difference, namely, whereas satisfaction continued to rise monotonically with number

---

*Among women, in fact, those few who reported educational activities (and who derived greater satisfaction from their spare-time activities) now report lower than average life satisfaction. Perhaps people who look to education as an activity in free time are either frustrated in other aspects of their lives or find educational activity itself a source of frustration; in any event, to the extent that education represents a form of spiritual renewal or contemplation, it certainly was not associated with more positive overall satisfaction.

of activities for men, it reached a peak for women engaging in only one activity, and did not increase for women participating in two or more activities. Much the same was true for ratings of life satisfaction, although the correlations between participation and life satisfaction again were not as great as for spare-time satisfaction, and they were not found at all for women.

Table 6.6 also examines some specific features of participation in spare-time activities, such as the number of organizations of which the person is a member (checked by the respondent from a list of 13 organizations), frequency of church attendance, number of friends, and number of children living at home. Among these four factors, number of friends clearly emerged as the most important predictor of both spare-time and life satisfaction. People reporting having "not too many friends" expressed far less spare-time satisfaction and life satisfaction than average, while greater than average satisfaction was found among people with "a good many" close friends. The differences, if anything, were larger for life satisfaction than for spare-time satisfaction and clearly point to extended networks of friendships as a crucial component of a more contented life style; such a result is consistent with visiting and other social activities being identified as the most satisfying parts of daily life in Chapter 5.

As seen earlier in this chapter, the presence of children was associated with somewhat less satisfaction with spare-time activities, and with no more satisfaction with life; and the optimal number of children for life satisfaction appeared to be one rather than two or more. Nor did satisfaction rise monotonically with more organizational memberships or more church attendance, although male members of organizations or attenders of church services expressed greater satisfaction, particularly at highest participation levels.

Table 6.7 examines a slightly different aspect of spare time, namely constraints that affect it. Responses to a question on overall perception that one's free-time activities were constrained for any reason were strongly associated with lower satisfaction with spare-time activities, and they related to significantly lower life satisfaction as well.

The three main constraints on free time examined for each respondent were money, time, and health. General questions about perceived problems with each were included in the survey and Table 6.7 shows that each was a highly significant correlate of satisfaction in the multivariate context. Even after other factors are taken into account, the more constrained the respondent felt due either to perceived financial worries, perceived state of health, or perceived amount of available time, the lower was their reported spare-time and life satisfaction.

Unfortunately, "objective" measurement of only one of these constraints, amount of income, was obtained in the study. Nonetheless, financial constraint was the major correlate of dissatisfaction among the three perceptions in Table 6.7. Thus, it is even more surprising to find income level being all but unrelated to satisfaction. In fact, other factors being equal, it was the lowest income groups who emerged as most satisfied with spare time and with life. Thus, the most dissatisfied groups in Table 6.7, were those men and women who claimed to worry often about financial matters, or who "quite often" had excess time on their hands, or who had major health problems that kept them "from doing a lot of things" they wished they could do.

Consistent with the findings in Table 6.4, then, it was excessive free time—or perception of too much free time—that was associated with lowest life satisfaction. Nonetheless, the correlation between time pressure and satisfaction was basically a curvilinear one with respondents who "always feel rushed even to do the things that have to be done" also expressing more dissatisfaction with spare-time activities and with life than those in the middle of the time-pressure scale.*

Table 6.8 examines the association between these satisfactions and the final set of variables included in this MCA, namely demographic and other satisfaction questions. These were introduced mainly as control variables in this analysis, but it is interesting that we find again subjective factors—here marital satisfaction and job satisfaction—correlating more strongly with spare-time and life satisfaction than the objective factors of education and life-cycle stage. These results also suggest a pronounced "spillover" from marital and job satisfaction to spare-time satisfaction, rather than a compensation mechanism whereby greatest spare-time satisfaction would be achieved by people otherwise frustrated in their work or family situations. Thus, individuals in unhappy marital situations, and to a lesser extent job situations, reported satisfaction levels from spare-time activities that were well below average. The multivariate nature of the analysis again precludes explanation of these differences solely in terms of "response set," that is, the tendency of people to be satisfied or dissatisfied with anything.

----

*In a separate MCA using only four predictors of life satisfaction (perceptions of being rushed, nonwork satisfaction, job satisfaction, and the tendency to give satisfied responses to all questions) the "rushed" question virtually disappeared as a predictor of life satisfaction. Satisfaction with spare-time activities, however, continued to predict significantly to life satisfaction in this context.

Table 6.8 shows it is also true that persons without marital partners and the unemployed also expressed less satisfaction with spare-time activities and with life. Of the three other "objective" variables in Table 6.8, education related to satisfaction more strongly than either age or age of one's children. Most intriguing was the great dissatisfaction with spare-time activities reported by college graduates; note also that men who had been to college, but who did not graduate, expressed more dissatisfaction with life than any other educational group in Table 6.8.

In summary, these data on satisfactory uses of free time show not only a correlation but a strong carry-over from spare-time satisfaction to life satisfaction. Factors that related to one consistently related to the other. While it is not clear from these analyses whether changes in one variable cause changes in the other, it does appear that the two variables are intimately interrelated (see also the evidence in the explanatory note on p. 171).

Overall, having too much time on one's hands was associated with higher dissatisfaction than having too little time, although having too little time was also associated with less than average satisfaction. This held for both actual available time and perception of available time. General perceptions of having one's choice of leisure activities constrained by either time, money, or health was even more strongly related to spare-time dissatisfaction, and money and health did act as more frustrating sources of constraint than time. However, despite the predominance of financial worries as a predictor, income itself was basically unrelated to spare-time satisfaction, reflecting the generally superior performance of "subjective" over "objective" variables as predictors.* These results also provided support for the "spillover" hypothesis, which postulates a direct correspondence between satisfaction derived from work and leisure.

In terms of the central question of our analysis, it was more the amount rather than the type of participation that seemed to result in more satisfying uses of leisure time. While amount of participation was not monotonically related to amount of satisfaction (particularly among women), the ability to identify oneself as a participant

------

*One objective factor that did relate to spare-time satisfaction was education, although it was surprising to find the relation being generally negative; the lower satisfaction achieved with spare-time activities reported by college graduates suggests that some portion of the college curriculum might be usefully devoted to exploring satisfying ways of spending time subsequent to the college experience.

in any activity—whether it be adult education or a creative hobby, home repairs or television viewing, sports or socializing—was a most important feature of satisfying use of one's free time.

TELEVISION

If there is any conclusion on which critics of the American culture can agree, it is the deplorable state of our television. Statistics on how many hours a day Americans spend in front of their television sets are used to comment on the sterility of our use of free time. The statistic, not fully documented by our standards, that children by age 18 will have spent more time with television than in the classroom or with parents is an example of the alarmist tone that pervades the debate about television.

Our own 1965–66 data did show television to be our most popular free-time activity, consuming 28 percent of the free time available and almost 40 percent if viewing as a secondary activity was included. Television was also the most widely used of the mass media, reaching 80 percent of our sample on the diary day compared to 78 percent for newspapers, 67 percent for radio, 25 percent for magazines, 17 percent for books and 2 percent for movies. Time devoted to television as a primary activity was double that on all these other media combined.

Television figured prominently in interpretations placed on various activities in Chapter 5. It was clearly the most "elastic" of all activities, being the first candidate nominated by respondents for replacement if something important arose and the most popular activity among people who felt that they had excessive time on their hands. It was also among the most discretionary of free-time activities. It was fairly often cited by respondents as the highlight of their day, and seldom listed as the least satisfying activity of the day. Nonetheless, when systematically compared to other activities, television was not rated particularly highly as a general way of spending time, and in fact was evaluated below average compared to other free-time activities.

As such a unique activity, then, television deserves closer scrutiny, and we shall examine certain questions about television in this section. Why did our time–use figures show less public use of television than the widely used data from commercial rating services, such as those of Nielsen, Roper, and Simmons? How much use was made of television as a daily source of news, and how did this compare to other media? How did use of television in the United States compare to that in other countries? Finally, what kind of impact has television made on other aspects of our daily lives?

Television Time

Despite the widespread citation of statistics on how much time Americans spend with television, it is surprising how little attention has been paid to the source of these statistics. Commercial rating services use two main approaches: (1) electronic devices attached to television sets, such as the Nielsen "audimeter," which records what channels are viewed when the set is on (Bogart, 1972), and (2) viewing logs in which people keep an account of all the programs they watch in a day. The electronic devices are kept by people in around 1,000 households across the country, while the logs are kept by much larger numbers of people for shorter periods of time, usually one or two weeks.

These two main methods of measuring time spent with television do provide a remarkable feedback service to keep broadcasters and advertisers aware of what television fare people prefer of the programs that are available. However, when one wants information on how much time Americans watch television, both methods are subject to a number of limitations. People who agree to keep the devices or logs are more likely to be heavier viewers of television than those who do not. Only limited information is provided on what else people are doing when the set is on, whether they are giving the set their undivided attention or are involved in other activities that may distract them. Finally, there may be a tendency for people to overestimate their viewing to oblige the sponsors of the study. If one agrees to provide information about one's television viewing, it is appropriate to have as much viewing as possible to report.

None of these limitations applies solely to television, of course. Our own research tends to show that, for any given activity, people tend to provide generous estimates of time devoted to it, be it housework, sports, or mass media activities. Thus, if one were to ask people to estimate time spent on all their daily activities, the total would far exceed 24 hours. One reason for this state of affairs is that respondents are often involved in more than one activity at the same time, and this is particularly the case for mass media usage. Another reason is that respondents have difficulty in constructing accurate estimates of time spent on a particular activity, or in understanding what behavior is to be included under the heading of a particular activity. If the question simply asks about "sports," for example, will the respondent think to include shuffleboard or chess?

The time diary frees the respondent of these ambiguities of definition since they are asked only to provide information concerning the daily activities in which they engage. Memory problems are also kept to a minimum, since only activities for a single day are examined; they are also recorded on an activity-by-activity basis and do capture multiple uses of time. Furthermore, people are not aware of any purpose of the study other than to record their time and have minimal expectations of what particular activities will interest or please the interviewer or research investigator.

In the case of television, the thorough inventory of activities in the diary illuminates the daily context in which television is viewed and the extent of television use as a secondary activity, a particularly American phenomenon as revealed by the multinational study.

The amount of television time recorded in the 1965-66 time diaries was considerably lower than that reported by the rating services. The hour and a half of viewing as a primary activity, and 35 minutes as a secondary activity, fall well short of the three hours per day that rating services estimated people spent in front of their sets.

The explanation for the difference may come from a separate validity study (Robinson, 1972b), in which the television viewing of people in their home was monitored by having them make estimates, by keeping viewing logs, and by filming their behavior by means of a video camera mounted on top of their television set that recorded what was happening in front of the set when it was turned on. Even though respondents in the study knew their viewing behavior was being monitored on videotape, they reported 25 percent more viewing in their Nielsen-type viewing logs than could be observed from the tapes. The camera recorded significant periods of time when the set was on and no one was watching; furthermore, the study subjects tended to record viewing an entire program in a television viewing log when they in fact watched only a portion of it.*

---

*By comparison, the daily estimate question employed by Roper (1971) yielded a viewing figure that was less inflated than that of Nielsen, but it suffered from the fact that the "typical days" framework of their question produced inflated figures. One important reason for this is that many people respond to the "typical day" question in terms of a "typical day during which you watched television." On a truly typical day, our diaries indicate that about 20 percent of the population did not watch television. Furthermore, even when asked about their viewing on a particular day (for example, yesterday), rather than for a general "typical day," the validation study found people overestimating their viewing times. Again the reason may be that people forget periods when they missed part of a program due to other outside interests and interruptions.

The lower proportion of daily time devoted to television in our
time diaries is also confirmed in our own observational studies of
how people spend their time (Robinson, forthcoming). Moreover,
daily viewing figures very close to ours are reported by Chapin
(1974), who also used the diary approach to the full day's activities.

Television News

Much has been made of the increasing public reliance on television as a source of news. The Roper organization surveys conducted
for the Television Information Office (see, for example, Roper, 1971)
have been finding for many years that Americans claim television to
be their major source of news. Supplemental information about
daily media use gathered in our 1965-66 time-use study raises some
unsettling questions about this widely accepted conclusion.

While daily television exposure was reported by 80 percent of
the respondents in our survey, only 46 percent said they had watched
a news program or documentary on that day. On the other hand,
virtually all of the 78 percent who read a newspaper on the diary
day should have been exposed to news of some sort, even if just by
glancing at the front page. Furthermore, the vast majority of
respondents in our sample who reported listening to the radio also
reported that they heard at least one news report, so that almost
60 percent of the sample were exposed to news through that source.
In fact, the proportion watching television news coverage was not
that much greater on a percentage basis than the proportions exposed
to magazines and books.

On a per-minute basis, television fared somewhat better as
news source, respondents estimating almost 20 minutes of news
viewing (or 40 minutes on a per-participant basis) compared to
15 minutes for all book and magazine reading and 33 minutes for
the newspaper. As compared to the time spent on printed media,
college-educated respondents spent no more time watching television
news. These average time estimates put the information seeking
of the better educated in interesting perspective. However, while
respondents who had not been to college devoted about a tenth of
their television time to news content, the college educated devoted
about a fifth.

Nonetheless, it is hard to reconcile our figures on daily news
media usage with the Roper findings about the public receiving most
of its news from television (see also Robinson, 1971). Perhaps
it reflects more on the amount and type of news information the
public is absorbing (Robinson, 1972a).

Viewing in Other Countries

Comparison of the television viewing habits of Americans with
the full set of multination data indicates that Americans are no more
addicted to television than are people in other countries. Americans
did report more television than people in any other of the 12 countries
surveyed, but that was a direct function of their higher set ownership.
When American set owners were compared to set owners in other
countries, the differences in viewing times across countries were
remarkably small, even though in many of these countries the broadcast day was only four or five hours long (Robinson et al., 1969).
As noted earlier, Americans did spend far more time with television
as a secondary activity, an indication of how television had become
incorporated into the routine of daily life here.

This finding of a virtual constancy of television time was supported
by other data. For example, we asked respondents the following
question to gauge their behavioral dissatisfaction with television
programming:

> Were there any times on (Diary Day) when you would have
> liked to watch TV, but did not because there were no
> programs worth watching on at that time?

Only 10 percent answered yes to this inviting question about boycotting television, indicating that American television did do a
remarkable job of reaching its potential audience, particularly
during "prime time" (Robinson, 1969). Longitudinal studies done
both in America and in England indicate that when an educational
channel was the only one available people watched no less television
than when more popular commercial channels became available.

The existence of large proportions of persons without TV sets
in other countries made it possible to document how drastically
television had affected the allocation of time in a society (Robinson,
1972b). Comparing set owners and nonowners in each of the countries
in the survey, certain consistent patterns emerged. First, set
owners spent more than twice as much time in contact with the mass
media. Second, other mass media appeared to be the main casualties
of television, particularly radio, movies, and the reading of books
and magazines (presumably fiction).

However, set owners consistently spent less time on certain
nonmedia activities as well. They spent much less time visiting,
for example, and less time on hobbies and in conversation. Particularly interestingly, they obtained an average of almost 15 minutes a
night less sleep, suggesting an interesting trade-off or functional
relation between television and sleep.

The use of television did differ by certain factors in a society, most interestingly by education. Better-educated people watched less television in the United States; we saw in Chapter 4 that college graduates reported less than half as much television viewing as a primary activity as those with only a grade school education. This difference was also regularly found for viewing in the other Western European countries in the survey.

No such differentials by education were found in Eastern European countries, however, where the available programming was much more akin to that on our public television channels. In some of these countries, in fact, the better educated watch more television. Historical data from the early days of American television suggest that the less educated have always watched more television in this country, so that the reverse pattern in Eastern European countries is not simply due to lack of sets among the less educated.

Conclusions

Their great familiarity with television may explain why for so many Americans television is a low-involvement activity. When asked which activity during the previous day they could most easily give up if the need arose, we have seen that television was by far the most popular candidate. Robinson (1972b) found that many programs viewed were seen simply because they were on a channel to which the viewer was already tuned. Combined with the above findings on how much television is combined with other activities, the low salience of television as an everyday activity is rather clear. Perhaps this is what McLuhan should mean when he describes television as a "cool" medium.

That is not to deny television's role as a source of considerable satisfaction. Occasions of boycotting television because of poor program selection are relatively rare. Few people describe programs they have just seen as a "waste of time" and even people who claim to watch over six hours of television a day do not think the amount they watch is "too much" (Robinson, 1972b).

What emerges from the results of these time-use studies, then, is a picture of a medium that has had a far more profound impact on how we spend our time than any other technological innovation in this century, be it the automobile, or all of the various home appliances combined. The amount of time people watch television once they purchase a set is highly predictable, as are the activities that television replaces. In this country television has had its major impact on the time use of people with less education, but this is not true in some societies where television stations mainly carry educational and cultural programs.

The available data do not tell us how much of the free time Americans devote to television represents a squandering of this precious human resource. Certainly, Americans are not any more addicted to their sets than people in other countries. Nor do many Americans themselves feel that the television programs they watch are a waste of time, even though that is the first daily activity they would sacrifice if something more important arose.

Television has become a vital fixture of American daily life, having developed into this country's dominant, but not dominating, leisure-time activity. It is a plausible (if not satisfying) and appropriate way of spending that time when there is nothing better to do. It is usually combined with a wide variety of other activities, which may explain why so little television content is intellectually demanding. It is likely to become more demanding only when the audience finds such other activities more pleasantly diverting than the current pictures which flash across this "window on our world."

SUMMARY AND CONCLUSIONS

SUMMARY

Our explorations into and interpretations of how Americans
spend their time have led us in many directions. At the outset,
reasons for the increasing interest in time among sociologists and
economists were discussed. Some unique features of the time
variable (for example, neutrality, ease of definition, equal distribution across the population) that make it a fascinating unit of analysis
for both economists and sociologists were also described, along
with some of the subtleties and ambiguities encountered in analysis
of time-use data.

Our first empirical results centered on evidence confirming
the reliability and validity of the central method of collecting time-
use data, the time diary. Applications of time-diary data, both from
previous research and from that reported in subsequent chapters of
this volume, illustrate four types of social indicator analyses:

1. Cross-time: How has American daily life changed over
the last 20, 50, or 100 years? This subject was examined most
extensively in Robinson and Converse (1972) with the conclusion
that television has clearly brought about the most important change
that can be documented, with its attendant declines in usage of other
media and in visiting. Increases in shopping, child care, and
travel were also apparent, with decreases in routine housework
and eating. Outside of television, other notable time-related innova-
tions of the twentieth century—the automobile, household technology,
and even the "shorter" workweek—showed surprisingly little ability
to affect time usage to any consistent or significant extent.

2. Cross-sectional: What are the major factors that distinguish
how people spend time? As the previous chapters have abundantly

attested, sex and employment status predominate as predictors of
time use. Social class variables mainly affect how free time is
spent, particularly time with the mass media, with education being
a more important predictor than income. Number and age of children
clearly affect household and family care, but only for women. Surprisingly little variation in time was found by age, religion, marital
status, season, weather, the ecological factors of urbanicity or
region of the country, by type of dwelling, and the availability of
household help or automobiles.

3. Cross-national: How does daily life in America differ from
that in other countries? These differences were identified most
extensively in Szalai et al. (1972, pp. 574-75) with reference to the
other Western and European countries that participated in the multinational study. While Americans had a shorter workweek than
Europeans, we spent no less time on housework than people in countries with far less household technology. Our time diaries revealed
uniquely American patterns of child socialization, that is, (a) more
time devoted to preschool children, (b) less time devoted to older
children, (c) more time spent in chauffeuring children, and (d) less
time spent in helping children with their schoolwork (Stone, 1972).
Despite our practically universal access to automobiles, we spent
no less (or more) time traveling than people in other countries;
however, our commute to work did tend to be shorter than in other
countries, even though we lived much further from the place of
work. While Americans did spend more time than Europeans watching television, this was not true on a per-set-owner basis; we also
spent more time reading newspapers but that too may have been
the result of their greater availability here. The greater attendance
at church services among Americans was particularly distinctive
as was our time spent visiting, playing sports, and helping friends
and relatives. Americans walked less for pleasure than Europeans,
and also spent less time mending clothing.

4. Cross-activity: One approach to understanding the dynamics
of trade-offs that take place between daily activities is to observe
systematic time-use differences as a function of whether more or
less time is devoted to a particular activity. Thus, in Chapter 3,
we found that people with longer workweeks did not reduce all
other activities equivalently, but spent disproportionately less of
their free time in organizational activity, watching television and
traveling to nonwork destinations. On the other hand, people who
spent more time watching television spent less time visiting, participating in organizations, and engaging in recreation and entertainment away from home. We did not find systematic differences using
less direct approaches to observing trade-offs in which the time
use of individuals in certain presumably time-bound situations was

compared to the time use of other individuals. Thus, individuals living further from work, without household help, or without access to an automobile differed little in their time-use patterns from other individuals. Even our comparison of workers on the four- and five-day workweeks provided little in the way of systematic differences in time use.

In an attempt to place these and other determinants of time use into systematic perspective, a general model of time-use factors was developed in Chapter 2. Following that general model, we proceeded to examine various daily activities in terms of the multiple factors that contributed to high or low participation in various activities.

The following discussion briefly summarizes the observations we have made about differential uses of time on an activity-by-activity basis using the various factors in the model* and incorporating relevant material from the last two chapters on the meanings associated with various activities.

Work

Respondents can give fairly accurate estimates of the time they spend at work and in commuting to work, at least when these estimates are compared to entries in their time diaries. Nonetheless, at least 12 percent of the time individuals record as "work" is spent on non-work activities and personal business done at the workplace. Less than 2 percent of all work can be classified as moonlighting, which amounted to less time than work brought home from the office in the 1965-66 study.

Of the several predictors of time use examined in our model, the major factor associated with work was sex, employed men recording almost a third longer workweek (51 hours including commuting) than employed women (39 hours). Even on a per-participant basis, the average workday for an employed man was an hour longer on the average than for an employed woman.

The only other factors that explained appreciable amounts of variance in work time were self-employment and experience of an unusual day. Self-employed people put in a much longer than average workweek; on the other hand, unusual days were associated with less than average work, since they required heavier than usual commitments of time away from work with voluntary organizations, on family business matters, or an unusual social visit.

———

*The major and obvious day-of-the-week differences are omitted from this discussion.

In terms of the satisfaction associated with daily activities, work rated higher than expected, only slightly below the average for all free-time activities. Nonetheless, it can be the source of considerable frustration, and work was cited most often by respondents as the least enjoyable aspect of their day in the 1965-66 study. While few workers specifically cited their work schedules or work hours as a source of such frustration, this has become a topic of increasing societal discussion.*

Housework

No activity has as clearly demarcated the sexual division of labor in our society as household care. Women performed over 80 percent of both the housework and child care in this country in the 1965-66 study. While the employed woman was able to complete her housework in about half the time required by the housewife, this still represented a considerable encroachment on what could

---

*National data from the Quality of Employment surveys of the Survey Research Center (Quinn and Shepard, 1974) do suggest a rising concern with work schedules among workers. In response to an open-ended question in a 1973 survey, 39 percent of the national sample reported some "problems or difficulties you run into concerning the hours you work, your work schedule, or overtime" compared to only 30 percent in a 1969 national survey. While there was little shift in the proportion describing this work problem as sizable or great (a little over a third of workers in both samples) there was an interesting shift in the problems cited in the four-year interim, namely, excessive hours had declined significantly as a source of difficulties, while interference with family activities (perhaps the opposite side of the coin) had increased significantly. That these increases in work scheduling problems were more prevalent among younger, better-educated, and male workers could signal a critical and articulate mass pushing for changes in societal work schedules in the future.

Questions about dissatisfactions with the hours and scheduling of work were asked of both men and women in our small 1973 Jackson sample. Three times as many employed women as employed men said they would like to work fewer hours per week than they did, and more women than men voiced support for the four-day workweek for themselves. More support for these changes was given in response to these specific questions than when respondents were asked a more abstract question earlier in the interview about expressed interest in switching their work hours in any way.

be free time for her. This was particularly true given that husbands
of employed women reported little more contribution to housework
than husbands of women not in the labor force.

Of the other factors that affect housework of women, age and
the number of children emerged from multivariate analyses as
most important. Other factors being equal, housework rose
monotonically with age and with number of children; less housework
than average was reported by better-educated women and by unmarried women. Perhaps the most significant finding, however, was
that only one of these four factors—age—held as a predictor of the
housework time of men.

This male insensitivity to the burdens of housework imposed
on women by marriage, children, and their entry into the labor
force, one would think, would be a major source of marital dissatisfaction. This is particularly true given that housework tasks clearly
fall at the bottom of the list of daily activities that provide satisfaction
and enjoyment. However, we found that while additional role burdens
did increase the woman's sense of being rushed, and that employment was the most important of them, this did become directly
translated into feelings of dissatisfaction with life. Relatively few
women (23 percent in a 1973 national survey), moreover, said they
wanted their husbands to help more with household chores, and the
demand was not that much greater among employed women than
among housewives. Consciously or unconsciously, women apparently
prefer not to turn to their husbands to resolve this inequitable state
of affairs.

Child Care

As noted above, women also reported the lion's share of the
child care in this country, spending four times as much primary
activity time on child care as men, and twice as much time in general
contact. Furthermore, most of women's child care was custodial
in nature (feeding, dressing, etc.), while most of men's child-
centered activity was interactional (playing with children, helping
with schoolwork, etc.)

We again found men's child care to be virtually unaffected by
the factors that profoundly affect the time women devote to children.
Age of children rather than number of children has most effect on
the time American women spend on child care. It was estimated
that, other factors being equal, employed women gave to child care
half as much primary activity time as housewives; marriage per se
seemed to bring with it no more or less time spent on child care on
a per-parent basis. The proposition that better-educated parents
invest more time in their children received only modest support.

Better-educated parents devoted more time to interactional activities with their children than less-educated parents and reported more time with children during the crucial preschool years. Overall, however, college-educated respondents in the 1965-66 study spent only slightly more time with their children than less-educated parents.

It was estimated that the arrival of the first child will consume eventually about 5 percent of the mother's primary activity time over the subsequent 18 years of the child's life and about 22 percent of her total waking life will be spent in the company of the child during that period; these figures can practically double if the number of children reaches four or more.

While the comparable figures for men are at most only half as large, and do not increase appreciably with additional children, we found, as in the case with housework, that relatively few mothers (29 percent in a 1973 national survey) expressed a wish for more child care from their husbands. One explanation here may lie with the considerable satisfaction that women derive from child-care activities, both interactional and custodial.

The effects of these various factors on children also need to be considered. Whereas the absence of a father may deprive the child of a third or a fifth of the time they would receive from both parents combined, the entry of the mother into the labor force could almost cut such parental access time in half; and there was little evidence of husbands of employed women making up for the loss. The single child also appeared to have his or her parental access time cut considerably with the arrival of a second child. However, it was with the third and fourth child that the children in the family seemed most deprived of parental time, since total child-care time of parents did not rise significantly when more than two children were present in the household. This reduced access to parental time may well be connected to the poorer performance of later-born children from larger families on academic achievement tests (Zajonc and Markus, 1975).

Personal Needs

In general, virtually constant amounts of time were expended on personal needs, even across sex and employment status categories. Some hint of the hectic life style of employed women was reflected here, however. Employed women averaged over 20 minutes less time per day eating than housewives, but spent more time washing and dressing, presumably readying themselves for the day's work. While employed women averaged only a half an hour less sleep per week than housewives, this was accomplished by almost an hour more sleep and naps on Sunday.

Sleep averaged remarkably close to the proverbial eight-hour-per-day figure. The most surprising finding with regard to sleep was that employed older people did not register more sleep in their diaries than younger people.

Travel

The time diary provided a unique opportunity to examine Americans' travel behavior in full perspective. Few transportation studies made of the public, for example, include time spent walking or riding a bicycle, which accounts for about 15 percent of all travel time. Some of the possibilities of using time-diary data to construct models of the American transportation system were illustrated in Chapter 3, in which data on commuting to work followed regular, but not linear, patterns for different distances to work, city sizes, and countries.

Men spent more time traveling per week (11 hours) than women (8 hours), if commuting to work was included, and almost half again as much as housewives (7 hours). The more affluent parents of school-aged children and those who lived furthest from work also spent more time on total travel and on nonwork trips as well. No clear pattern could be found relating the presence or number of automobiles to the time spent traveling.

Free Time

By the time all of the above "obligatory" activities were taken into account, only about 20 percent of time remained as "free". Men and women had almost equal amounts of free time, about 35 hours per week, but that figure was obtained because housewives have over five hours more free time per week and employed women five hours less. While both marriage and children appeared to cut into the free time of men, as it did for women, husbands had more free time if their wives were employed.

There were not enough differences in free time by income or education to support descriptions of "harried leisure classes" or leisure-deprived underclasses. However, striking social class differences did emerge in how leisure time was used. The less affluent watched more television and rested more, the more affluent were involved more in adult education courses, formal organizations, reading, and frequenting places of entertainment.

Older people had less free time than younger people, particularly people under age 25. Free time varied, but not on a direct one-to-one basis, with length of the workweek, that is, for every extra hour of work, about .6 hours of free time were given up, the remainder going to personal care and family care. Some evidence was reviewed in Chapter 6 that suggested that people who had more free time used that time to engage in active and social pursuits rather than spectator-type activities (such as movies or concerts), household hobbies, or helping others.

Free-time activities, in general, were felt by respondents to provide more satisfaction than work or housework, but the differences between work and leisure on this dimension were not pronounced. People who generally felt rushed did in fact report less free-time activity in their diaries than those who felt they had time on their hands, but data from a 1971 Quality of Life survey indicated it was the latter group that reported least life satisfaction. Individuals in that survey who felt constraints on their money or health also reported well below average satisfaction, as did people who claimed to have few close friends and people who could not list a single pleasurable free-time activity. A strong correlation in the 1971 study was found between satisfaction with free-time activities and satisfaction with life. More extensive analysis indicated this could not be adequately explained as a methodological artifact; these analyses also provided support for the "spillover" hypothesis of leisure.

Organizations and Education

Empirical evidence in Chapter 5 was presented to corroborate our concern that these three activities (organizational participation, religion, and education) qualify more as "semi-leisure" than as free-time activities. Nonetheless, inclusion of the small amounts of time devoted to these activities (less than three hours per week) did not greatly inflate the figures on free time. Roughly equivalent amounts of time were devoted to organizations, religious practice, and adult education.

The amount of time devoted to organizational activity was lower than we expected on the basis of the voluminous sociological literature on the organizational participation of the American public. The higher participation in organizational activity by housewives, and particularly more affluent housewives, provided further testimony to its "obligatory" nature. Moreover, organizational participation was considered by respondents to provide far less satisfaction than any free-time activity. It was noted that relatively little of the organizational activity reported was of benefit to persons outside of the respondent's immediate family; from the time-diary perspective, far more philanthropic or helping behavior was accomplished through informal channels than through formal organizations.

Housewives also reported more religious devotion than employed women or employed men. Most reported religious activity was in

the form of attendance at Sunday services. There was definitely a
higher rate of religious observance reported by older people, although
it is not known whether this was a cohort effect or simply functional
preparation. Religious activity was not seen as particularly satisfying in the context of free-time activities, although it provided far
more satisfaction than organizational participation.

Our sampling criteria excluded the possibility that many full-
time students would fall into our 1965-66 sample so that our data
greatly underestimate the extent of academic activity in this country.
As was the case with organizational participation, additional education was mainly reported by the better educated. About as much of
this educational activity was in the form of homework as in attendance
at classes.

Mass Media

Almost half of all free time as a primary activity in the 1965-66
study was devoted to one of the mass media, and as much secondary
activity use of the media was reported as primary activity use.
More primary activity time was devoted to television than to the
other mass media combined. Television also was clearly the most
distinctive and elastic of all daily activities as noted in the previous
two chapters.

Television appears to be the most likely recipient of the time
in which individuals have nothing better to do with their time. While
it provided less satisfaction than other free-time activities, it was
still a source of considerable satisfaction to many people, being
noted with some frequency as the highlight of one's day.

Almost 80 percent of our sample reported watching television
on an average day. The strongest correlate of viewing was education,
which in multivariate context reduced the bivariate relations between
viewing and income and between viewing and race. Men reported
more viewing as a primary activity than women, but women reported
more viewing as a secondary activity.

Television time as reported in our respondent diaries was
considerably less than that estimated by the commercial media-
rating services and several plausible reasons for the discrepancy
were discussed. Some corroborating evidence was presented for
our more conservative viewing figures and for the contention that
television was reaching close to its maximum audience.

Supplementary time-use questions called into question the
contention that television was the main medium Americans depended
on for their news. Close to 80 percent of Americans also read a
newspaper on an average day and close to 70 percent listened to a
radio news broadcast, compared to less than 50 percent who watched

a television news program. Like television, more newspaper reading
was reported by men than by women. The better educated also spent
slightly more time reading the newspaper, but they spent considerably
more time reading magazines and books; older people also spent
more time reading. News and women's content predominated the
magazines read, while the books read dealt equally with fiction,
analytic nonfiction, and religion (particularly the Bible).

Over 90 percent of all radio listening was done as a secondary
activity, with the better educated listening more to mood and classical
music and the less educated listening more to top-40 and country-
western stations. Slightly less aggregate primary activity time
was devoted to the movies than to radio, and most movie going was
reported by the 20 to 29 age group and the college educated.

Recreation-Social

If organizational participation can be said to be an overstudied
sociological phenomenon on a time-use basis, then visiting would
be the prime candidate as an understudied phenomenon. Although
there is evidence that visiting time in this country has suffered with
the advent of television, it was still the second most prevalent free-
time activity in the 1965-66 study, consuming over 20 percent of
free time. Moreover, in our various approaches to measuring the
satisfaction and enjoyment derived from daily activities, it consistently emerged at or near the top of such dimensions.

More socializing was reported by women than men, by housewives than employed women, by single than married people, by
parents of preschool children than of older children, by blacks than
whites, by people reporting their day was unusual rather than normal,
and by people expressing a more gregarious attitude toward making
new acquaintances.

Women, particularly housewives, reported more time in conversation than men. Housewives were also more likely to report
engaging in interesting conversations than employed women or men.
The topics of such interesting conversations tended to follow traditional sex-role lines, women's conversations dealing more with
family-centered topics, men's with work and news events; the same
division was found when respondents were asked to report important
plans or problems that were on their minds during the diary day.
Differences in interesting conversations or important plans by
educational level were surprisingly small.

Better-educated (and higher-income) respondents did tend to
report greater participation in recreation and entertainment away
from home. The major variable that distinguished such participation,
however, was sex, men reporting over twice as much such activity

as women. There was only a minor tendency for such away-from-home activity to be restricted by advanced age or the presence of children.

Women, on the other hand, reported far greater participation in the final two free-time activities examined, hobbies and resting. With two-thirds of hobby activity being in the form of needlework and food preserving (rather than crafts, collections, or art or music practice) the large sex difference in hobby activity becomes more understandable, as does the greater hobby time reported by older women and women with fewer children in the household.

FUTURE DIRECTION OF
TIME-USE RESEARCH

Data from the 1965-66 study and the follow-up studies in this volume represent a significant start in our understanding of how Americans use their time and what their daily activities mean to them. The survey analytic techniques employed here have allowed us to separate daily activities that are either constants of human behavior (such as personal needs and travel) or about which much is already known from other sources (such as work time or movie attendance) from those that represent more dynamically variable and interesting behaviors, such as child care, religion, television, reading, and visiting. It has also allowed us to separate those variables that profoundly affect almost all aspects of how time is spent (such as sex, employment status, ownership of television sets, and day of the week), from those that have strong effects but only on certain activities (such as education and presence of children), from those that have surprisingly little influence (such as age, marital status, geographic location, and availability of household technology). These data also form a solid benchmark from which it will be possible to gauge clearly and accurately how daily life in the United States will change in future generations.

In retrospect, there are several ways in which the 1965-66 study could have been done better or more efficiently. The cost of the "tomorrow" diary approach would not seem to warrant the relatively small gains in recording detail that were obtained. Diaries should be collected from all members of the family, including children, in order to capture the dynamics of family interaction. Even though other activity surveys show minimal rural-urban differences, a full national sample ought to be used, including the unemployed and retired. Such a data set could be considerably enriched by having these individuals keep daily diaries for more than one day of the week or one season of the year. A larger number of

activity-coding categories and more specific codes could be employed
to increase coding reliability, particularly for organizational activity
and recreation. Having respondents in such a sample describe the
satisfaction or enjoyment they derive from each activity would intro-
duce the crucial meaning component of time use. We have seen in
Chapter 5 that this is not only technically feasible but gives intriguingly
different results than when respondents are asked about the satisfaction derived from these activities in general.

Such a data set would provide better perspective on the psychological factors underlying everyday life. We have already seen that
the traditional demographic and sociological survey variables
explained surprisingly little of the variance in daily activities. In
contrast, rather strong relations were found in Chapter 5 between
the satisfaction that individuals derive from activities and their
participation in that activity. This might simply represent another
example in which the theory of cognitive dissonance could be said to
apply; that is, individuals somehow derive satisfaction from whatever
it is they have to do or whatever daily routine they fall into (much in
the manner that even slaves "hug their chains"). The activities for
which the relation is strongest, however, are loosely structured
free-time activities over which the individual has considerable
discretion on a daily basis—television, reading, hobbies, and so on.

We suspect, therefore, that even daily routine evolves from a
process in which individuals selectively find those activities that
are psychologically rewarding and arrange their lives in such a
way that participation in these activities can be scheduled more
frequently. Although the issue may be too subtle ever to resolve
definitively, the availability of data on both daily activities and their
associated satisfactions for two or more days would allow analysis
for causal connections between the two variables via such techniques
as cross-lag correlation or path analysis.

We have seen evidence in Chapter 6 that links life satisfaction
with total amounts of free time. The evidence is less clear on the
larger question of whether participation in particular free-time or
work activities provide individuals with greater satisfaction in their
lives. In Chapter 6, we uncovered support from the 1971 Quality
of Life study for the notion that types of activities were less important than number of activities in providing life satisfaction, or spare-
time satisfaction. Few consistent or plausible linkages between
life satisfaction and daily time expended on various activities, however, were found in the 1965-66 study as shown in Tables 2.2 and
2.4-2.8 of Chapter 2; for example, men who were more dissatisfied
with life spent more time on second jobs, visiting, and television,
while dissatisfied women spent more time on nongrocery shopping
and hobbies and less time on organizations. This failure to identify

activity patterns related to life satisfaction is reinforced employing
a different analytic approach with the 1965-66 data. Responses to
a question on life satisfaction asked in that survey were correlated
with respondent estimates of yearly frequency of participation in 18
activities (see Chapter 6). The average correlation across activities
was only .02 for men and .08 for women (Robinson et al., 1969).*
On the other hand, when the 18 items were combined into an index
of total participation, there was a significant correlation with life
satisfaction for women (r = .23), although it was much lower for
men (r = .07).†

There was, of course, a definite tendency for greater life satisfaction to be found among people who expressed satisfaction with
other aspects of their lives. In Chapter 6, for example, we noted
the significant correlation between life satisfaction and nonwork
satisfaction in the 1971 Quality of Life study. The correlation
between life satisfaction and satisfaction derived from 19 activities
and aspects of life in the 1965-66 study are presented in Table 7.1,
separately for men and for women. In this table the "positivity"
factor in satisfaction ratings is clearly evident with only 4 of the
37 correlations being negative. The only activities for which no
relation is found for either men or women are the passive leisure
activities: television, reading, and relaxing.

Nonetheless, certain items in Table 7.1 stand out as particularly
strong correlates of life satisfaction for both men and women. These
are the "basics" of life, namely work, housework, marriage, and

---

*Frequency of participation in two activities, religion and
organizations, was correlated significantly with life satisfaction
for both men and women. Interestingly, both activities ranked near
the bottom of satisfactory free-time activities in Chapter 5. Note
also that in Table 7.1 of this chapter, satisfaction with religious
and organizational participation correlate consistently with life
satisfaction. This suggests that the ability to derive satisfaction
from generally unsatisfying activities, or from those free-time
activities with a work or obligatory component, can contribute to
an individual's overall satisfaction with life.

†Correlations with life satisfaction were also calculated for
the following subindices of participations: home-centered activities,
energetic activities, activities with things, activities with people,
age-related activities, cultural activities, and sex-role activities.
In line with the above findings, very little differentiation was apparent
in the ability of these subindices to predict to life satisfaction, each
of them showing slightly lower correlations than the total activity
index.

TABLE 7.1

Correlation between Life Satisfaction and
Satisfaction Derived from 19 Activities
and Components of Life

Satisfaction Derived from	Men (N = 497)	Women (N = 637)
1. Television	-.01	.01
2. Sports	-.01	.11
3. House	.26	.23
4. Shopping	.05	.08
5. Religion	.13	.12
6. Reading	.05	.01
7. Politics	.13	.05
8. Preparing food	.02	.17
9. Making things, repairs	.04	.13
10. Children	.10	.00
11. Car	.11	.00
12. Relaxing	.01	.04
13. Helping others	.15	.07
14. Being with relations	.23	-.01
15. Being with friends	.17	-.05
16. Clubs	.12	.10
17. Marriage	.19	.24
18. Job satisfaction	.33	.26
19. Housework satisfaction	NA*	.18

*NA = No activity.

Source: Compiled by the author from the Study of Americans'
Use of Time (1965-66).

house. Note that, although the differences are not striking, Table 7.1
does provide support for the contention that marital satisfaction is
more important for women than men and that job satisfaction is
more important for men than women; women's life satisfaction is
also more tied to food preparation, and men's to politics, automobiles,
and children. Note also that, while children rated near the top of
their satisfaction scale in Chapter 5, satisfaction with children did
not correlate at all with satisfaction with life among women.

In general, however, there is not enough convergence and
consistency in these various analyses to warrant any general conclusions about what specific activities make one person's daily
schedule or life style more satisfying than another's. While more
active participation in leisure activities does seem to provide a more

satisfying daily life, it would appear that general states of life (such
as work, marriage, and living quarters) have much more to do with
achieving a satisfying way of life than particular activities per se.
Nonetheless, this question is important enough to justify replication
and extension of these analyses with an updated, larger, and fuller
national sample. It will also be useful to see whether the curvilinear
relations between life satisfaction and amount of free time continue
to hold as we move toward a society in which more information is
disseminated about the beneficial potentials of leisure.

One most fruitful area for further research would be the area
of verifying the extent of overlap between time use and measures of
individual energy expenditure. Indeed, it has perhaps been the
expectation that time-use data could provide insights about how
individuals distribute their energies across daily activities that has
spurred the interests of economists and sociologists. The attractiveness of time in this research context has been that, although only a
surrogate measure of energy expenditure, time can be measured
with far greater confidence and objectivity than human energy. Even
the social-psychological study of satisfaction may find its ultimate
value in the clues time use provides about the things that attract
people's energies or that "energize" them.

The conception of man or society as an energy-distribution
system is a prominent one in the theories of Freud, Erikson, and
Lewis, among many others. The outlines of such an energy model
are greatly aided by the time-use data provided in this volume.
Most Americans probably expend their energy in rough proportions
to those waking activities that are most time-consuming, such as
work, friendship networks, and child care. This is further reflected
in the frequency with which respondents brought up such topics in
important conversations or planning (Chapter 5). Similarly, a
rough idea of the energy levels expended during leisure time can
be gained by comparing the amount of time spent on active sports
or education activity with that spent on television or resting.

However, these aggregate time-use figures are much less
satisfying in helping us understand daily behavior at the level of the
individual. For example, it is obvious that for some people the
40-hour workweek can drain virtually all of their energy, while for
others work represents the least energy-demanding part of their
week. In the small methodological sample in Jackson, Michigan,
we asked a question about how much energy their jobs required.
Only about a quarter of the sample said their jobs required them to
"work really hard all the time," although in hourly terms, this
sample did estimate they had to put in about 30 hours of hard work.
However, not one respondent in the sample said that he usually
came home from work "completely exhausted," and only about half

of the sample said they were somewhat exhausted. Furthermore, less than 20 percent of the sample said they were usually so tired from a day's work that all they could do after work was relax and recuperate for the next day's work. Anecdotal evidence at least indicates that if the question had been asked of a similar sample 25, 50, or 75 years ago, work would have represented a far higher drain on individual energy than it does today. If measures of productivity could be shown to have increased over the same period, the ability of workers to expend as much energy on family-related and leisure activities as on work would constitute a truly significant way in which a higher quality of life has been achieved in this country.

Parallel to data on work productivity, measures of the "output" from housework (as well as other activities) will be needed before the values of these measures of human energy can be put in proper perspective. At many points in our analyses, it would appear that people under great time constraints were able to allocate their energies more efficiently, that is, to accomplish the same output with less time input. For example, the employed woman may have done less housework than other housewives before entering the labor market, or may have been more experienced in combining the burdens of work and housework through previous job experience. However, the fact that she is able to complete her housework in about half or two-thirds of the time needed by housewives probably does not mean that her house is only half as clean or well organized or that her family is half as well cared for or well fed.

Nonetheless, the fact that roughly the same proportional reduction occurs for primary activity child-care time among employed women gives much more cause for alarm. Data from working and nonworking mothers on output measures from child care, such as academic achievement, self-esteem, or juvenile delinquency, will be needed before one can say that such alarm is justified. Some early results from data on the academic performance of primary school children show little relation with mother's time investment on outside employment (Natali and Goldberg, forthcoming).

Time data, then, need such elaboration to move from being simply social indicators to being linked to measures of social or economic welfare, or to becoming useful in social planning. Some of the more obvious dimensions of the meaning of time have been explored in this volume, and undoubtedly others will arise, and become even more prominent, in the future. There seems little question that increasing reliance will be placed on time-use data for social policy purposes. At least as much thought and effort need to go into maximizing the social-psychological interpretation of gross time-use figures. The expectation here is that this can be best accomplished through relating individuals' time both to some measure of energy they expend and to some output they hope to achieve.

Complete two-digit activity code

Code		Abbreviation	Code number in reduced 37 categories
Working time and time connected to it (00-09)			
00	Normal professional work (outside home)	Regular work	1
01	Normal professional work at home or brought home	Work at home	1
02	Overtime if it can be specifically isolated from 00	Overtime	1
03	Displacements during work if they can be specifically isolated from 00	Travel for job	1
04	Any waiting or interruption during working time if it can be isolated from work (e.g., due to supply shortage, breakdown of machines, etc.)	Waiting, delays	1
05	Undeclared, auxiliary, etc. work	Second job	2
06	Meal at the workplace	Meals at work	15
07	Time spent at the workplace before starting or after ending work	At work, other	3
08	Regular breaks and prescribed non-working periods etc. during worktime	Work breaks	3
09	Travel to (resp. from) workplace, including waiting for means of transport	Travel to job	4
Domestic work (10-19)*			
10	Preparation and cooking of food	Prepare food	5

*Such activities (especially gardening and animal care) are to be recorded as "domestic work" only if not part of professional work or gainful employment.

Information for this appendix was taken from Szalai et al. (1972).

11	Washing up and putting away the dishes	Meal cleanup	6
12	Indoor cleaning (sweeping, washing, bed-making)	Clean house	6
13	Outdoor cleaning (sidewalk, disposal of garbage)	Outdoor chores	6
14	Laundry, ironing	Laundry, ironing	7
15	Repair or upkeep of clothes, shoes, underwear	Clothes upkeep	7
16	Other repairs and home operations	Other upkeep	11
17	Gardening, animal care	Gardening, animal care	9
18	Heat and water supplies upkeep	Heat, water	11
19	Others (e.g., dealing with bills and various other papers, usual care to household members, etc.)	Other duties	11

Care to children (20-29)

20	Care to babies	Baby care	12
21	Care to older children	Child care	12
22	Supervision of school work (exercises and lessons)	Help on homework	13
23	Reading of tales or other non-school books to children, conversations with children	Talk to children	13
24	Indoor games and manual instruction	Indoor playing	13
25	Outdoor games and walks	Outdoor playing	13
26	Medical care (visiting the children's doctor or dentist, or other activities related to the health of children)	Child health	13
27	Others	Other, baby-sit	13
28	Not to be used	Blank	
29	Travel to accompany children including waiting for means of transport	Travel with child	17

Purchasing of goods and services (30-39)

30	Purchasing of everyday consumer goods and products	Marketing	8
31	Purchasing of durable consumer goods	Shopping	10
32	Personal care outside home (e.g., hairdresser)	Personal care	14

33	Medical care outside home	Medical care	14
34	Administrative services, offices	Administrative service	10
35	Repair and other services (e.g., laundry, electricity, mechanics)	Repair service	10
36	Waiting, queuing for the purchase of goods and services	Waiting in line	10
37	Others	Other service	10
38	Not to be used	Blank	
39	Traveling connected to the above mentioned activities, including waiting for means of transport	Travel service	17

Private needs: meals and sleep etc. (Private and non-described activities) (40-49)

40	Personal hygiene, dressing (getting up, going to bed, etc.)	Personal hygiene	14
41	Personal medical care at home	Personal medical	14
42	Care given to adults, if not included in household work	Care to adults	11
43	Meals and snacks at home	Meals, snacks	15
44	Meals outside home or the canteen*	Restaurant meals	15
45	Night sleep (essential)	Night sleep	16
46	Daytime sleep (incidental)	Daytime sleep	16
47	Nap or rest	Resting	36
48	Private activities, non-described, others	Private, other	14
49	Traveling connected to the above mentioned activities, including waiting for means of transport	Travel, personal	17

Adult education and professional training (50-59)

50	Full time attendance to classes (undergraduate or post-graduate student), studies being the principal activity	Attend school	19

---

*A number of special types of meals outside home and the canteen have special codes, different from 44 (see under "Spectacles, Entertainment, Social life," especially codes 71, 76-78).

51	Reduced programs of professional or special training courses (including after work classes organized by the plant or enterprise in question)	Other classes	19
52	Attendance to lectures (occasionally)	Special lecture	19
53	Programs of political or union training course	Political courses	19
54	Homework prepared for different courses and lectures (including related research work and self-instruction	Homework	19
55	Reading of scientific reviews of books for personal instruction	Read to learn	19
56	Others	Other study	19
57-58	Not to be used	Blank	
59	Traveling connected to the above mentioned activities, including waiting for means of transport	Travel, study	18

Civic and collective participation activities (60–69)

60	Participation as member of a party, of a union, etc.)	Union, politics	21
61	Voluntary activity as an elected official of a social or political organization	Work as officer	21
62	Participation in meetings other than those covered by 60 and 61	Other participation	21
63	Non-paid collective civic activity (e.g., volunteers)	Civic activities	21
64	Participation in religious organizations	Religious organizations	20
65	Religious practice and attending religious ceremonies	Religious practice	20
66	Participation in various factory councils (committees, commissions)	Factory council	21
67	Participation in other associations (family, parent, military, etc.)	Misc. organization	21
68	Others	Other organization	21

| 69 | Traveling connected to the above mentioned activities, including waiting for means of transport | Travel, organization | 18 |

Spectacles, entertainment, social life (70-79)

70	Attending a sports event	Sports events	34
71	Circus, music-hall, dancing, night club (including a meal in the entertainment local)	Mass culture	34
72	Movies	Movies	28
73	Theatre, concert, opera	Theatre	35
74	Museum, exhibition	Museums	35
75	Receiving visit of friends or visiting friends	Visiting with friends	29-30
76	Party or reception with meal offered to or offered by friends	Party, meals	29-30
77	Cafe, bar, tearoom	Cafe, pubs	29-30
78	Attending receptions (other than those mentioned above)	Other social	29-30
79	Traveling connected to the above mentioned activities, including waiting for means of transport	Travel, social	18

Sports and active leisure (80-89)

80	Practice a sport and physical exercise	Active sports	32
81	Excursions, hunting, fishing	Fishing, hiking	33
82	Walks	Taking a walk	33
83	Technical hobbies, collections	Hobbies	37
84	Ladies' work (confection, needle work, dressmaking, knitting, etc.)	Ladies hobbies	37
85	Artistic creations (sculpture, painting, pottery, literature, etc.)	Art work	37
86	Playing a musical instrument, singing	Making music	37
87	Society games	Parlor games	29-30
88	Others	Other pastime	37
89	Traveling connected to the above mentioned activities, including waiting for means of transport	Travel, pastime	18

Passive leisure (90-99)

90	Listening to the radio	Radio	22
91	Watching television	TV	23
92	Listening to records	Play records	37
93	Reading books	Read book	27
94	Reading review, periodicals, pamphlets, etc.	Read magazine	26
95	Reading newspaper	Read paper	25
96	Conversations, including telephone conversation	Conversation	31
97	Writing private correspondence	Letters, private	37
98	Relaxing, reflecting, thinking, planning, doing nothing, no visible activity	Relax, think	36
99	Traveling connected to the above mentioned activities, including waiting for means of transport	Travel, leisure	18

ACTION. 1975. Americans Volunteer. Washington, D.C.: U.S. Government Printing Office.

Andrews, Frank, James Morgan, and John Sonquist. 1969. Multiple Classification Analysis. Ann Arbor, Mich.: Survey Research Center.

Andrews, Frank, and Stephen Withey. Forthcoming. Social Indicators of Well-Being in America: The Development and Measurement of Perceptual Indicators. New York: Plenum.

Becker, Gary. 1965. "A Theory of the Allocation of Time." Economics 75 (September): 493-517.

Bell, Daniel. 1975. "Clock-watchers: Americans at Work." Time 106 (September 8): 55-57.

____. 1973. The Coming of Post-Industrial Society: A Venture in Social Forecasting. New York: Basic Books.

Bevans, G. 1913. How Working Men Spend Their Spare Time. New York: Columbia University Press.

Bogart, Leo. 1972. The Age of Television. New York: Ungar.

Bower, Robert. 1973. Television and the Public. New York: Holt.

Campbell, Angus, Philip Converse, and Willard Rodgers. 1976. The Quality of American Life. New York: Russell Sage Foundation.

Chapin, F. Stuart, Jr. 1974. Human Activity Patterns in the City: Things People Do in Time and Space. New York: Wiley.

Converse, Philip. 1972. "Country Differences in Time Use." In The Use of Time, edited by A. Szalai et al. The Hague, Netherlands: Mouton.

_____. 1968. "Time Budgets." In International Encyclopedia of the
Social Sciences, Vol. 16, edited by David Sills. New York:
Macmillan Company and The Free Press.

Festinger, Leon. 1957. A Theory of Cognitive Dissonance.
Evanston, Ill.: Row, Peterson.

Gold, Martin. 1963. Status Forces in Delinquent Boys. Ann Arbor,
Mich.: Institute for Social Research.

Goodman, Leo and William Kruskal. 1959. "Measures of Association for Cross-Classification II: Further Discussion References."
Journal of the American Statistical Association 54: 732-64.

Gutenschwager, Gerald. 1973. "The Time-Budget-Activity Systems
Perspective in Urban Planning and Research." Journal of the
American Institute of Planners 39 (November): 378-87.

Heirich, Max. 1964. "The Use of Time in the Study of Social
Change." American Sociological Review 29: 386-97.

Hill, C. Russell, and Frank Stafford. 1974. "Allocation of Time
to Preschool Children and Educational Opportunity." Journal
of Human Resources 9 (Summer): 323-41.

Juster, F. Thomas, ed. Forthcoming. Studies in the Measurement
of Time Allocation. Ann Arbor, Mich.: Institute for Social
Research.

Katz, Elihu, and Paul Lazarsfeld. 1955. Personal Influence.
Glencoe, Ill.: Free Press.

Lansing, John. 1966. Residential Location and Urban Mobility.
Ann Arbor, Mich.: Survey Research Center.

_____ and Gary Henricks. 1967. Automobile Ownership and Residential Density. Ann Arbor, Mich.: Survey Research Center.

Leibowitz, Arleen. 1974. "Home Investments in Children."
Journal of Political Economy 82 (March-April): S111-31.

Linder, Staffan. 1970. The Harried Leisure Class. New York:
Columbia University Press.

Lindert, Peter. Forthcoming. Fertility and Scarcity in America.
Princeton, N.J.: Princeton University Press.

Lundberg, George, Mirra Komarovsky, and Mary Alice McInerny.
    1934. Leisure: A Suburban Study. New York: Columbia
    University Press.

Maklan, David. 1976. "The Four-Day Workweek: Blue-Collar
    Adjustment to a Nonconventional Arrangement of Work and
    Leisure Time." Ph.D. dissertation, University of Michigan.

Meissner, Martin, Elizabeth Humphreys, Scott Meis, and William
    Scheu. 1975. "No Exit for Wives: Sexual Division of Labor
    and the Cumulation of Household Demands." Canadian Review
    of Sociology and Anthropology 12: 424-39.

Melbin, Murray. 1976. "Time Territoriality." Unpublished
    manuscript. Department of Sociology, Boston University.

Moore, Wilbert. 1963. Man, Time and Society. New York: Wiley.

Morgan, James, Ismail Sirageldin, and Nancy Bacrwaldt. 1966.
    Productive Americans. Ann Arbor, Mich.: Survey Research
    Center.

Natali, Daniel, and Roberta Goldberg. Forthcoming. "Parental
    Time and Children's Academic Performance." In Studies in
    the Measurement of Time Allocation, edited by T. Juster.
    Ann Arbor, Mich.: Institute for Social Research.

Nerlove, Marc. 1974. "Household and Economy: Toward a New
    Theory of Population and Economic Growth." Journal of
    Political Economy 82 (March-April): S200-218.

Parkinson, C. Northcote. 1957. Parkinson's Law. New York:
    Ballantine.

Quinn, Robert, and Linda Shepard. 1974. The 1972-73 Quality
    of Employment Survey. Ann Arbor, Mich.: Institute for Social
    Research.

Reiss, Albert. 1959. "Rural-Urban and Status Differences in
    Interpersonal Contacts." American Journal of Sociology 75:
    182-95.

Robinson, John. 1967. "Time Expenditure on Sports Across Ten
    Countries." International Review of Sport Sociology 2: 67-87.

_____. 1969. "Television and Leisure Time: Yesterday, Today and (Maybe) Tomorrow." Public Opinion Quarterly 33: 210-22.

_____. 1971. "The Audience for National TV News Programs." Public Opinion Quarterly 35: 403-05.

_____. 1972a. "Mass Communication and Information Diffusion." In Current Perspectives in Mass Communications Research, edited by Gerald Kline and Philip Tichenor. Beverly Hills, Calif.: Sage Publications.

_____. 1972b. "Television's Impact on Everyday Life: Some Cross-National Evidence." In Television and Social Behavior, Vol. 4, edited by Eli Rubinstein, George Comstock, and John Murray. Washington, D.C.: U.S. Government Printing Office.

_____. Forthcoming. "Methodological Studies into the Reliability and Validity of the Time Diary." In Studies in the Measurement of Time Allocation, edited by T. Juster. Ann Arbor, Mich.: Institute for Social Research.

_____, Robert Athanasiou, and Kendra Head. 1969. Measures of Occupational Attitudes and Occupational Characteristics. Ann Arbor, Mich.: Survey Research Center.

_____, Philip Converse, and Alexander Szalai. 1972. "Everyday Life in Twelve Countries. In The Use of Time, edited by A. Szalai et al. The Hague, Netherlands: Mouton.

_____, and Philip Converse. 1972. "The Impact of Television on Mass Media Usage." In The Use of Time, edited by A. Szalai et al. The Hague, Netherlands: Mouton.

_____, and Philip Converse. 1972. "Social Change as Reflected in the Use of Time." In The Human Meaning of Social Change. edited by A. Campbell and P. Converse. New York: Russell Sage Foundation.

Roper, Burns. 1971. An Extended View of Public Attitudes Toward Television and Other Mass Media. New York: Television Information Office.

Sears, David, and Ronald Abeles. 1969. "Attitudes and Opinions." Annual Review of Psychology 20: 253-58.

Sheldon, Eleanor, and Robert Parke. 1975. "Social Indicators."
    Science 188 (May): 693-98.

Sorokin, Pitrim, and Clarence Berger. 1939. Time-Budgets of
    Human Behavior. Cambridge, Mass.: Harvard University
    Press.

Staikov, Zahari. 1972. "Time-Budgets and Technological Progress."
    In The Use of Time, edited by A. Szalai et al. The Hague,
    Netherlands: Mouton.

Steiner, Gary. 1963. The People Look at Television. New York:
    Knopf.

Stone, Philip. 1972. "Child Care in Twelve Countries." In The
    Use of Time, edited by A. Szalai et al. The Hague, Netherlands:
    Mouton.

Szalai, Alexander. 1966. "Trends in Comparative Time Budget
    Research." American Behavioral Scientist 9 (May): 3-8.

Szalai, Alexander, Philip Converse, Pierre Feldheim, Erwin
    Scheuch, and Philip Stone. 1972. The Use of Time. The
    Hague, Netherlands: Mouton.

Tunstall, Daniel. 1975. Social Indicators 1973. Washington, D.C.:
    U.S. Office of Management and Budget.

U.S. Bureau of Outdoor Recreation. 1972. The 1970 Survey of
    Outdoor Recreation Activities. Washington, D.C.: Department
    of the Interior (preliminary report).

U.S. Office of Management and Budget. 1973. Social Indicators
    1973. Washington, D.C.: U.S. Government Printing Office.

Walker, Kathryn. 1969. "Homemaking Still Takes Time." Journal
    of Home Economics 61: 621-24.

_____. 1970. "Time Spent by Husbands in Household Work."
    Family Economics Review ARS (June): 8-11.

Walker, Kathryn, and William Gauger. 1973. "Time and Its
    Dollar Value in Household Work." Family Economics Review
    ARS 62-5 (Fall): 8-13.

Walker, Kathryn, and Margaret Woods. 1976. Time Use: A Measure of Household Production of Family Goods and Services. Washington, D.C.: American Home Economics Association.

Wilensky, Harold. 1964. "Mass Society and Mass Culture: Interdependence or Independence." American Sociological Review (April): 173-97.

_____. 1961. "The Uneven Distribution of Leisure: The Impact of Economic Growth on Free Time." Social Problems 9 (Summer): 32-56.

Zajonc, Robert, and Gregory Markus. 1975. "Dumber by the Dozen." Psychology Today (January): 37-43.

Zehner, Robert, and F. S. Chapin, Jr. 1974. Across the City Line: A White Community in Transition. Lexington, Mass.: D. C. Heath.

Zuzanek, Jiri. 1974. "Society of Leisure or the Harried Leisure Class?" Journal of Leisure Research 6 (Fall): 293-304.

JOHN P. ROBINSON is Professor of Communication and Director of the Communication Research Center at Cleveland State University. Until 1975, he had been Study Director for the time-use project at the Survey Research Center of the University of Michigan and at various times had taught in the departments of Journalism, Sociology, Psychology, and Political Science at that university.

Professor Robinson has published widely in the areas of social science methodology, with particular emphasis on attitude measurement and the effects of mass communication. He is the senior author of the three attitude measurement reviews, Measures of Social Psychological Attitudes, Measures of Political Attitudes, and Measures of Occupational Attitudes and Occupational Characteristics; he also authored the Statistical Appendix to the multination work, The Use of Time. His articles have appeared in Public Opinion Quarterly, Journalism Quarterly, Social Science Quarterly, Journal of Communication, Journal of Personality and Social Psychology, and Psychology Today, among other journals.

Professor Robinson holds a B.A. from St. Michael's College of the University of Toronto, an M.S. from Virginia Polytechnic Institute and a Ph.D. in Mathematical Psychology and Social Psychology from the University of Michigan. He was Research Coordinator for the U.S. Surgeon General's Committee on Television and Social Behavior in 1969-70. He has acted as Conference Chair for the American Association for Public Opinion Research and for the World Association for Public Opinion Research and is on the editorial board of Public Opinion Quarterly.